J. I. Packer and the
Evangelical Future

SAMFORD UNIVERSITY

Beeson Divinity Studies
Timothy George, Editor

Beeson Divinity Studies is a series of volumes dedicated to the pastoral and theological renewal of the Church of Jesus Christ. The series is sponsored by the faculty of Beeson Divinity School of Samford University, an evangelical, interdenominational theological school in Birmingham, Alabama.

J. I. Packer and the Evangelical Future

The Impact of His Life and Thought

Edited by

Timothy George

Timothy George

Baker Academic

a division of Baker Publishing Group
Grand Rapids, Michigan

© 2009 by Timothy George

Published by Baker Academic
a division of Baker Publishing Group
P.O. Box 6287, Grand Rapids, MI 49516-6287
www.bakeracademic.com

Printed in the United States of America

Library of Congress Cataloging-in-Publication Data
J. I. Packer and the evangelical future : the impact of his life and thought / edited by Timothy George.
    p.   cm. — (Beeson divinity studies)
    Chiefly proceedings of a conference held Sept. 25–27, 2006 at Beeson Divinity School.
    Includes bibliographical references (p.   ) and index.
    ISBN 978-0-8010-3387-2 (pbk.)
    1. Packer, J. I. (James Innell)—Congresses. 2. Evangelicalism—Congresses. I. George, Timothy.
    BX5199.P22J26 2009
    270.8′2092—dc22   2009022735

Sacred to the memory
of
Father Richard John Neuhaus
(1936–2009)

We travel together still

Contents

Preface   9
   Timothy George
List of Contributors   13

1. The Great Tradition: J. I. Packer on Engaging with the Past to Enrich the Present   19
   Alister E. McGrath

2. The Gifts of J. I. Packer: A Cool Head, a Warm Heart, and the Great Tradition   29
   Edith M. Humphrey

3. Pumping Truth: J. I. Packer's Journalism, Theology, and the Thirst for Truth   43
   David Neff

4. J. I. Packer's Theological Method   55
   Donald J. Payne

5. God Has Spoken: The Primacy of Scripture in J. I. Packer's Ministry   69
   Paul R. House

6. J. I. Packer and Pastoral Wisdom from the Puritans   87
   Mark E. Dever

7. Retrieval and Renewal: A Model for Evangelical Spiritual Vitality   99
   D. Bruce Hindmarsh

8. J. I. Packer: An English Nonconformist Perspective   115
   Carl R. Trueman

9. Packer, Puritans, and Postmoderns   131
   Charles W. Colson

10. Christ without Culture   143
    Richard John Neuhaus
11. On Knowing God   155
    James Earl Massey
12. *Unde, Quonam, et Quemadmodum?* Learning Latin (and Other
    Things) from J. I. Packer   163
    Timothy George
13. Reflection and Response   171
    J. I. Packer

    Appendix A: Bibliography of the Works of J. I. Packer:
    July 1952–August 2008   187
    Appendix B: A Tribute to J. I. Packer   231
        Gary A. Parrett
    Notes   233
    Index   249

Preface

TIMOTHY GEORGE

The genesis of this book goes back to a conversation Alister McGrath and I had at Oxford about our friend, J. I. Packer, his influence on us, and the role he has played in the revitalization of evangelicalism as a living tradition within the world Christian movement. We wanted to bring together a symposium where friends, colleagues, and former students could express their gratitude and respect to him on his eightieth birthday, but we knew that Packer, with his natural British (and perhaps also Canadian?) reserve, would balk at the idea. He did. It took some time for us to convince him that this gathering was meant not only to celebrate a life well lived to the glory of God (the life of one, let it be said, who is still going strong and shows no signs of diminishment at age eighty-three), but more importantly to exalt J. I. Packer's God—the great, awesome, three-personal God of joy and grace, the God of creation and redemption we meet in the pages of the Bible and see most clearly in the face of Jesus Christ.

In time, this long-planned conference did in fact take place on September 25–27, 2006, at Beeson Divinity School on the campus of Samford University, in Birmingham, Alabama. Most of the essays in this volume were first given at that conference and retain something of the verve and color of their original presentation. Some who were invited to speak at the conference were not able to be present on that occasion, including Sir Fred and Lady Elizabeth Catherwood, whose friendship with J. I. Packer goes back to his student days at Oxford. Several other scholars have since contributed fresh material for this publication. Together, these essays present a mosaic of some major aspects of J. I. Packer's life and thought and also a prism through which we may learn

9

something about the future of the evangelical church—its opportunities, dangers, disciplines, and direction.

It needs to be said at once that the influence of J. I. Packer far exceeds the range of issues and personalities represented in this volume. In preparing the bibliography included at the end of this book we came across translations of Packer's writings in many languages: including Estonian, Hindi, and Urdu. It is a measure of Packer's modesty that he was not even aware of some of these. His writings are so voluminous that it is hard to imagine that they have come from the pen of one person. We did discover an unusual title by a certain James I. Packer, *Characteristics of Absent Father Families Receiving Aid to Needy Children in California*, done in partial fulfillment for an MA thesis in social work at the University of Southern California in 1952. After some investigation, it became clear that this was not our man. Who, then, is the real J. I. Packer?

James Innell Packer was born July 22, 1926, in Gloucestershire, England. The son of a clerk for the Great Western Railway, Packer grew up in a modest, working-class, nominally Anglican family who encouraged their bookish son by giving him a typewriter. At age seven, he survived a violent collision with a bread truck that left him physically scarred for life and something of a "speckled bird" among his student peers. Packer received a scholarship to Oxford University, where he heard the famous apologist C. S. Lewis speak and was influenced by his writings, especially *The Screwtape Letters* and *Mere Christianity*. But it was in meetings of the Oxford Inter-Collegiate Christian Union, a British version of InterVarsity, that Packer found a living relationship with Jesus Christ and committed his life to Christian service.

After teaching Greek and Latin at Oak Hill Theological College in London, Packer enrolled in Wycliffe Hall, Oxford, where he studied theology and was ordained a priest in the Church of England. Packer served as a lecturer at Tyndale Hall, Bristol, from 1955 to 1961, and as librarian then principal at Latimer House, Oxford, from 1961 to 1969. He was principal of Tyndale Hall in 1970, and associate principal of Trinity College, Bristol, from 1971 to 1979.

Having found the writings of John Owen helpful in his own spiritual life, he worked closely with Martin Lloyd-Jones to encourage a revival of interest in the Puritans and their writings. Packer's own writings, especially *"Fundamentalism" and the Word of God* and *Evangelism and the Sovereignty of God*, established him as a formidable theological voice for the evangelical movement. In 1973, he published *Knowing God*, a modern theological classic.

In 1979, Packer moved to Vancouver to assume his position at Regent College, where he serves as the Board of Governors' Professor of Theology. From this base, he has had a deep and encompassing influence on many renewal movements within North American Christianity and beyond. Through his many books and lectureship around the globe, he has become a highly regarded leader in the world Christian movement. In 2000, he chaired the theological track at the World Conference on Evangelism convened by Billy Graham in Amsterdam. He has long been associated with *Christianity Today* as a visiting scholar and senior editor. In recent years, he has garnered much attention through his participation in the movement known as Evangelicals and Catholics Together.

He also has been involved in theological conversations with Orthodox believers, charismatic Christians, and mainline Protestant theologians. In all these contexts, he has promoted a vigorous spiritual theology, faithful to the Holy Scriptures, and in keeping with the Great Tradition. Packer has been ever mindful of the maxim of Richard Baxter, on whom he wrote his Oxford doctoral dissertation:

> *in necessariis Unitas,*
> *in non-necessariis Libertas,*
> *in utrisque Caritas.*[1]

Despite his charitable spirit and his desire to foster a unitive, irenic evangelicalism, Packer has not been able to avoid the effects of the deep ruptures within the world Anglican Communion. In June 2002 the Anglican Diocese of New Westminster in Vancouver voted to approve the blessing of same-sex unions. Packer, among other synod members, saw this action as a flagrant abandonment of the authority of Scripture and walked out in protest. In February 2008 Packer's church in Vancouver voted to seek episcopal oversight from an orthodox Anglican bishop. In response to charges brought against them by the bishop in Vancouver, Packer and other evangelical clergy declared their determination to continue their ministry "under the jurisdiction of and in communion with those who remained faithful to historic, orthodox Anglicanism and as part of the Anglican Communion worldwide."[2] In the midst of controversy that continues to unfold, Packer has received acclaim for his courage and commitment in the face of what by all accounts must be considered one of the great tragedies in contemporary church history.

It has been my privilege to know and work closely with J. I. Packer for the past twenty-five years, only a fraction of his long and still amazingly productive career. I have seen him buffeted by adversity and criticized unfairly, but I have never seen him sag. His smile is irrepressible and his laughter can bring light to the most somber of meetings. His love for all things human and humane shines through. His mastery of ideas and the most fitting words in which to express them is peerless. Ever impatient with shams of all kinds, his saintly character and spirituality run deep. I love to hear him pray. Again and again, he has reminded us that we live our lives *coram deo* and in the light of eternity. He has taught us that theology is for doxology and devotion, that theology is always at its best "when it is consciously done under the eye of the God of whom it speaks, and when it is singing to his glory."[3]

Contributors

Charles W. Colson is an internationally known commentator, columnist, and author, and the founder of Prison Fellowship. His radio broadcast, *Break-Point*, airs daily to two million listeners. Former counsel to President Richard Nixon, Colson was converted to Christ before spending time in prison on a Watergate-related charge. In the last thirty-three years, Colson has visited more than six hundred prisons in forty countries and, with the help of nearly fifty thousand volunteers, has built Prison Fellowship into the world's largest prison outreach. In recognition of his work, Colson received the prestigious one million dollar Templeton Prize for Progress in Religion in 1993, which he donated to Prison Fellowship, as he does all speaking fees and book royalties. *Born Again*, Colson's first book, was published in 1976 and became the first of many international bestsellers. In 2008, he published *The Faith* described by Timothy George as "a contemporary statement of the apostolic faith—articulate, persuasive and winsome."

Mark E. Dever serves as the senior pastor of Capitol Hill Baptist Church in Washington, DC. He is also the executive director of 9Marks Ministries and has taught at a number of seminaries, including Beeson Divinity School, The Southern Baptist Theological Seminary, and Trinity Evangelical Divinity School. Dever has authored several books and articles, including *Nine Marks of a Healthy Church* (Crossway, 2000, 2004), *The Deliberate Church* (Crossway, 2005), *Promises Kept: The Message of the New Testament* (Crossway, 2005), and *Promises Made: The Message of the Old Testament* (Crossway, 2006). His latest book, *In My Place Condemned He Stood: Celebrating the Glory of the Atonement* (Crossway, 2008) was written with J. I. Packer.

Timothy George is the founding dean of Beeson Divinity School. He is currently serving as senior editor for *Christianity Today* and on the editorial advisory boards of the *Harvard Theological Review*, *Christian History*, and *Books & Culture*. A prolific author, he has written more than twenty books and regularly contributes to scholarly journals. His book *Theology of the Reformers* is the standard textbook in many schools and seminaries on Reformation theology and has been translated into several languages. He has been active in the evangelical dialogue with the Roman Catholic Church and is a highly sought after preacher and conference speaker. He is also the general editor of the *Reformation Commentary on Scripture*, a multivolume work of sixteenth-century exegetical commentary. As founding dean, George has been instrumental in shaping the character and mission of Beeson Divinity School. An ordained minister in the Southern Baptist Convention, he has served as pastor for churches in Tennessee, Alabama, and Massachusetts.

D. Bruce Hindmarsh is the James M. Houston Professor of Spiritual Theology at Regent College, Vancouver. He has a broad interest in the history of Christian spirituality and a particular research interest in evangelical spirituality. Hindmarsh has published and lectured widely on the early evangelical movement in the age of John Wesley and Jonathan Edwards, and is the author of *John Newton and the English Evangelical Tradition* (Oxford, 1996) and *The Evangelical Conversion Narrative* (Oxford, 2005). The recipient of numerous research awards, he was a Meyers Research Fellow at the Huntington Library in San Marino, California, in the summer of 2005, and was awarded the Henry Luce III Fellowship in Theology for 2006–7. A lay member of the Anglican Church of Canada, Hindmarsh serves with J. I. Packer at Regent College.

Paul R. House is associate dean and professor of divinity at Beeson Divinity School. He joined the Beeson faculty in 2004 after serving at Taylor University, The Southern Baptist Theological Seminary, Trinity Episcopal School for Ministry, and Wheaton College. He oversees all aspects of academic programming. House is the author or editor of fifteen books, including *The Unity of the Twelve* (Sheffield, 1990), *Old Testament Survey* (Broadman, 1992), *Old Testament Theology* (InterVarsity, 1998) and *Lamentations* (Word Biblical Commentary, 2004). He has been pastor of churches in Missouri, Indiana, and Kentucky.

Edith M. Humphrey is the William F. Orr Associate Professor of New Testament at Pittsburgh Theological Seminary. She began her walk with Christ in the Salvation Army and then was confirmed in and became a member of the Anglican Communion, where she has served as a layperson for over fifteen years: as director of music at St. George's Anglican Church (Ottawa), in service on the Primate's Theological Commission (Canada), and in various teaching ministries. Humphey attends Church of the Ascension in Pittsburgh and serves on the Commission on Ministry in that Episcopal diocese. She has taught in various institutions in Canada, including McGill, Bishop's, Carleton, and St. Paul Universities; Regent and Augustine Colleges; and Toronto School of Theology. Humphrey is the author of numerous academic and popular writings, including: *The Ladies and the Cities: Transformation and Identity in Four Apocalypses* (Sheffield, 1995), *Ecstasy and Intimacy: When the Holy Spirit Meets the Human Spirit* (Eerdmans, 2005), and a recent book titled *And I Turned to See the Voice: The Rhetoric of Vision of the New Testament* (Baker Academic, 2007).

James Earl Massey is dean emeritus and distinguished professor-at-large of the Anderson University School of Theology, honors bestowed on him after more than twenty-five years of service in theological education on that campus. From 1984 to 1990 and 1997 to 1998 he was dean of the chapel and university professor of religion and society at Tuskegee University. A native of Detroit, he is pastor emeritus of Metropolitan Church of God, a congregation of which he was the founding pastor and served from 1954 to 1976. Massey has preached and lectured in America, the Caribbean, England, Europe, Egypt, Australia, and Japan and on the campuses of more than one hundred colleges, universities, and seminaries worldwide. A productive scholar, Massey has published twenty-three books including: *Designing the Sermon: Order and Movement in Preaching* (Abingdon, 1980), *Sundays in the Tuskegee Chapel: Selected Sermons* (Abingdon, 2000), and *The Burdensome Joy of Preaching* (Abingdon, 1998), which was named by *Preaching* magazine as its 1998 book of the year. Most recently he published his autobiography, *Aspects of My Pilgrimage* (Anderson University Press, 2002). Massey has served on the editorial boards of *Preaching*, *Leadership*, and *Christianity Today*.

Alister E. McGrath is head of the Centre for Theology, Religion, and Culture, King's College, London, England. Previously, he was president of the Oxford Center for Evangelism and Apologetics and served as professor of historical theology at Oxford University. He has served as curate at St. Leonard's Parish Church in Woolaton, Nottingham, and as principal of Wycliffe Hall, Oxford. He is one of the most widely read and influential Christian writers in the world and travels extensively to speak at conferences and missions. McGrath has written a number of important works on Reformation history and theology and on the development and prospects for evangelicalism. He has published over thirty-five books, including his acclaimed book on apologetics, *Bridge-Building* (InterVarsity, 1982) and the bestselling *Christian Theology: An Introduction* (Blackwell, 2007), which has been translated into nine languages. He is an expert both on the history of Christian thought, especially in the sixteenth and early seventeenth centuries, and systematic theology in general, and has been featured regularly in radio and television programs in England and abroad.

David Neff is editor-in-chief of *Christianity Today* and the Christianity Today Media Group. He also serves as director of the Robert E. Webber Center for an Ancient Evangelical Future at Northern Seminary. In his twenty years at *Christianity Today*, he has written on topics as diverse as physician-assisted suicide, Palestinian statehood, English evangelicalism, and sexual addiction. Before coming to *Christianity Today*, Neff served as editor of *HIS*, InterVarsity Christian Fellowship's erstwhile magazine for college students. He was involved as business and promotion manager for the launch of the *Journal of Christian Nursing* for Nurses Christian Fellowship.

†Richard John Neuhaus (d. 2009) was acclaimed as one of the foremost authorities on the role of religion in the contemporary world and served as president of the Institute on Religion and Public Life, a nonpartisan interreligious research and education institute in New York City. He was editor-in-chief of the institute's publication, *First Things: A Monthly Journal of Religion and Public Life*. Among his best known books are: *Death on a Friday Afternoon: Meditations on the Last Words of Jesus from the Cross* (Basic Books, 2001), *Freedom for Ministry* (Eerdmans, 1992), and *The Catholic Moment: The Paradox of the Church in the Postmodern World* (Harper & Row, 1987). His most recent book is *Catholic Matters: Confusion, Controversy, and The Splendor of Truth* (Basic Books, 2006). Prior to his conversion to Roman Catholicism, he served for seventeen years as a Lutheran pastor of a low-income parish in Brooklyn, New York. He played a leadership role in organizations dealing with civil rights, international justice, and ecumenism. Father Neuhaus held presidential appointments in the Carter, Reagan, and Bush administrations. In a survey of national leadership, *U.S. News and World Report* named him one of the thirty-two "most influential intellectuals in America."

Donald J. Payne serves as associate dean and professor of theology and ministry at Denver Seminary. He joined the faculty in 1998 as director of the suburban and rural training centers in the training and mentoring department. In his current position he provides overall leadership for the training and mentoring program and teaches in the areas of systematic theology. Prior to coming to Denver Seminary, he was a pastor for many years—first as a church-planting pastor in Chattanooga, Tennessee; then as associate pastor at Southern Gables Evangelical Free Church in Littleton, Colorado. He taught at Colorado Christian University, Colorado State University, and Moody Bible Institute's extension school. His book *The Theology of the Christian Life in J. I. Packer's Thought* was published in 2006 by Paternoster.

Carl R. Trueman has served as a council member of the Alliance of Confessing Evangelicals since 2004 and has been professor of historical theology and church history at Westminster Theological Seminary since 2001. He also served as editor of the journal *Themelios* from 1998–2007. He has written many books including *Luther's Legacy: Salvation and English Reformers, 1525–1556* (Oxford University Press and Clarendon, 1994).

1

The Great Tradition

J. I. Packer on Engaging with the Past to Enrich the Present

ALISTER E. MCGRATH

J. I. Packer identifies himself on a map of Christian possibilities using a multiple series of coordinates: he is, he affirms, "an Anglican, a Protestant, an evangelical, and in C. S. Lewis' sense a 'mere Christian.'"[1] The agenda underlying this volume is both honorific and analytical—setting out to celebrate the achievements of this major evangelical theological and spiritual writer (and there is much to celebrate) while at the same time asking how he helps evangelicalism, Protestantism, and what I like to call "Great Tradition Christianity" strategize for the future. Neither I nor any of the distinguished contributors will be able to do justice to Packer's immense literary output, the quality of his theological analysis, and the shrewdness of many of his judgments in the limited space that is available to us. I shall have to content myself with scratching the surface.

I count it both a personal and professional privilege to address this topic. As one who taught historical and systematic theology for more than twenty years at Oxford, primarily but not exclusively to those who would enter pastoral ministry or serve as missionaries, I have often reflected on how difficult it is to teach theology in a way that maintains its integrity as an academic discipline while at the same time stimulating, guiding, and nourishing the life of faith. I can only claim modest success, I think, in my attempts to do so. Yet if one speaks to students who attended Tyndale Hall, Bristol, during the 1950s; Trinity College, Bristol, during the 1970s; or Regent College, Vancouver, at just about any point during the last quarter of a century, one will hear them acclaim Packer as a master of this art. There is a popular saying in England that is partly born of cynicism and partly out of the dreadful reality of experience: "Those who can, do; those who cannot, teach." Packer is a rare example of an original thinker with a genuine gift for teaching who confounds this piece of popular wisdom.

Packer and I also have one or two shared areas of experience. We both served as principals of leading theological colleges of the Church of England. Perhaps I should not say too much about this, save to remark that running such institutions is not particularly conducive to either one's sanity or one's capacity to get some serious research done. I take great comfort from the fact that Packer went on to achieve so much after moving on from such a position.

My professional admiration for Packer as a historical theologian is grounded not simply in his excellent historical analyses but in the use to which he puts history. When I first read his doctoral thesis on Richard Baxter, I was gripped by the rigor of Packer's analysis but also sensed the importance that he attached both to the questions that Baxter was handling and to Baxter himself as an important (though far from infallible) guide to these issues.[2] Packer is able to popularize from profundity; his accessible accounts and applications of leading theological and spiritual themes are grounded in a deep knowledge of the issues.

While not agreeing with Packer at every point, I find in him someone whose views are so well biblically and theologically grounded, so well defended, so well articulated, and so well applied that one could wish for no better dialogue partner in wrestling with the great theological issues of our own age as well as of the past. This is one of the reasons that I suspect future generations will continue to find him a significant resource. In my view, Packer shares a combination of properties I also see in George Whitefield and Charles Haddon Spurgeon—a commitment to a clear Reformed theological position along with a personal graciousness that enables dialogue and collaboration with others.

In this essay, I want to focus above all on one topic: Packer's distinctive and, in my view, critically important insight that evangelical theology is both enriched and stabilized by attentiveness to the past. I have chosen to focus on this topic for a number of reasons. Perhaps very obviously, it resonates strongly with my professional interest as a historical theologian. It is always nice to find someone else who thinks that the study of the past might actually be theologically useful. My second reason is perhaps equally obvious; having read J. I. Packer's works over many years, I have noticed and respected his engagement with the past, and his capacity to enrich our own grasp of God's glory and greatness by a principled dialogue with those who made that discovery before we were around. But my third reason is perhaps the most significant, and it requires a little further discussion. I believe that evangelicalism as a whole needs to listen to Packer's approach to theologizing—and I use the verb deliberately—in the light of the present challenges that face the movement.

One of the most interesting themes that I discern within evangelical history during the past fifty years is its growing interest in issues of theology. The acceleration of such interest reflects a number of factors. One such factor is the existence of role models who have demonstrated the utility of theology and its capacity to illuminate and inform the life of faith. Evangelicalism has always been somewhat pragmatic in its evaluation of individuals and methods. To put it rather crudely, the core criterion used in this process of evaluation has often been: Will this work? Will this make any difference? Will this help me grow in faith? Will this help the ministry of my church? And while I would wish to enter a note of caution about these concerns, I think they must be respected. Through his writings, and especially through his classic work *Knowing God*, Packer has demonstrated the utility of theology to a rising generation of evangelicals, who had hitherto tended to see their intellectual commitment to the gospel as restricted to reading a few biblical commentaries.

Perhaps this is an idiosyncrasy on my part, but I am firmly convinced that an integral part of the walk of faith is a "discipleship of the mind." Paul talks about renewing our minds (Rom. 12:1–4), and this seems to me to be an integral part of our conversion—the reshaping and recalibration of our ways of thinking in accordance with the patterns of reality disclosed in Christ. At this point, I would like to offer a case study, drawn from an early point in Packer's rich and varied career, which seems to me to help us appreciate his insistence on the importance of theology in relation to faith and, above all, to engagement with the Great Tradition.

The example is Packer's 1955 critique of certain aspects of the "victorious living" theology associated with the Keswick Convention.[3] This critique was prompted by a specific occasion—the publication of a book promoting this approach that seemed to Packer to be seriously deficient. Packer's early love of the Puritans, which developed in the 1940s, had persuaded him that there were already approaches available to address the problems of personal holiness that were considerably more realistic than the one he found in the Keswick teaching.

Yet such was the influence of this school of thought in England at the time that Packer believed it needed to be criticized at a much deeper level—not so much its pastoral effectiveness as its fundamental theological ideas. He had no doubt that Keswick's fatal weak spot lay in the idea of the human ability to make the critical decisions necessary to facilitate sanctification. For Packer, this was an uninformed Pelagianism, based on a hopelessly optimistic view of fallen human nature. For Packer, the Keswick teaching offered an understanding of salvation that is "attenuated and impoverished," resting on a theological axiom that is both "false to Scripture and dishonouring to God."[4]

Most important of all was Packer's suggestion that a theologically naïve Pietism inevitably lapsed into a Pelagianism of this kind. "Pelagianism is the natural heresy of zealous Christians who are not interested in theology."[5] Although Packer later took a more conciliatory attitude toward the Keswick school,[6] this early criticism shows his passionate awareness of the pastoral and spiritual importance of theology. Well-meaning pastoral approaches and well-intended spiritual techniques may actually harm the life of faith if they are not securely grounded in theology. It is a theme that we find throughout Packer's writings and one that I believe is not only important in itself but of particular importance within an evangelical culture that tends to regard validation as resting on practical outcomes.

Yet Packer's emphasis on the importance of theology does not lead him into the somewhat dry and dusty approaches to theology that treats it as essentially abstract theorizing about God. The noted American Presbyterian writer James Henley Thornwell (1812–62) had no doubt of the danger of these kinds of excessively rationalist or cerebral approaches to theology. His comments bear repeating:

> It gave no scope to the play of Christian feeling; it never turned aside to reverence, to worship, or to adore. It exhibited truth, nakedly and baldly, in its objective reality, without any reference to the subjective conditions which, under the influence of the Spirit, that truth was calculated to produce. It was a dry digest of theses and propositions—perfect in form, but as cold and lifeless as a skeleton.[7]

Such an approach to theology divorces it from the realm of experience—and hence from the reality of everyday Christian life, especially among believers who did not find intellectual analysis natural or easy.

Packer's approach to theology is grounded in the Puritan tradition, that particularly English variant of Reformed theology that so often showed an exquisite sensitivity to the pastoral needs and spiritual realities of fallen human life. While his understanding of theology is perhaps best seen in *Knowing God*, I would like to single out his 1989 inaugural lecture as the first Sangwoo Youtong Chee Professor of Theology at Regent College, in which he reflected on the nature of theology and its relation to spirituality. The lecture offers an important vision of the nature of theology and above all a corrective to excessively rationalist understandings of theology that severely truncate its scope. Theology and spirituality, he argued, are intimately connected, not because of the will of theologians to try and make artificial connections with the totally different discipline of spirituality, but because theology, when rightly understood, leads into spirituality. Theology is to be understood, he writes, as "a devotional discipline, a verifying in experience of Aquinas' beautiful remark that theology is taught by God, teaches God, and takes us to God."[8]

There is, Packer rightly maintains, a real need for systematic theology within the church, synthesizing the biblical witness to God into a seamless garment. Biblical exegesis is to be commended—and also correlated. All the data about God that exegesis has established must be brought together in a single coherent scheme. Packer commends such an enterprise but counsels against any understanding of theology that is *limited* to the cataloging and indexing of revealed truths about God. Theology cannot, and should not, be detached or dissociated from the relational activity of trusting, loving, worshiping, obeying, serving, and glorifying God.[9] Yet reaction against an inadequate vision of theology must not lead us to reject what is right in such an impoverished account—and to construct another that is equally impoverished, yet in diametrically opposed ways. "Reaction against dry and heavy theology has made some of us woolly and wild, valuing feelings above truth, depreciating 'head knowledge' by comparison with 'heart knowledge' and refusing to allow that we cannot have the latter without the former, just as reaction against overheated emotionalism has made others of us cool, cerebral and censorious to a fault."[10]

So how did Packer develop this interest in the role of tradition in theologizing? I suspect that we probably cannot point to any one defining moment when this appreciation of the significance of the theological past for nourishing the present was crystallized, although it is certainly possible to point to some landmarks in the process. One of these dates from Packer's days as an undergraduate at Oxford, studying "Greats"—Oxford's term for the literature, language, and philosophy of the classical world—at Corpus Christi College. He became a Christian a few weeks after his arrival, as a result of hearing a sermon that helped him appreciate the importance of saving faith.

Everyone who comes to faith has a certain amount of mental readjustment to do. Packer found his thinking on a number of issues undergoing significant development—for example, in relation to the authority of the Bible. He also found himself reflecting on one of the great problems of Christian spirituality: how do we deal with the ongoing presence of sin in the life of the believer? Oxford undergraduate evangelicalism in those days was heavily influenced by what is known as "the Keswick teaching," a matter on which we have already touched. The slogan "let go and let God" was certainly easy to remember; its theological basis and practical benefits seemed rather more elusive.

I am not sure whether we can say that Packer was actively seeking an alternative; yet, there is no doubt that he found one during the academic year 1945–46. While sorting through piles of old books that a generous retired cleric had given to the Oxford Inter-Collegiate Christian Union, Packer came across the writings of the great Puritan John Owen. As he flipped through the volumes, he found himself struck by the titles of some of the treatises— above all, "On Indwelling Sin" and "On the Mortification of Sin." He began to read them. Immediately, he found himself challenged by the realism of Owen's analysis of both the problems arising from "indwelling sin" and the means of dealing with it (which Owen termed "mortification"). This was clearly transformational for Packer. So impressed was he with the approach that he went on to type out a twenty-page précis of Owen's arguments, which he circulated to his friends.[11]

We see here the roots of Packer's love for the Puritans, born not out of antiquarian curiosity but out of a burning conviction that there was gold in the Puritan hills. At the academic level, this led to what was easily the best scholarly analysis of Richard Baxter's soteriology; at the popular level, it lay behind Packer's superb popularizing of the Puritan vision in works such as *A Quest for Godliness*[12]; at the institutional level, it led to the establishment of the "Puritan and Reformed Study Conferences," through which Packer and Martyn Lloyd-Jones were able to shape a rising generation of clergy who were looking for serious theological roots for their ministries and preaching.

It is impossible to read Packer—or to write about him—without appreciating his deep love for the Puritans; this, I suggest, is an excellent illustration of the deeper principle of the value of tradition for today's church and today's Christians. The importance of this point is now well established within evangelicalism as a whole. The new—and, I must say, very welcome—interest in Jonathan Edwards within evangelicalism can be seen as a continuation of this tradition of engagement with excellence.[13] Positively, it represents a retrieval and reappropriation of wisdom from the past; negatively, it represents an implicit critique of some trends within evangelicalism that cause some concern, most notably the quest for cultural significance, which can so easily, despite the best of intentions, degenerate into cultural concession.

Yet Packer's growing interest in the notion of tradition also took a more explicitly theological form. Packer has seen himself as an attentive, appreciative, yet critical participant in the great conversation about how best to articulate and defend the gospel that has continued throughout history. As he put it in 1996, "I theologize out of what I see as the authentic biblical and creedal mainstream of Christian identity, the confessional and liturgical 'great tradition' that the church on earth has characteristically maintained from the start." On this view of things, the Protestant reformation of the sixteenth century is to be seen offering "corrections" that "took place within the frame of the great tradition, and did not break it."[14]

I share this approach, which I believe represents an important corrective to a vulnerability within contemporary evangelicalism.[15] In celebrating the movement's great strengths, it is also important to ask what can be learned to make it stronger through being more faithful. Packer's answer is, in part, to listen to others who have sought to be faithful to God in their own generations and passed down to us their insights. But what of Packer's diagnosis of the problem?

Packer sets out with clarity and compassion a concern he has about trends in his 1992 essay "The Comfort of Conservatism," which is a highly accessible account of the potential role that tradition might play in the stabilization of evangelicalism.[16] Packer's intimate knowledge and experience of North American evangelicalism led him to appreciate the dangers of individualism, which seemed to him to engender a dangerously superficial and ephemeral form of Christianity. For Packer, tradition is an antidote against precisely such an individualism. North American evangelicalism, steeped in individualism, often seems to have no real sense of historical "belonging" or rootedness. As such, it is radically prone to destabilization. Too often, as Packer comments, the North American evangelical has been "a spiritual lone ranger who has proudly or impatiently turned his back on the church and his heritage"—a development that Packer suggests is "a surefire recipe for weirdness without end!"[17] Rediscovering the corporate and historic nature of the Christian faith reduces the danger of entire communities of faith being misled by charismatic individuals and affirms the ongoing importance of the Christian past as a stabilizing influence in potentially turbulent times.

Packer articulates an approach by which he believes that what is wise, good, and true from the past can be discerned and gladly and joyfully reappropriated by today's church. Rediscovering the historic and corporate dimensions of our faith makes the great treasures and resources of the Christian past accessible and available to the present, thus enriching the life and witness of modern evangelicalism. We are enabled, as Packer puts it, to "receive nurturing truth and wisdom from God's faithfulness in past generations."[18]

In commending the recovery of tradition as an antidote to this trend, Packer is aware that the notion is open to a series of misunderstandings. A concern for tradition is not, he stresses, equivalent to "traditionalism"—that is to say, a nostalgic and backward looking approach to the Christian faith that "can quench the Holy Spirit and cause paralysis and impotence in the church"[19] by demanding that we blindly and uncritically repeat exactly what evangelicals did and said back in the 1950s, the 1920s, the 1820s, or the 1730s (or whatever period in evangelical history happens to be regarded as a "golden age" by its advocates).

Packer is quite clear that a concern for tradition does not violate the evangelical emphasis on the sole and supreme authority of Scripture. Tradition serves in a ministerial mode and does not rule magisterially. It is there to help and to guide, not to command. "Scripture must have the last word on all human attempts to state its meaning, and tradition, viewed as a series of such human attempts, has a ministerial rather than a magisterial role."[20] In the end, all interpretations of Scripture must be judged in the light of Scripture itself, recognizing that the church—including evangelicals—has misunderstood the Bible on occasion in the past. "We are all beneficiaries of good, wise, and sound tradition, and victims of poor, unwise, and unsound traditions. This is where the absolute 'last word' of Scripture must sort the wheat from the chaff. Hence, the apostle Paul's counsel: '. . . test everything; hold fast what is good' (1 Thess. 5:21 ESV)."[21]

Tradition, for Packer, is thus something that must be judged. It can too easily shape our readings of Scripture, highlighting some ideas and obscuring others. All Protestants, Packer reminds us, stand within traditions—whether Anglican or Baptist, Pentecostal or Dispensationalist, Reformed or Lutheran, Methodist or Mennonite—that open our eyes to some things and close them to others. "All traditions function as blinders, focusing our vision on some things at which we have been taught to look constantly and that we therefore see clearly, but keeping us from seeing other things that other traditions grasp better."[22] There is an important corollary of this: Christians of different traditions should talk to each other so that we can help each other eliminate our blind spots and ensure that the totality of Scripture is illuminated and applied to life and thought.

As a historian, Packer is aware how tradition predisposes us to read the Bible in certain ways without realizing how that seemingly "obvious" or "self-evident" interpretation of the Bible actually gains its power or plausibility from tradition. A time-honored way of reading the Bible is not necessarily right. Perhaps just as importantly, Packer points out how past controversies cast their long, lingering shadows over contemporary readings of the Bible. Many Protestants, Packer suggests, have reacted against Roman Catholic sacramentalism in such a way that they mistrust the sacraments and deny their importance in practice.

Engaging properly—that is, positively and critically—with tradition opens the way to proper biblical interpretation and theological reflection. Packer suggests that there are three ways in which this process can take place.

1. *By liberating us from our own thoughts.* We need to be challenged by alternative perspectives. "We need the discipline of learning with the saints, past and present, in the ways noted above, to counterbalance our lopsidedness and to help us break out of the narrow circle of our own present thoughts into a larger vision and a riper wisdom."
2. *By being set free from being locked into today's ways of thinking.* Packer argues that attentiveness to the past liberates us from "chronological snobbery" and alerts us to the richness of past readings of Scripture. "Keeping regular company with yesterday's great teachers" opens our eyes to wisdom that is otherwise denied to us.
3. *By setting us free from the limitations of our own traditions.* Developing his earlier argument, Packer stresses that "the tradition that shaped us had a narrowing as well as an enriching effect on us." Illustrating this from his own Anglican heritage, Packer urges his readers to value what

is good yet identify what is weak—and that means listening to other perspectives, past and present.[23]

We see here an approach that has much to offer evangelicalism. It encourages a process of respectful yet critical dialogue with the past, determined as a matter of principle to learn from the wisdom of the past, while being liberated from mechanical and wooden repetition of its judgments. Its vision of theology is corporate rather than individualistic, yet creates space for individuals to make a difference in how the community perceives and articulates its foundational beliefs and judgments. It is rigorously grounded in Scripture on the one hand, while taking into account the long history of faithful Christian engagement with the Bible on the other. Perhaps it seems paradoxical to look backward before moving forward. But it is an important corrective to our natural tendency to rush ahead, act precipitately, and make snap judgments. Packer's vision of theology will challenge those whose spiritual hunger leads them to the theological equivalent of fast food outlets. Yet we must ask ourselves, in all seriousness, whether the prefabricated, processed, and predigested approaches to theology that are so often encountered within the evangelical world really can sustain it as it confronts the future.

I end with an apposite reminiscence. When I was researching my biography of Packer some ten years ago, I received many letters from former students at Tyndale Hall, Bristol, who had been taught theology by Packer during the late 1950s. Some described how they would ask him theological questions over breakfast. The answers, they recall, took some time in coming. Why? Because Packer insisted on showing them how he arrived at his answers. He refused to give short, snappy answers, instead going through the process of explaining how one might arrive at an answer in the first place. As those students realized, they were being taught how to think theologically—how to *theologize*, as Packer would have it. We need to learn from this in an age in which people want to learn the answers without the inconvenience of going through the reflective process that led to them in the first place.

himself at the center of the church's teaching, with transparency, all the time using common sense to "state firmly" those things that are common to the faith of Christians, and particularly to his Reformed and Anglican understanding of that faith. In a time of flux, he has reminded both those of us who are tempted to despair and those who are seduced by revisionism that "the great tradition will most surely survive."[2] In this he is on firm ground, for we have it on the very best authority that not even the gates of hell, let alone the schemes of man, will prevail against God's people.

Packer commends to us the hard path as the "going gets tough." He neither directs us to the quietism of the ostrich, as some have done in these fiery times, nor sounds a note of panic that suggests everything depends on an urgent and immediate response. This balance is clear in the way that he has continued, both publicly and behind the scenes, to foster health in the church's thinking, while always remembering that God the Holy Spirit is our physician and our strengthener. There has never been the "J. I. Packer" project, an idiosyncratic and focused campaign, something that is the perennial great temptation of many other faithful academics. For me he stands in the line of "unflashy" servants of God such as Elizabeth Achtemeier, who tirelessly and faithfully continue in that long obedience of using mind and strength and fearlessly telling the truth. His is the courage of a long-distance runner and the tranquility of the cool head, as he has tackled first the spirit of modernism, and then postmodernism in its turn, with efficiency and without hysteria. Indeed, in waxing eloquent on the difficulties particular to preaching and teaching in our postmodern climate, he has been known to stop himself short by commenting, "our present agenda is not . . . to develop jeremiads."[3] Instead, his agenda has always been to commend to his brothers and sisters what he has understood to be the very core of the faith and to do this while also recognizing where there are significant differences in opinion, particularly in the areas of ecclesiology. His is the role of the spiritual watchdog, as he exemplifies that charisma of the Reformation that he dubs "theological watchfulness"[4]—a gift of ongoing importance but of special significance today, where "whimsy" would supplant "wisdom."[5]

From the cool head of Packer has come a consistent sounding of significant theological themes, for he is convinced (with others like James Orr) that Christian truth is organic, knit together as a living thing. First, he points us to the rational coherence of the Christian story and how this story is interconnected with the Christian mind and Christian way. That coherence comes by insisting on "trinitarian theocentricity," by telling the whole story of God the Son (from the incarnation, through to the resurrection, ascension, and promised return) and by rejoicing in the power of God to transform lives.

This he has commended to those outside and inside the church, all the while longing for God to bring us back together as an international church, undivided by cultural tensions.

Within my own Anglican Communion, we have been indebted to Packer for works of love and clarity such as his *Commentary on the Montreal Declaration: Anglican Essentials* in which he carefully clarifies and expounds on the brief consensus statement of those who sought in the 90s to reform the Anglican Church of Canada.[6] With humility and care, he has offered this very helpful booklet, full of Scripture and creedal, theological, and social context, and insisted that this was a "personal interpretation" in which he claimed "only to be putting on paper things that I myself see . . . that the [Lord of the church] may use it to his glory."[7] A reading of its pages will show how, with perspicuity, Packer has directed faithful readers to look *back* unashamedly to the traditions handed down to us, *around* unflinchingly at the "rapid drift" away from those things, and *ahead* resolutely with confidence in the renewing and enlivening power of the Holy Spirit. There are many riches in the course of his treatment here, but I would like to single out two.

First, the *Commentary* was not simply an uncritical encouragement to the coalition of faithful evangelicals, charismatics, and Anglo-Catholics that comprised the Essentials movement. True to style, Packer spoke a word of gentle correction to his own constituency in that group, encouraging the faithful of the Essentials movement to put worship first, even above evangelism.[8] This emphasis that he draws out of the Declaration remains for us today a prophetic and salutary word. Indeed, many of us in the reform movements of the church find ourselves in a setting where evangelicalism threatens to tyrannize, thus crushing or deforming the very truth it seeks to proclaim. So he speaks a word *into* the group represented by the Declaration. Second, he also speaks a word of warning outside. In his *Commentary* is found a careful contrast between two tendencies that are frequently and dangerously confused, especially in mainline Protestant churches. The celebrated genius of Anglicanism is that it has been able to hold together a certain amount of dogmatic diversity, by differentiating between what is "essential" and what is more at the periphery of the faith. But with that genius has come, as has become clear in the past crisis, a matching danger. Some have come to understand Anglicanism's "middle way" as a laissez-faire toleration for everything, an eclectic approach that leads to doctrinal and ethical indifference. Packer makes a clear divide between the growing tendency to privilege "diversity" in an uncritical manner and the characteristic Anglican discernment between essentials and nonessentials. It is one thing to recognize that some matters may be in the area of theological opinion,[9] or *theologoumena*, it is quite another to allow the realm of "opinion" to take over like a cancer, so that truly doctrinal matters are placed under the not-so-tolerant reign of Lady Diversity.

These two principles—Packer's insistence on the primacy of worship among evangelicals and his refusal to collapse nuanced and charitable discernment into a religion of diversity—are potent points that will keep faithful Anglicans clearheaded and that will also (it seems to me) lead them to a place where they can enter into fruitful discussion with Christians outside their own tradition. To allow worship to take its rightful place above evangelism will prevent fervent Anglicans from reducing the church to a mere service organization, though it is certainly this. To plead that the "middle way" of Anglicanism cannot be made into a religion of sheer toleration or unbridled diversity is to open the door to discussion with other Christian bodies who do not place the boundaries between "essential" and "nonessential" exactly where we do. In both cases, Packer commends "humility" to his readers: humility before the living God in worship, humility before other Christians as we acknowledge that there is a realm of human theological opinion, and humility before the real world as we hold on to the unequivocal revelation that *has* been given to us. To me these very points represent the "growing edges" of my own Communion as we yearn to see God in all his fullness (something that deepens as we worship) and as we struggle to understand the fullness of revelation while still welcoming the pneumatic liberty that God simultaneously bestows on the "holy, catholic, and apostolic Church." It is as we worship, cleaving to what we know to be God's unchanging truth and acknowledging in charity that there are some disputed matters among God's children, that we best allow the Spirit to draw us closer to the Father and closer to each other. The mind that is set on worship, humble with regard to what it can see is disputable and settled with regard to those things once given, is a promising starting point for a vulnerable and probing discussion with others who name Christ and who practice these same disciplines.

It is a cause of great lament that even among faithful, creedal, and searching Anglicans, there is great difficulty in even coming to a point of discussion about those issues that still divide us, things such as worship styles, sacramental realities, the nature of the church, and women in ministry. This is true also of the larger evangelical or creedal Christian community, which tends to—when meeting ecumenically—avoid these matters and speak only of our agreements. It seems incredible to me that we continue to sweep these divisions under the rug for fear that we will be swallowed up by internal discord and render ourselves unable to face the deeper and more dangerous issues of our institutional churches or of a hostile secular world. We are, in the words of the song, "by schisms rent asunder, by heresies distressed," and fear that the world outside will look on us in "scornful wonder" if we dare to admit that we are not united on every point.[10] This, it seems to me, is faithless. Indeed, an admission of our failures as well as our strengths may in itself speak volumes to a world that knows little of Christ's humility. Let us remember that even the Gospels do not whitewash the sins of the apostles nor the tensions of the early church; moreover, the first step to health is to admit where there is illness. Here the wisdom of Packer indicates to us a way forward. Things seem bleak at this point for many of the bodies of which we are a part: but if, with cool heads, we admit our disputes while standing firmly on the foundations that are indisputable, we will patiently brave the theological and social cyclones that assault us. And who knows what God, in the end, will do. Realism and humility are spectacles by which we can, in Packer's words, "see what God will do," as we "work and wait together."[11]

So far we have considered the bracing gift of a cool head, given to the church by God, and freely offered by Packer himself, in his characteristic unassuming manner. Sobriety, realism, and faithfulness are the watchwords here. There is great value in what the ancient theologians called the *neptic* ("watchful") approach that eschews the fashions of the day, joined with a realism that balances an appreciation of the current situation with a faithfulness to what has been delivered to God's people, and governed by a concentration on the One who has called and will continue to guide us. God's people find here a healthful model: the careful articulation of God's revealed Word, open eyes to the present and perennial dangers that we face, and the cultivation of a steadfast hope for the future. In all the vicissitudes and debates, the Reformed emphasis on God's sovereignty serves as a constant assurance that it is not those who are departing from the faith, or attacking it, who are in control of the situation, but rather God himself.

The "Warm Heart"

We move on from a consideration of J. I. Packer's "cool head" to "the warm heart." By its very title, Packer's best known book, *Knowing God*, sets out the importance of "heart religion." It is not titled *Knowing about God* or *Understanding Christianity* but *Knowing God*. As such, Packer answers to the same yearning that is addressed by many of the spiritual pundits of our day, including Marcus Borg, whose *Meeting Jesus for the First Time* has made such an unfortunate impact on mainline Christianity—I say unfortunate because such approaches insinuate that creedal Christianity cannot warm the heart and that a doctrinal emphasis is deadening. In contrast, Packer's book, written years before the contemporary fetish with individual experience, signaled to the Western world that our God is personal and our faith is therefore person-centered. To place the Triune God at the foundation of all that we are, all that we believe, and all that we do, though once in the thinking of the church a commonplace, has now become a corrective to the deformed or skewed depictions of Christianity so characteristic of our day.

Seen through the eyes of one who yearns to know more and more of the One who makes all knowing possible, doctrine may be transformed into prayer. The Eastern Christian adage, "a theologian is one who prays, and one who prays truly is a theologian," ceases to be a surprising statement when we consider the experience of those who have read Packer's works. John Stott, for example, speaks of the "frustration" that he encountered in trying to read *Knowing God*—because he was continually moved to prayer and had to stop frequently throughout the reading. I am indebted to a particular insight of this book, which made its impact on me in a practical way that I had not expected. As a young mother, I was interrupted during the singing of a particularly emotive contemporary song in our evangelical Anglican Church: "You've broken chains that bound me, you've set this captive free, I will lift my voice unto your throne for all eternity, And, I worship you! I give my life to you! I fall down on my knees!"[12] My five-year-old was evidently struck by the fervency and expressive praise around her, and she tugged on my sleeve. Imagine my surprise (and concern!) when she said, on the verge of tears, "Mom, I don't know if I love God." Perhaps some will think that I lost an evangelistic opportunity at that moment, but I did not sense that my daughter was requiring that I outline to her the plan of salvation in a few easy steps. Indeed, I suspected that she was not asking a spiritual or theological question but was disturbed that she did not have the same emotional response as those around her to the song we were singing. In a flash, I knew what to say to those pleading eyes: "Alexandra, don't worry about that right now. Because what is more important is that God knows and loves *you*!"

My reply, I am quite certain now though I did not remember its source at the time, came directly from Packer's book, which I had read at least fifteen years previously during my late teens:

> What matters supremely therefore is not, in the final analysis, the fact that I know God, but the larger fact that underlies it—the fact that *he* knows me. I am graven on the palm of his hands. I am never out of his mind. All my knowledge of him depends upon his sustained initiative in knowing me. . . . He knows me as a friend, as one who loves me.[13]

Of course, the twinned concepts of God's initiative and love are not novelties. But it is the ease with which Packer weaves careful theological insight with commonsense and scriptural allusion that lends the words their wings. This particular insight is laced with potent phrases ingested from the bread of life, delivered without pomp or ceremony, and innocent of any attempt to manipulate the feelings of the reader.

In the end, it is at those moments when we display integration that others will be warmed in heart when we speak, live, and act. Without a coherent center, or *heart* where all is brought together, our words and actions fall flat and our lives cease to be the God-bearing icons that the Holy Spirit yearns to make of us. A transparency is afforded our words, however, when they come from the center that God is forging in us. It is there that they are joined with all the other words that God has spoken to us and in us and through us, and it is because of a growing integrity of our person, the new creation of the Holy Spirit, that we can admit to those enigmas or mysteries not yet illumined for us.

Moreover, our healing does not take place in isolation, but in communion with brothers and sisters. So it is that a luminous word spoken is frequently informed by the life and the characteristic phrases of others—especially those phrases familiar to us from the context of common worship. There are many examples of such practiced verbal and conceptual communion in the teachings of Packer. We find an interesting example in an unlikely place—the corporate work entitled *Across the Divide*, authored by R. T. Beckwith, G. E. Duffield, and J. I. Packer as a response to "The Open Letter on Relations between Evangelical Churchmen and Roman Catholics, Orthodox and Old Catholics." In this work that comments on the fruit of this ecumenical discourse, and in commending the particular significance of justification, the warm heart of Packer is evident, alongside his characteristic concern for truth. He writes:

> It is easy to see—at least, it should be easy, though some have stumbled here—how repentance as a life-style, and works of love to God and men, will spring from faith spontaneously, as expressions of gratitude for grace received and of the joy that is felt at being "ransomed, healed, restored, forgiven"; but believers know better than to suppose any of these things meritorious, whatever well-meaning men and even theologians may say to the contrary. When Richard Baxter, the saintly and seraphic Puritan pastor, was on his deathbed, a sententious visitor told him: "Your works will follow you." "Not works," whispered the dying man; "not works."[14]

I suspect that this moving paragraph made its mark most naturally on those Anglicans among the pamphlet's ecumenical readership, since its climax is borrowed from the great hymn *Praise my soul, the King of Heaven*—"ransomed, healed, restored, forgiven, who like thee his praise should sing?" Here, Packer's natural language of worship comes to his aid: he works through the relationship of faith and fruit, making clear the objections that a conscientious evangelical Protestant would have regarding doctrines of merit through human effort; he also speaks exuberantly and with evocative family language regarding the "many-colored" wisdom of God, whose grace overflows so that the redeemed can display God's glory (cf. Eph. 3:10). In the course of his argument, Packer also refers to a well-known theologian of the Anglican Communion: even if Baxter is no household name, the seventeenth-century Puritan divine was beloved and continues to be beloved by many. Indeed, it is through Baxter that the Anglican Essentials movement in Canada adopted the English translation of that Christian motto found first conceptually in Augustine, and precisely in the Latin of Meldinius: "In necessary things, unity; in doubtful things, liberty; in all things, charity." The story told by Packer regarding Baxter's last moments reflects both Baxter's theological convictions and the humility and God-centeredness of many a great saint. Though the theological question on which it centers is decidedly Protestant (faith and *not* works), Baxter's dying words are surprisingly reminiscent of the ancient desert father St. Sisoes, a

the Reformation who naïvely imagine that they can leap directly from the Scripture to the present without showing much awareness that the Bible is the book of the church."[21]

Packer's own self-designation is that of "a catholic Christian protesting against what appear as uncatholic specifics."[22] Even those who will not agree in every particular as to what constitutes an "uncatholic specific" will be appreciative of Packer's candor and grace—a remarkable combination. So then, while I would most certainly find my own ecclesiology roundly critiqued in his discussion concerning the grounds proposed for intercommunion between Anglicans and Methodists in the 1960s, I find much of value there.[23] Specifically, his critique of the ambiguous and woolly use of language or of worship services of reconciliation to cover over significant theological differences is trenchant—it should be required reading for anyone engaging in ecumenical discussion. Packer has a fine way of noticing when "the camel has his nose in the tent," and if we heed his wisdom, we will learn to remove the camel before the beast supplants the occupants of the tent entirely.

In his dealings with Christians from other communions or ecclesial bodies, Packer is led by two competing, though sometimes complementary, concerns—his sense that our divisions are not God's first purpose for the church and his conviction that truth must not be obscured. So he considers the schismatic and divided nature of the twenty-first-century Christian community to be an abnormal situation and insists that "to regard emergency arrangements as the normal order of things is defective thinking."[24] In this sense, ecumenical discussion is not born simply of British gentility nor of Canadian niceness but of conviction that Christians should talk together and ideally live and worship together. At the same time, Packer commends the Protestant ideal of prophetic witness as something inherent to the faithful community and indeed essential to its health. Hence, he argues that "theological watchfulness . . . is itself part of the great tradition"![25]

His construal of the Great Tradition has been consistent throughout the years, including such themes as the primacy of the canonical Scriptures, the sovereignty of God, the importance of faith in Christ, the description of the church as a family of forgiven sinners indwelt by the Holy Spirit, his understanding of the church as a "supernatural" organism nourished by the two sacraments recognized in Protestantism, a stress on godly practice of the faith, a recognition of personal evil in the universe, and a clear articulation of the future hope of the Christian, which includes an expectation of the bodily return of Christ. More recently, he has also stressed the transcultural nature of the church and the deep desire that Christ's "High Priestly" prayer (John 17:11) for our unity will be realized in both theological and concrete terms.

I would like to add a postscript to this matter of Packer and the Great Tradition from the position of privilege that is afforded me as a woman in the twenty-first-century church. It would be easy to stay with the general themes that I outlined above, which are, in their basic outline, not so very controversial—or, if they are not agreed on by the whole Christian church, they are explicable by reference to Packer's theological context and formation. It would be easy not to mention that he has also, when it seemed necessary or advisable, tackled more knotty theological and social issues, including debates over the holiness movement, charismatic gifts, Calvinism versus Arminianism, substitutionary atonement, inerrancy, and the like. Here is no faint heart but a brother who is willing to wade into cold water and swim. More recently Packer has continued, despite the current climate, to question the wisdom, indeed, the validity of women's ordination. I am appalled that in the church we seem unable to hear his words on this subject without rancor. Here, as in the newfound liberty of some churches to offer an open table, there is a smugness and a hegemony among the "tolerant" that is hard for me to fathom. Do we forget that until recently Packer's position was the position of the whole church? Do those who censor him, either verbally or by a dismissive attitude, not realize that in doing so they also are casting a judgment against the historic church and against the continuing historic churches of Rome and Constantinople? No, our brother's courage in continuing to speak on this, despite the chilly response, should be applauded and embraced. We need this voice, as a community running pell-mell into all sorts of novelties without careful consideration. Whether in the end we will agree with Packer on this or not, we must listen and not suppress what he has to say. For we have much still to learn about the nature of male and female, about the nature of the priesthood or ordained ministry, about the full nature of the church. We are a people with short memories and pulled up roots, and Packer's voice on this very current debate reminds us that the church universal has not yet received this new thing. Packer's concern for this issue is consonant with his embrace of Scripture and his concern for truth. Though a hot-button issue, it is of a piece with the more central creedal matters that he constantly stresses.

Packer's continuous presentation of these themes and others interconnected with them, coupled with his determined refutation of substandard, heretical, and worldly presentations of the gospel, have served our current generation in ways that we can hardly imagine. Especially his combination of sobriety and imagination has stood the test of time, both exposing facile, consumer-driven, or feel-good construal of the faith and chastening those rigid, driven forms of Christianity that forget the grace of the living God and major in minors. Packer's many friends, his numerous brothers and sisters in Christ, will find in his spirited and sensible words and in his life much to emulate and to celebrate, even where they would demur, or speak otherwise on certain issues. I look forward myself to a frank and bracing discussion with my older brother concerning the relationship between Scripture and tradition, for I yearn for less of a minimalist approach to our faith and am not content to describe as "theologically non-significant"[26] longstanding catholic traditions that are not "biblically prescribed."[27] As a one-time Salvationist whose doctrine pleaded *sola scriptura* but whose practice did not include the sacraments, I have learned the hard way, and early, that we all read Scripture from within the context of tradition. As a longstanding member of the Essentials movement, I have come in the past few years to ask myself, "essential for what?"—bare escape from judgment, or do we look for full salvation, health, and life?

I suspect the answer to this question "essential for what" will lead me to recognize the wisdom of reading God's wonderful and vibrant written Word *within* the context of that living tradition passed down by centuries of Christians—both Eastern and Western. This I see not as a danger to enslavement but as a hopeful promise that we can learn about *all* the graces that God has given through Christ and by his Holy Spirit, without leaving some of these on the rubbish pile of history marked by the signs "papal" or "high-church" or "ascetic" or "murky mystery." For me, as for many of my generation, the big and pressing questions are those connected with ecclesiology. I am certain that the answers are not to be found in the ecumenical movements of the last century, with their compromising approach to dogmatics and liturgics. Rather, they are to be found in the robust discussion, clear thinking, fervency of heart, and charitable living displayed by our dear brother, to whom I would now sing, as a friend borrowing from the tradition of those Orthodox brothers and sisters whom Packer has also befriended: "God grant you many years!"

In recognition of his constant blending of true belief with true worship, in celebration of this *ortho-doxy*, may I request that we close with the Doxology, with which Packer so often introduced his classes at Regent College?

> Praise God from whom all blessings flow!
> Praise Him all creatures here below!
> Praise Him above, ye heavenly hosts!
> Praise Father, Son, and Holy Ghost!
>   Amen.[28]

3

Pumping Truth

J. I. Packer's Journalism, Theology, and the Thirst for Truth

DAVID NEFF

When Timothy George approached me about delivering a paper at this conference, I demurred, saying (as I often say) that I am not a scholar. But, he said, since he wanted me to talk about J. I. Packer as a journalist, he expected me to draw on my experience of working with Packer at *Christianity Today*.

That experience has been a joyously rewarding one over two decades, and so I happily write in a personal way about J. I. Packer and journalism.

Packer is not a journalist in the ordinary sense of the word. But much of his writing is for periodicals, and much of it is ad hoc, that is to say, keyed to the issues of a particular historical moment.

J. I. Packer's first article for *Christianity Today* appeared in 1958 in volume 2, no. 25. And it was journalistic—even reportorial and ad hoc. Most of Packer's journalistic efforts have not been reporting as such but theological responses to current trends or ideas, offering a theologically-based prescription for the ailments of our times. But his first article was indeed a report.

In the article, entitled "Fundamentalism: The British Scene," Packer recounted the retreat of British evangelicalism in the face of higher criticism and liberal theology, and the fond hope of those retreating evangelicals who had "withdraw[n] from the theological battlefield," that "liberalism must sooner or later discover its own inadequacy and burn out, after which there would surely be a return to the old paths."[1]

While liberalism had perhaps not *discovered* its own inadequacy, it had indeed *demonstrated* its inadequacy, and now Packer claimed was the time "to make a constructive re-entry into the field of theological debate." What made this possible was the strength of the Inter-Varsity Fellowship and other interdenominational youth movements as well as the influence in Britain of Billy Graham's evangelistic efforts.

But Packer is ever the clear-eyed realist. To call for theological reengagement is not the same as to achieve it. And he could not envision the reinvigoration of evangelical theology and the extending of its influence without addressing the weaknesses of late 1950s British evangelicalism.

"Two prevalent weaknesses" needed correction. Both he attributed to "flabby pietism." "The effect of this pietistic conditioning was to focus concern exclusively on the welfare of the individual soul, and to create indifference both to the state of the churches and to the ordering of society."

In the case of the first weakness (i.e., evangelical individualism), Packer blamed not only "flabby pietism," but also the way that "evangelicals regard interdenominational organizations as filling the center of the ecclesiastical stage." Thus, he concludes, "the reinvigorating of the local church as an aggressive witnessing community is strategic priority number one in the present British situation."

For the second weakness (i.e., "a sublime insensitiveness to the implications of the Gospel for social, political, economic, and cultural life, and shirking the responsibility of bearing a constructive Christian witness in these fields")— for this weakness he prescribed Puritanism. He means, of course, not those mores that are called "puritanical," but the "consuming concern for the glory of God in all things" that was characteristic of such great Puritan leaders as Baxter, Owen, and, on this continent, Edwards.

What I find remarkable about this first J. I. Packer article for *Christianity Today* is its combination of timeliness and timelessness. The weaknesses of evangelicalism in 1958 are its fundamental stress points today. The challenges facing a numerically stronger evangelicalism in 1958 are the challenges facing a numerically stronger evangelicalism today. Other observers might have seen flaws closer to the surface rather than fault lines that run deep. Others might have prescribed activity that had more flash or fashion. But Packer is a man who thinks about basics and calls attention back to basics, and thus his timely prescription for what has turned out to be a perennial pair of problems.

The kind of journalism practiced by J. I. Packer is an example of what those of us in the journalism business call "advocacy journalism." That is to say, while we hope to be fair to all the parties in a conflict, we nevertheless hope to advance a point of view and even, at times, a program.

Within the guild, advocacy journalism comes and goes from favor. The problems it faces are, first, maintaining credibility (because it doesn't pretend to be neutral) and, second, upholding high ethical standards (because the lack of neutrality carries with it temptations to shortchange the truth in the service of a noble cause). In today's highly polarized political atmosphere, the ethics of reporting are often subordinated to the achievement of ideological advantage. This need not be the case, but it is the constant temptation of journals and journalists that advocate a point of view.

Christianity Today advocates a point of view. J. I. Packer advocates a point of view. And both journal and journalist work to maintain balance and fairness while also offering clear-eyed criticism and arguments for solutions.

In her 2004 doctoral dissertation, Bethel College journalism teacher Phyllis Alsdurf examines the way the tension between ideology and journalistic values plays out in the history of *Christianity Today*.[2] The phrase *journalistic values* covers a wide variety of concerns. They range from how readable and engaging is the prose (here *journalistic* carries connotations the opposite of *academic* and *ivory tower*) to how careful writers and editors are to maintain accuracy, fairness, and balance. (Note that older ideals of empiricist objectivity have disappeared in journalism just as they have in historiography.) Alsdurf assesses how well journalistic values fared in their necessary tension with "ideology" (as she puts it) in the era of Carl Henry's editorship and the era of Harold Myra's presidency. In both eras, the magazine's leaders strongly testify to their commitment to journalistic values, but Alsdurf judges the Myra era magazine as having better embodied those values.

What does this have to do with J. I. Packer? An examination of Packer's contributions to *Christianity Today* in both eras demonstrates a keen sense of how to hold the "ideological" and the "journalistic" in creative tension. His prose is imaginative, engaging, readable, credible, realistic—and yet clearly devoted to the "ideology" the magazine was founded to promote.

We will look further at these characteristics of Packer's magazine contributions and illustrate them as well. But first, let us consider another aspect of Alsdurf's thesis and the role that Packer played and continues to play. Alsdurf asserts that it was the mission of *Christianity Today* (as articulated by its editors Carl Henry and Nelson Bell) to "construct" and "reconstruct" evangelicalism. In choosing this language of "construction," Alsdurf interacts with American church historian Darryl Hart who argues that evangelicalism lacks a certain reality because it is an artificial construct. Alsdurf tells us we do not need to agree with all of Hart's argument in order to recognize that the very real movement that came to be known as the New Evangelicalism had to be constructed and that *Christianity Today* was one of the primary agents of that construction. Graham, Ockenga, Bell, Henry, and their friends were engaged in an effort to create a sense of identity and a web of communication for a widely dispersed group of pastors and lay Christians. In a 1955 address to those he hoped would help him found and fund *Christianity Today*, Graham said, "We seem to be confused, bewildered, divided, and almost defeated in the face of the greatest opportunity and responsibility possibly in the history of the church."[3] It was the job of *Christianity Today* to help them realize that indeed there was an evangelical resurgence under way, that there were strategies to be considered, and that the classic Christian message could be propounded with intellectual strength. To be an evangelical was not to be an aimless dunderhead. It was to be part of a purposeful and well-thought-out movement.

As we can see from Packer's first *Christianity Today* article, he was contributing to that very act of construction by announcing new numerical strengths, clearheadedly analyzing weaknesses, and proposing a direction in which to move. He has not varied much from that basic pattern in the past nearly fifty years.

Now let us consider J. I. Packer's approach to journalism (broadly conceived). The first concern of journalists is truth. The fundamental goal of journalism is creating an informed citizenry. And an informed citizenry is an equipped citizenry, and that makes for a healthy community.

Telling the truth is a fundamental value for journalists: this means taking risks by holding a mirror up to a community of readers or revealing the truth about a corrupt mayor or providing information about the likely effects of a piece of legislation.

Citizens of God's kingdom need information in much the same way that citizens of Chicago or Birmingham need information. A journalist who desires to serve God's kingdom will thus take truth-telling risks in order to increase the health of the community.

Packer shares this journalistic value. In the mid-1980s, he was part of a new group of senior editors impaneled to advise the magazine's leadership. I was only an associate editor then and was not invited to those early meetings. But reports came back to the staff of a speech Packer delivered in one of those meetings in which he urged *Christianity Today* to "pump truth." It was, by all accounts, a stirring speech. And both Christianity Today International president Harold Myra and *Christianity Today* managing editor Harold Smith regularly invoked the slogan "pumping truth."

Truth in Packer's thinking is not merely about accuracy (though accuracy, both of intention and representation, is very important). Truth is about life and health and vitality, for both individuals and communities.

In a 1989 column titled "Hype and Human Humbug," Packer treats the subject of book endorsements (or blurbs), of which he has written many. He has been solicited for many more, and given the chance (as have others here present) to take a shortcut in endorsing a friend's book.

Packer has refused such shortcuts, despite the rationalization that such shortcuts are intended to "encourage the use of good Christian teaching material." But, he writes,

> Surely the means to any end has a moral quality of its own. Surely I am not respecting God's image in my neighbor if I conspire to bamboozle him. Surely

David Neff

51

Even when discussing terrorism and terrorists shortly after the events of September 11, 2001, Packer wants us to understand the other.

> We need to be clear [he writes] that terrorism, whether religiously, politically, or ideologically motivated, begins as a mindset—what the Bible calls a thought of the heart. In this case, alienated persons are driven by bitterness at real or fancied wrongs, by some form of racial or class hatred, and by utopian dreams of better things after the present order has been smashed. This is an explosive mix.
>
> Terrorists think of themselves as both victims and avenging angels. They act out their self-justifying heartsickness in a way that matches Cain killing Abel. They see themselves as clever heroes, outsmarting their inferiors by concealing their real purpose and by overthrowing things they say are contemptible. So their morale is high, and conscience does not trouble them. Gleeful triumphalism drives terrorists on; they are sure they cannot lose.[14]

Packer writes these things not to create sympathetic feelings for terrorists, but to steel us for the difficult times ahead. "This is what the anti-terrorism coalition is up against. It is only realistic to anticipate that ridding the world of terrorism will be a long job."[15] I suspect that Packer understood that better than George Bush did, and his clarity on this matter comes in the same way G. K. Chesterton's Father Brown's does—that is, from a keen understanding of the human heart, which begins with a regular examination of one's own heart. In his 1986 column, "A Bad Trip," Packer is most revealing of his own self-awareness.[16] The bad trip of the title was an airplane ride to England in which everything that could go wrong did go wrong. After outlining a Reformed understanding of the virtue of patience, he writes: "I had always taken it for granted that patience was something I was good at. (You always fancy yourself good at that of which you know the theory.) But look at what happened."

He then tells the tale of the bad trip, punctuated by references to these failings: self-pity and grumbling; resentment; cold contempt; cynical gloom; seething anger, which kept me awake all night; petty greed. Packer says he "flunked the course." Only a person with that level of insight and self-awareness can understand the motives of others, and when their motives are bad or irrational, remain charitable.

Once, in writing about his own experience of being criticized, he made this sage observation:

> There are good and bad ways of fulfilling the ministry of criticism among Christians. This ministry is important, for all we who seek truth and wisdom take up from time to time with wrong ideas and need correction. But discussion and debate ordinarily achieve more than gestures of denunciation. To think of sustained denunciation as the essence of faithful witness, and of the mindset that will not see any good in what is not totally good as a Christian virtue, is very wrong. Denouncing error has its place, but since it easily appears arrogant

and generates much unfruitful unhappiness, anyone who feels drawn to it should take a lot of advice before yielding to the urge.[17]

Those words came from a 1993 column entitled, "Packer the Picketed Pariah." What was he being picketed for? Essentially for regarding "Roman Catholics who love the Lord Jesus as real Christians." Packer is in no way soft on some of the distinctive Roman teachings and practices. But he has often been open to recognizing fellow Christians and the work of the Spirit wherever they are to be found. In his 1989 column reporting on the Lausanne II meeting in Manila, he not only noted the important events of the Lausanne Congress but also a parallel congress run by Filipino Pentecostals and a Roman Catholic "Bible rally attended by tens of thousands, featuring testimonies to conversion . . . and raising funds to buy Bibles for the destitute." His conclusion? "Surely the Holy Spirit . . . is busy in Manila."[18]

That was in 1989, but four years later, in the wake of his signing the initial statement from the group Evangelicals and Catholics Together (ECT), he had a lot of explaining to do and fences to mend. He explained privately and in public (see his 1994 apologia "Why I Signed It"[19]), and he mended fences by engaging in the writing of some distinctly Protestant evangelical manifestos. With Michael Horton, he drafted a clarifying document, "Resolutions for Roman Catholic and Evangelical Dialogue," and he later participated in the drafting of "The Gospel of Jesus Christ: An Evangelical Celebration."[20] I was privy to some of the drafting and present for some of the horse trading that went into that document, and I can say that the first half of the Celebration, with its positive and constructive tone, was initially drafted by John Woodbridge and was then heavily redrafted by Packer. The second half of the document, with its contrasting precisionist and anathematizing tone was largely the work of others whose friendship it was important to retain in order to avoid splitting the evangelical movement further over this issue.

There were multiple sources of pain in the events following from ECT, and I believe that comes from Packer's desire to see God at work—and yes, join God in his work—wherever God's Spirit sovereignly stirs people to health-giving activity. Unfortunately, that means building and maintaining connections with people who do not always appreciate the extent to which God may be working in and through those with whom they disagree. Packer's ability to see the praiseworthy and the blameworthy on all sides puts him in difficulty. But it is a gift that makes his journalism clearheaded and that ultimately makes for deeper understanding.

I have so far spoken of journalistic values such as truth, engaging communication, and fairness. I wish to raise one more journalistic value, that of context. In the case of J. I. Packer, that context is often historical. And most often, when Packer thinks of history, he thinks of Puritans. He has, of course, written extensively about the Puritans in nonjournalistic contexts, but he can't help writing about them when he writes for magazines as well. He has alluded to them in *Christianity Today* (citing Baxter's *The Saints' Everlasting Rest* when writing a column about heaven)[21] and also given them more extended attention (writing with Timothy Beougher an essay on the three-hundredth anniversary of Baxter's death).[22]

But Packer's historical resources are much broader than that, and so when evangelicals were engaged in the so-called Lordship Salvation controversy, he wrote a brief item about the mid-eighteenth-century Scot Robert Sandeman, whose intellectualist notion of saving faith "dampened evangelism."[23]

Similarly, after the attacks of September 11, 2001, Packer synthesized wisdom for wartime from the writings and experiences of Oswald Chambers and C. S. Lewis. He summarized eight points of convergence in their wartime insights and passed along the best of their words: "Human life has always been lived on the edge of a precipice" (Lewis); "If the war has made me reconcile myself with the fact that there is sin in human beings, I shall no longer go with my head in the clouds. . . . It is not being reconciled to the fact of sin that produces all the disasters in life" (Chambers); "Don't worry about being brave over merely possible evils in the future. . . . If and when a horror turns up you will then be given Grace to help you" (Lewis); "The remarkable thing about fearing God is that when you fear God you fear nothing else, whereas if you do not fear God you fear everything else" (Chambers).[24]

No person without a usable past has a real identity. Some of our historians have helped us recover useful elements of the Christian past. I think of the late Timothy Smith, who helped us relive in our imaginations a time when Christian holiness meant not only keeping oneself unstained by the world but also serving the most abject of the world's unfortunates. I think of Mike Gorman's wonderful little study on *Abortion and the Early Church*, which helped us Protestants realize that abortion was not merely a Roman issue but was there at the earliest Christian thinking about good and evil. And I think about J. I. Packer, who helped us realize that Puritans like Owen and Baxter were as committed or more so to holy living as any Keswick teacher. These thinkers help us understand ourselves as part of something larger and longer than our era of entrepreneurial innovation and parachurch activism.

Let me conclude by briefly summarizing what journalists call the "take-away value" of an article. What is the "take-away value" of this essay about J. I. Packer as a journalist? What does he model that should be taken to heart by church and parachurch leaders who, like Packer, wish to promote biblical truth and build up the body of Christ?

Quickly then, a few propositions:

• We must be "pumping truth." Truth is health-giving, and it should be the main drug in our pharmacopoeia, as well as the main course on our menu.

- Truth must be tempered, however, by wisdom and charity. Remember his words about the ministry of Christian criticism? "To think of sustained denunciation as the essence of faithful witness, and of the mindset that will not see any good in what is not totally good as a Christian virtue, is very wrong."
- Truth must also be communicated with imagination and impact. If God's Word is a gleaming, two-edged blade, why should our communication dull its edge? Truth must be a fire alarm to the sleeping soul and the savory aroma of a boeuf bourguignon to a hungry spirit.
- Bridge-building is better than bomb throwing.
- We must appreciate the good in those with whom we disagree, and understand the motives of those whose deeds are evil.
- We must remember the evil in our own hearts.
- We must know our place in history. That means, first, remembering the struggles and achievements of those who have gone before in order to avoid reinventing what doesn't need invention, and to appropriate the wisdom and emulate the courage that allowed them to meet their challenges so that we can meet the challenges that God in his providence has set before us.

An evangelicalism that would take those ideas to heart would be less easily seduced by the present age, more faithful to the gospel, less given to endless innovation, more humble in its "ministry of criticism," and better anchored, able to ride out "every wind of doctrine."

The admonition to know our place in history invites us to ask about J. I. Packer's place in history. He himself has done so, though it was fifteen years ago that he wrote about it in *Christianity Today*.[25] A friend asked him the awkward question, "How would you like to be remembered?"

One thing Packer was clear on is this: he wants to be remembered for calling into question the personality cult among evangelicals. No matter how worthy the personality, evangelicals have a tendency to say, "So-and-so says it; I believe it; that settles it."

"This," says Packer, "is a lapse from the Protestant appeal to Scripture into a more-than-papal traditionalism." He hopes instead to be remembered as a "voice . . . encouraging people to think, rather than as a personality whose felt status and charisma stopped them thinking."

He was clear on another thing: he wants to be remembered for calling into question evangelicalism's short memory. "What I live on is what I have learned from yesterday's giants," he said. Then he listed some giants: Augustine, Bernard, Luther, Calvin, the Puritans, Whitefield, Wesley, Edwards, Spurgeon, Ryle.

Perhaps these two things are also his most important contributions as a journalist: to teach people to think rather than merely to follow the call of our charismatic personalities and to expand our memory and put our history to use as we meet the challenges of the hour.

4

J. I. Packer's Theological Method

Donald J. Payne

J. I. Packer has been among the most influential English-speaking theologians in shaping the character of late-twentieth-century North American evangelical thought.[1] In a Festschrift to Packer, David F. Wright commends him as "one of the most powerful theologians of the twentieth century."[2] Roger Steer describes Packer as "one of the most influential Anglican Evangelicals of the twentieth century," noting that "by 1997 Packer's books had sold almost three million copies worldwide."[3] The context of North American evangelicalism has provided a fertile opportunity for his Reformed theological perspectives to wield influence across a spectrum of denominations.

The scope and nature of his influence can only be fully appreciated, however, by examining both his overt theological emphases and the undercurrents of his theology. That is, *how* does Packer do theology? What is his method? The recent proliferation of studies in theological method suggests a growing awareness that belief systems are intertwined with the methodologies that produce and uphold them. Questions of theological method may seem irrelevant to those who assume that appropriate attention to literary genre and grammatical, historical, and contextual canons of interpretation constitute all the method one needs in order to adequately and accurately understand Scripture.

Nevertheless, attention to method has uncovered the significance of even more basic, if unnoticed, factors in the process of interpreting Scripture and in the nature of the theological task. This range of factors includes the organizational paradigms for our theological systems and why we construct our paradigms as we do, how various doctrines relate to other doctrines in our systems and which ones have controlling influence over others, and the epistemological assumptions that shape what we mean by "knowing God" (to admiringly borrow Packer's words). This chapter attempts only a modest overview of Packer's theological method, propelled by a deep appreciation for his thought (including both affirmation and critique) and with the desire to benefit even more richly from his work by understanding in some small measure why his theology works as it does.

In his own definition of theological method, Packer refers to the procedures by which theology is done and the justification for those procedures.[4] He observes two general types of theological method. The first gives priority to the text of the Bible as "the revealed Word of God" that provides authoritative guidance as that text is progressively understood through research and the illumination of the Holy Spirit.[5] The second type prioritizes "the historical institutional church" as the guide for "infallibly identifying and interpreting the Scriptures."[6]

These alternatives differ, according to Packer, primarily with respect to the locus of interpretive responsibility and capability. From this basic distinction emerge other distinctions such as differing views on the nature of biblical authority and the focus of the Holy Spirit's ministry. Packer unashamedly advocates and utilizes the first of these approaches. Thus, his theological method is marked first and foremost by an unwavering commitment to biblical inerrancy and authority.

Packer's commitments regarding the nature and role of Scripture are, however, only starting points. Consideration of his theological method must begin with his evolving attitude toward the discipline of hermeneutics. Alister McGrath records Packer's early ambivalence toward the field of hermeneutics, prompted largely by Anthony Thiselton's address to the National Evangelical Anglican Congress at Nottingham in 1977. Packer left the congress disappointed that it had not attempted to generate relevant biblical answers to contemporary questions. Rather, in his opinion, it opened further questions.[7] McGrath observes, "Packer never discounted the importance of hermeneutical questions; however, he felt that the approach adopted by Thiselton risked generating a relativistic mindset, which could pervade every aspect of theology."[8]

Since that time Packer has authored numerous monographs on hermeneutics that reflect a broadened, if selective, appreciation for various contributions made by Hans-Georg Gadamer,[9] Anthony Thiselton, and a host of thinkers outside evangelicalism.[10] His later writings give evidence that he has grown to value the challenges and the necessity of hermeneutics, offering critical analysis on a wide range of theological questions.[11]

Those who have influenced Packer's theological method are the same people he credits for influencing the broader strokes of his theology. Commenting on purpose of God's revelation by making that coherence evident. In a personal reflection on his theological work, Packer states,

> I am first and foremost a theological exegete. My constant purpose was and is to adumbrate on every subject I handle a genuinely canonical interpretation of Scripture—a view that in its coherence embraces and expresses the thrust of all the biblical passage and units of thought that bear on my theme—a total, integrated view built out of biblical material in such a way that, if the writers of the various books knew what I had made of what they taught, they would nod their heads and say that I had got them right.[41]

Canonical interpretation, like the covenantal framework, speaks to the internal coherence of the biblical writings. More specifically, it involves developing the implications of Scripture in a manner that is congruent with the author's original intent.

The Christological Focus of the Bible

The internal coherence of Scripture, on which Packer's theological method depends, is reflected in his commitments to the inerrancy, covenantal framework, and canonical character of Scripture. Each of these features, for Packer, culminates in Jesus Christ, who is the innermost principle of Scripture's internal coherence.[42] Christology sustains the commitment to inerrancy in three ways for him. First, it demonstrates the credibility of belief in inerrancy. Second, it demonstrates the essential relationship between inerrancy and authority. Third, it provides an essential hermeneutical criterion.

Packer defends the notion of an inerrant written Scripture on the basis of the affirmation that Jesus was both fully divine and fully (though sinlessly) human. Jesus's moral perfection is sustained by the dominance or definitive role of his divinity in the relationship between his divine and human natures. Likewise, Packer argues for the perfection (inerrancy) of the biblical text because its divine origin defines the nature of its divine/human character.[43] Inerrancy and authority, while deriving ultimately from the mind of God, are expressed in and validated by the divine/human nature of Jesus Christ. Jesus Christ not only constitutes the plausibility of inerrancy but also the content of inerrancy. He is the supreme expression of God's verbal or propositional revelation. Jesus's teachings constitute the ultimate form of God's self-revelation.

Thus Packer understands the revelatory function of the incarnation in a primarily linguistic and rationalistic manner. The incarnation directs Packer's attention back to the technical precision and rational accessibility of the scriptural text for epistemological access to God's revelation. But Packer clearly emphasizes Jesus Christ as the focal point and interpretive criterion for Scripture. He observes, "The person and place of the Christ of space-time history is the interpretative key to all Scripture; the Old Testament is to be read in the light of its New Testament fulfillment in and by him, just as the New Testament is to be read in the light of its Old Testament foundations on which that fulfillment rested."[44] The salient feature of Packer's methodology at this point is that the validity and epistemological reliability of Jesus Christ presupposes an inerrant Bible.

Christology also influences Packer's thought about the task of identifying the contemporary and personal implications or applications of Scripture. The legitimacy of application depends on the incarnation as the bridge between the universal and the particular.[45] The function of Christology in application is dramatically reflected in Packer's view of preaching, where he insists that the preacher "never let his exposition of anything in Scripture get detached from, and so appear unrelated to, Calvary's cross and the redemption that was wrought there."[46] This specific angle of focus on redemption constitutes Packer's way of presenting Jesus Christ as the comprehensive criterion for both interpreting and applying Scripture.

A christological approach to Scripture has similar hermeneutical effects as a canonical approach to Scripture. But when Packer equates a canonical approach with the theological task itself he refers more broadly to "theism" as the framework for theology, thus appearing vague about the specific way in which Christology would define a theistic framework for theology. Stephen Neill draws attention to this subtle but significant distinction when he observes that in *Knowing God* Packer is not sufficiently "Christo-centric in his approach." He goes on to say, "To be fair to Dr. Packer, Jesus Christ always does come in somewhere in his presentation of each theme, but sometimes at the end of an argument, where we would bring him in at the beginning."[47] This feature raises a question concerning whether Packer's theological method is thoroughly as christological as he claims.[48]

At this point Packer reflects an intriguing combination of values in his theological method. On the one hand, he emphasizes that Scripture has not accomplished its purpose nor can the truth of God be known until it is has been obeyed. On the other, his stated hermeneutical methodology makes it appear that the meaning of Scripture can, in practice, be discerned apart from obedience to that text. This division between meaning and response is possible because he operates with a predominantly descriptive understanding of the nature of language.[49] This limitation on the way Christology actually functions in his hermeneutic results from the particular manner in which he distinguishes the acts of interpretation and application in hermeneutics.[50]

Interpretation, Application, and the Role of the Holy Spirit

One highly salient feature of Packer's approach to hermeneutics is his assumption that the original, intended meaning of the scriptural text (authorial intent) is at least theoretically ascertainable through an abstract or objective process of exegesis that precedes contemporary, personal response to (application of) the text. He describes this methodology as moving sequentially from exegesis to synthesis to application.[51]

In the starting point of this process, Packer makes the possibility of application contingent on the prior work of discerning the essential meaning of the text, though he is clear that the work of interpretation is not complete apart from application.[52] He commends Gadamer's two-horizons approach, in which the situation of the original text and the situation of the interpreter inform each other as the twin foci of an elliptical process.[53]

Interestingly, Packer considers his approach to be an integrated view of biblical hermeneutics, insisting that "understanding is never abstract and theoretical; it is always understanding of the work and will of the living God who constantly demands to change us."[54] This integrated process is depicted as a hermeneutical spiral in which the activities of exegesis, synthesis, and application produce a theology that, in turn, determines the integrity of those activities.[55]

Nevertheless, he states, "the first task is always to get into the writer's mind by grammatico-historical exegesis of the most thoroughgoing and disciplined kind, using all the tools provided by linguistic, historical, logical, and semantic study for the purpose."[56] Yet he differentiates between the approaches needed for the interpreter to discern what the text *meant* and what it *means*. The latter requires the Holy Spirit's enlightenment.[57]

In this hermeneutical paradigm the overall hermeneutical act is incomplete without personal application of the text. But by dividing the process into two parts—one that depends on the unassisted rational process and the other that depends on the Holy Spirit's illumination—Packer appears to introduce into hermeneutics a distinction that makes the full apprehension of the Word of God less than fully dependent on God.

Scriptural revelation, for Packer, functions primarily in a descriptive rather than performative capacity. The performative character comes from the work of the Holy Spirit through the written Word of God.[58] This methodological cleavage between the original meaning of God's Word and the contemporary power of God's Word seems to indicate a dilemma in which the text's original meaning is somewhat less than direct, timeless self-revelation from God until it passes through the second stage of the process (i.e., application).

Packer begins the hermeneutical spiral with the static, crystallized meaning of the text in the mind of the original author. The meaning inherent in the text may or may not be fully grasped by any particular interpreter, but the assumption of its existence and accessibility to the canons of reason undergirds the application step. Though he insists that these aspects of the hermeneutical process must go together, an innate tension exists in his classification of the exegetical process as a merely rational exercise and his assignment of the

Holy Spirit's work to the applicational aspect. He points to the *"clarity* and *perspicuity* of the entire collection [the canon], as a body of intrinsically intelligible writings that demonstrably belong together and constantly illuminate each other."[59] But he does not link this "intrinsic intelligibility" to any direct involvement of the Holy Spirit in the act of interpretation. He states, "It is in application specifically that we need divine help. Bible commentaries, Bible classes, Bible lectures and courses, plus the church's regular expository ministry, can give us fair certainty as to what Scripture meant . . . but only through the Spirit's illumination shall we be able to see how the teaching applies to our own situation."[60] His tendency to emphasize the Spirit's role in the applicational phase of hermeneutics gives the impression that the Spirit's role is not necessary (or at least *as* necessary) prior to that phase.

Indeed, this focus on personal response as innate to the Word of God avoids the deadening risk of a historically encrusted Word that fails to speak contemporaneously. But by suggesting that the task of application is discrete from and subsequent to the task of exegesis, he seems to permit the preliminary interpretive tasks to be undertaken in abstraction from the God whose Word is being interpreted.

The experiential character of application is the object of Packer's greatest suspicion. On one hand, his "spiral" allows the hermeneutical process to be theoretically self-correcting. On the other hand, his caveats about the subjectivity of experience undermine the formative influence that application or experience could have in exegetical interpretation. Inasmuch as he sees the Spirit's role most dominant in this experiential aspect of hermeneutics, it may be questioned whether he indeed acknowledges the Spirit's role in hermeneutics as much as he desires or thinks that he does.

The subject of the Holy Spirit's role in hermeneutics provides an important case study for examining the *functional* orientation of Packer's theological method; the extent to which it is theocentric or anthropocentric. He contends that the Spirit certainly validates the divine origin and authority of Scripture in the believer's experience. Moreover, the Spirit guides the submissive believer to the meaning/application of the text that is consistent with God's will. In these claims Packer attempts to avoid the danger of a rationalism that makes the meaning of the text accessible apart from the God of the text. Yet his separation of the hermeneutical process into phases of which the Spirit's role is more prominent in application than in exegesis suggests strains of a tacit, anthropocentric rationalism.

The Nature of Theology

Theology, for Packer, must be propelled and guided by pastoral intentions. He states, "It is vital to realize that truth is for people, and therefore, the pastoral function of theology is ultimately primary."[61] Theology is the premier expression and means of the applicational intent and pietistic trajectory of Scripture. It is an activity as much as a deposit. "The supreme skill," Packer claims, "in the art and craft of theology is to link the theoretical and cognitive aspects of God's revealed truth with its practical and transformative aspects in an unbreakable bond."[62] The pastoral and pietistic intentions of Scripture and theology can be summarized, he claims, in the biblical notion of wisdom.[63]

On a general level, Packer suggests "five principles that should guide our practice of theology in the twenty-first century."[64] The first principle is to "maintain the trajectories," that is, keep the pietistic concerns of godliness at the center of focus. Second, he recommends resisting the tendency of specialization to fragment the work of theology and thus create unbalanced spirituality. Third, theology must remain anchored in the Bible as God's divine Word. Fourth, it must stay in dialogue with the culture for the sake of meaningful, persuasive encounter. Finally, he encourages continual dialogue with nonevangelical traditions in order to learn from all who claim to belong to Jesus Christ.[65]

The specific work of theology is related to the work of hermeneutics for Packer. He uses the analogy of a rising spiral to describe theology just as he described hermeneutics.[66] Theology and hermeneutics are related, though not identical, and function in much the same manner by utilizing a mutually informing dialectic. Theology and hermeneutics are distinct, however, in that theology encompasses the work of hermeneutics, extending the fruit of hermeneutics into the comprehensive mission of the church.

Packer identifies and distinguishes ten disciplines within the overall scope of theology: exegesis, biblical theology, historical theology, systematic theology, apologetics, ethics, missiology, spirituality, liturgy, and practical theology.[67] Systematic theology constitutes the functional core of this sequence, building on the work that precedes it, then extending and determining the work of what follows. Though Packer depicts both the hermeneutical process and theology as rising spirals, he also speaks of theology as functioning in a linear fashion, much like a prism for the other disciplines before and after it on this continuum. It is, he describes, "a stockpiling discipline that gathers and combines all the resources of knowledge about God. The six following disciplines draw upon it, interact with and put to work its findings."[68]

Overall, Packer's theological method reflects his anthropological assumptions about the fundamentally rational nature shared by God and humanity. Though he describes the heart of the *imago Dei* as relational righteousness, both relationship and righteousness are dependent on rationality.[69] He portrays this dependency when he states that "theology pursues revealed truth about the Creator in order to know him relationally in a life of worship and obedience, thus using truth for his glory and for the correcting and directing of our thoughts and ways in his service."[70] Relationship and righteousness (the essence of the *imago Dei*), then, depend on rationality through the act of theology.

Interestingly, Packer seeks to avoid an anthropocentric orientation to the Bible by appealing to its "God-centeredness" that theology is intended to safeguard.[71] Theology protects the theocentrism of the Bible by preserving the message of God's rational, propositional self-revelation.[72] But it is not clear in Packer's theological method *how* theology does this when it depends on an exegetical process that assumes a rather unaided rational process. He presents Christ as the lens and the ultimate object of focus for all biblical revelation but stops short of showing how this works, especially in his own exegesis. The method he actually demonstrates could easily lead to the very anthropocentrism he strives to avoid.

A theological method driven by the anthropological assumption of a rational self as the ontological commonality between God and humanity leads, furthermore, to the notion that theology is reliable because it is static in nature. Theology is a repository of truth about God that never changes (though human comprehension of that truth may grow) because God never changes. Theology, then, is a process for identifying, collecting, and organizing the various aspects of that truth in the manner that most accurately reflects the nature of the truth. Packer affirms Thomas Oden's return from liberalism to historic orthodoxy, extolling the virtue of those who stay "at home" and build defenses against assaults by honoring the time-tested perspectives of historical theology. This he calls the "evangelical method."[73] He compares his theological vocation to that of a "sewage man" whose "goal in dogmatics is to find pure streams and to strain out sewage."[74] This image connotes a discomfort with all interpretations of biblical phenomena that do not immediately display the inner harmony of biblical revelation.

Packer's view of theology as a static repository of divine truth is reflected in his treatment of theological paradox. He defines paradox as "the unexpected and seemingly irrational or impossible."[75] He acknowledges the existence of verbal and logical paradoxes but expresses the greatest interest in what he calls "ontological paradox," which "is the seeming incompatibility of statements describing reality, or inferences drawn from those statements."[76]

Commending "neo-orthodox" theologians for dealing with paradox in a manner that recognizes the immeasurable distance between Creator and creature, he nevertheless finds fault with their approach for their "unwillingness to be bound by the consistent rationality of Scripture."[77]

Packer's portrayal of theology as static does not, however, imply a complete ontological correspondence between theology and the truth that it signifies. In order to describe the distinction, he draws on Aquinas's doctrine of analogy.[78] The integrity of this theological model is determined directly (even if

tion will endure the passing of time because Packer has rightly understood that the key to sound, enduring theology and thus to Christian obedience is a proper commitment to the Bible as God's written Word. This insistence on the Bible as the irreplaceable source for all adult catechesis in academic and church settings is arguably Packer's most important legacy to the future of evangelicalism. Without this emphasis Packer's catechesis makes little sense and will have little continuing impact, and the same is also true for evangelicalism.

This essay explores Packer's biblically insistent legacy by surveying his contributions to the doctrine of Scripture. To do so, it divides his adult life and his writing on the Bible into four parts. Each stage testifies to Packer's conviction that God has spoken and people need to hear and obey. The first part includes 1944 through 1954,[8] years in which Packer converted to Christianity, discovered the Puritans, began to contribute to scholarly meetings, and received his university degrees. In this era Packer recognized the importance of the internal witness of the Holy Spirit in the doctrine of Scripture and the importance of having models for interpreting Scripture. The second part spans 1954 through 1976, or the years between Packer's first major article on the Bible and the beginning of the International Council on Biblical Inerrancy. In these years Packer underscored the fundamental importance of the phrase "God has spoken" for a correct understanding and use of the doctrine of Scripture. The third part, 1977 though 1996, encompasses the beginning of that council to the publication of his most recent book on the Bible. Those years found Packer exploring biblical hermeneutics in keeping with his views on the nature of Scripture, which for him meant determining how best to pursue canonical (whole Bible) interpretation. The final stage includes 1997 though 2006, years in which Packer translated the Bible and contended for its centrality for church unity. Of course there is much overlap in these years and these categories, especially between the first three eras and the last. As will be argued below, Packer has maintained a very consistent approach to his catechetical ministry. Thus all divisions of his work are more for convenience than to demonstrate seismic changes.

God Has Spoken through the Holy Spirit's Internal Witness (1944–54)

Packer became a Christian as an Oxford undergraduate in 1944 through the ministry of evangelical Christians. He adopted a high view of Scripture almost from the outset of his Christian life, chiefly because of what he later described as the internal witness of the Holy Spirit. This appreciation for the Holy Spirit's role in confirming confidence in the Bible and in prompting Christian obedience has been a staple of his writing since that time. Concerning his early experiences he writes,

Having been brought to faith in Jesus Christ out of empty religious formalism, I began devouring Scripture devotionally. When I had read it before, it had seemed uninteresting, but now it glowed and spoke. At the close of a Bible exposition forty-one days after my conversion, I found myself certain, quite suddenly, that the Bible was not, as I had previously thought, a mixture of history, legend and opinion, requiring selective treatment as other human miscellanies do. I knew now that it was in its own nature a divine production as well as a channel of divine communication, triggering insight and praise.[9]

He adds, "Years later, when I found Calvin saying that through the Holy Spirit every Christian experiences Scripture speaking authoritatively as from God, I rejoiced to think that, without any prior human instruction and certainly without any prior acquaintance with Calvin, I had long known that experience."[10]

He concludes this autobiographical account by asserting, "The truth is that one element of the universal Christian experience into which the Bible leads is precisely the experience of the Bible challenging our thought and will with God's authority, and of our own inward inability to deny its divinity as it does so. That experience, by grace, has been mine throughout my Christian life—and is so still."[11] This personal testimony is important because it indicates that Packer's entire ministry has been based on acceptance of the truthfulness and usefulness of the Bible. His subsequent academic and ecclesiastical work has been a matter of "faith seeking understanding," and the Bible has been at the core of that faith-induced search.

Packer read classics during his undergraduate years (1944–48), a choice that allowed him to develop excellent proficiency in Greek, Latin, ancient philosophy, and ancient history.[12] It is hard to calculate how important this experience was to Packer's interpretative methodology and his appreciation for original language exegesis, for these studies required him to learn to translate, place in historical context, and determine the philosophical background of many ancient texts. His facility in Greek and Latin also led to his first academic job, a one-year post teaching those languages at Oak Hill College in London during the 1948–49 school year.[13] Greek stayed with Packer, for he could still virtually sight-read the Greek New Testament over fifty years later during translation committee meetings.

During his undergraduate years Packer also discovered Puritan writers. These authors provided him with a model for biblical interpretation leading to spiritual growth he found more helpful than the Keswick spirituality prominent among the people who led him to faith in Christ.[14] This Puritan model included close inspection of personal and congregational spiritual health through the lenses of Scripture. As Packer later wrote,

For Puritanism was, above all else, a Bible movement. To the Puritan the Bible was in truth the most precious possession that this world affords. His deepest conviction was that reverence for God means reverence for Scripture, and serving God means obeying Scripture. To his mind, therefore, no greater insult could be offered to the Creator than to neglect his written word; and, conversely, there could be no truer act of homage to him than to prize it and pore over it, and then to live out and give out its teaching. Intense veneration for Scripture, as the living word of the living God, and a devoted concern to know and do all that it prescribes, was Puritanism's hallmark.[15]

His appreciation for the Puritans grew as he continued his academic preparation. As was stated above, he chose Richard Baxter (1615–91) as the subject of his doctoral research, which he pursued from 1950 to 1952. The degree was conferred in 1954 while Packer was completing his curacy as part of his preparation for Anglican ordination.[16] Furthermore, he helped found the Puritan Studies Conference, a group that first met in 1950. Over the next two decades these conferences became a major resource for the rediscovery of the Puritans.[17] Clearly, Packer hoped that others would find the same sort of biblical/experiential help he had encountered as they read the Puritans. His pastoral and scholarly concerns had already begun to mesh.

By the time he began his teaching career Packer was convinced that he came to Christ because God has spoken in Scripture and confirmed that fact by speaking to him through the Holy Spirit. This internal witness of the Holy Spirit assured him that God's Word could be trusted and that God's Word shaped believers. He had embarked on a pursuit of how one's faith leads one to greater understanding, and he had found historical precursors to his own search. The fact that the Holy Spirit confirmed his faith also helped him understand that all that one can understand about the Bible begins and ends with the grace of God.

God Has Spoken though His Written Word (1954–76)

The decade of Packer's academic and ministry preparation coincided with British evangelicalism's early efforts at buttressing its intellectual foundations in a context in which liberalism and liberal evangelicalism were the predominant theological viewpoints.[18] Through the auspices of Inter-Varsity Christian Fellowship, the Biblical Research Committee (which later became Tyndale Fellowship) had been formed in 1938 "to nurture evangelical scholars and foster evangelical biblical scholarship."[19] One of the committee's goals was to publish books that would express evangelical theology in a scholarly fashion and thus wed evangelical piety to sound thinking. Among the first efforts in this direction was *The New Bible Commentary*, which first appeared in 1953. The response to this volume was so positive that a second edition was released in 1954, and Packer wrote the article "Revelation and Inspiration" for this edition.[20]

In this article Packer offers a tightly argued analysis of revelation and inspiration and its implications for Christian life. At least five major principles emerge that appear repeatedly in his subsequent work. First, a proper understanding of inspiration flows from a solid grasp of revelation.[21] Second, theology is a unitary discipline, so the entire Bible must be considered as a whole through unitary exegesis when addressing revelation and inspiration.[22] Third, whole Bible exegesis that includes historical-grammatical exegetical scrutiny of individual passages and whole cloth synthesis of all passages indicates that the Bible's authors assert that God's character guarantees the Bible's complete truthfulness and comprehensive usefulness. Read on its own terms the Bible offers a clear, unified, and pure revelation of God and his redemptive work.[23] Fourth, "inspiration" means "breathed out by God" (2 Tim. 3:16), so the nature of God as revealed in the entirety of the Bible determines the type of "inspiration" the Bible exhibits. Fifth, one's view of the Bible is crucial for one's Christian growth and maturity.[24]

The first point indicates Packer's commitment to sound traditional theological method; the second point reveals his primary hermeneutical convictions; the third and fourth points set forth his most essential theological conclusions on the subject; and the fifth point presents the core conviction that guides his spiritual theology. In 1954 the last three assertions were more controversial than the first two. Thus, Packer spends the most space arguing that the "fundamental truth" about the Bible is that it is "a divine product, whose *auctor primarius* is God,"[25] that Jesus's teaching about the full authority, unity, and finality of the Bible (see John 10:35, 39; Matt. 5:17–20; 19:4–6) should settle the issue for his followers, that the apostles write with Jesus's authority,[26] that the Holy Spirit gives internal witness to the Bible's complete truthfulness and daily usefulness for believers,[27] and that those who do not affirm the Bible's full reliability and usefulness cut themselves off from the guidance God gives for the church. Indeed, such a person "either does not possess or has not understood the *testimonium Spiritus Sancti internum*."[28] This strong language evidences Packer's pastoral concern that God's Word shape God's people. At the same time, his careful analysis demonstrates that he believes it is important to give intellectual reasons why the faith he prescribes is not irrational. Faith seeks and finds understanding, but faith deserves priority.

Having spent the majority of the article's space on revelation, Packer moves to inspiration. Again he bases his claims in exegesis, though he recognizes that *inspiration* is not a biblical word. He writes that a good definition of *inspiration* is "a supernatural influence of God's Spirit upon the biblical authors which ensured that what they wrote was precisely what God intended them to write for the communication of His truth."[29] He believes this definition embodies what 2 Timothy 3:16 means when it claims Scripture is *theopneustos*, "breathed out by God." Because the Bible is "breathed out by God" the positive affirmations of God's character, Jesus's attestation, and the Spirit's confirmation (see above) apply in the matter of inspiration as well.[30]

After dealing with some misconceptions about inspiration,[31] Packer concludes the article by writing that no doctrine is without problems that sometimes bedevil the mind. Thus faith is needed to accept revelation and inspiration on the Bible's terms and care must be taken to avoid pitfalls that indicate a lack of focus on the Bible's definition of these terms.[32] Packer identifies two primary ways believers often lose this focus. First, some believers accept that the Bible conveys revelation yet think God did not protect it from the errors associated with human authors writing the words. Second, some believers think internal difficulties in the Bible's individual stories or statements make belief in its total accuracy and reliability impossible. On the first issue Packer counsels accepting that God was fully able to achieve what the Bible claims. To the second issue Packer once again advises the embracing of a full-orbed biblical theology. He writes:

> Principles of biblical theology must interpret, as they are in their turn illustrated by, facts of biblical history and biography. Scripture must interpret scripture. Once it is grasped that the Bible is an organic unity, that the Word of God is its doctrine as a whole, and that each passage must be understood in the light of, even as it throws light upon, the truth as it is in Jesus, the grounds for this kind of objection vanish.[33]

Adhering to this fundamental interpretative principle will bolster faith and make new insights into the depths of Scripture possible.[34] Further theological research will make the most notable progress when it stays on the path Jesus and the apostles walked in these matters.

Packer's next work on the subject of biblical revelation, inspiration, and interpretation built on and developed each of the concerns that led to and were expressed in the 1954 article. By 1955 Packer had begun teaching at Tyndale Hall in Bristol, a post he held until 1961. Besides the signs of renewal associated with the Puritan Conference and other ministries, the Billy Graham London Crusade of 1954 had aided growth in conservative churches and led to a large influx of persons training for ministry in the Anglican Church.

Evangelicals considered such developments positive evidence of the Holy Spirit at work. But persons outside these circles believed that the traditional theology of Graham and other evangelicals was shallow and subjective to the point of being anti-intellectual and dangerous to Christians' spiritual health. These critics argued that historical-critical methods of biblical interpretation had made it impossible to accept traditional views such as the inerrancy and infallibility of the Bible, Mosaic authorship of the Pentateuch, and Pauline authorship of the Pastoral Epistles. They questioned the necessity of specific faith in Jesus for salvation and other traditional doctrines such as the penal substitution theory of Christ's atonement. Like evangelicals they believed that the gospel needed to be declared in an understandable way to modern hearers. Unlike evangelicals they thought doctrines that offended modern sensibilities ought to be downplayed or treated as earlier, superseded versions of Christian doctrine.

In an effort to treat evangelicalism as a legitimate part of ecumenical Christianity many critics claimed that evangelicals were basically sound in their overall Christian theology, just deficient at some major points. Thus, in their opinion the theology expressed in the evangelical movement deserved the label *fundamentalism*, which then as now was viewed in a most unfavorable light in most people's minds. Still, their critics believed fundamentalists could reform their doctrine of Scripture and become full partners in the Christian mainstream. Gabriel Hebert's 1957 volume *Fundamentalism and the Church of God* crystallized many of these concerns.[35]

In response, Packer published *"Fundamentalism" and the Word of God: Some Evangelical Principles* in 1958. He begins by noting that recent critiques of evangelicalism deserve answers because they are offered in good faith. More importantly, they deserve a response because they imply evangelical belief "is founded on a false principle—the exploded notion of biblical inerrancy. This is to say, in effect, that Evangelicalism is a form of Christianity that cannot honestly be held today."[36] He rejects the notion that evangelical theology is basically like that of its critics at its core but in need of repair. Instead, he claims that evangelicalism's critics operate on the basis of false analysis. That is, they "treat every theological tradition as no more than a loosely linked collection of isolated insights, brought together by mere accident of history." Doing so misses the point that "the evangelical faith is a systematic and integrated whole, built on a single foundation; and it must be understood and assessed as such."[37] He believes there are deeper issues that divide evangelicals and the critics he addresses.

Indeed, Packer asserts, the chief difference between evangelicals and their detractors lies in differing views of authority, and "there can be no stable agreement on anything between those who disagree here."[38] The word *stable* is quite important, for Packer desires that all Christians hold a truly catholic and apostolic theology that will stand the test of time. He recognizes that Christian groups have much to learn from one another, that no single individual or group grasps all of God's truth, and that one can learn much from those with whom one disagrees.[39] Yet he believes the only unity that can last requires each person "to bring all views—one's own as well as those of others—to the touchstone of Scripture."[40] Only what the Bible approves can be accepted.

Given this introduction, Packer pursues two basic aims.[41] His first is to discuss *fundamentalism* as a movement and as a term.[42] While doing so he states that the term stems primarily from American theological struggles that he believes needed to occur. Nonetheless, since evangelicalism has a longer

history and since the use of the term *fundamentalism* was basically intended
to shock and insult in current discussions he prefers *evangelicalism* as the most
appropriate description of the theology he defends. His second aim is to assert
that the evangelicalism he describes is in truth historic Christian orthodoxy,
which requires an unconditional submission to God's written Word revealed
in the Bible through a faith that does not negate reason. To achieve this second
aim he analyzes the nature of biblical authority,[43] Scripture,[44] faith,[45] and reason.[46] He also juxtaposes evangelicalism with liberalism, which he considers
the two main options open to his audience at the time.[47]

As his subtitle indicates, Packer operates from a specific set of principles in
this volume, the first three of which appeared in his 1954 article reviewed above.
First, since Jesus is the head of his church, his followers ought to adopt his
views on the Bible. Jesus submitted himself fully to the authority of Scripture,
and his apostles teach readers to do the same in their writings. Second, the
primary way Jesus teaches his followers today is by the Holy Spirit through the
Bible, his written Word. Third, "Anything short of unconditional submission
to Scripture, therefore, is a kind of impenitence; any view that subjects the
written Word of God to the opinions and pronouncements of men involves
unbelief and disloyalty towards Christ."[48] These are once again quite strong
words, but once again they testify to Packer's pastoral concern that believers
grow in Christ. Fourth, the Bible's authority exceeds that of tradition and
other forms of human authority.[49] Fifth, adopting the Bible's full authority
does not close one's mind. Rather, it opens it to the things God teaches and
guards one against transitory theological trends. Clearly, Packer developed
the principles in the 1954 article more fully in this book. His methodology
for biblical interpretation was in place.

In 1961 Packer became warden of Latimer House, Oxford, an institution
dedicated to aiding evangelical causes in the Anglican Church. He held this
position until 1970, when he rejoined the faculty of Tyndale Hall, Bristol.
During this decade Packer wrote several articles and tracts on subjects related to church renewal. His main publication on Scripture was *God Has
Spoken*, which appeared in 1965 and underwent subsequent revisions in
1979, 1993, 1998, and 2005. This work explicated Packer's core conviction
that the Bible is God's Word that must be heard and obeyed. It did so while
addressing mainly an Anglican audience using Scripture and key historical
Anglican documents such as the Book of Common Prayer and the Books of
Homilies. In the foreword to the 1993 edition Packer admits that the book's
tone is one of "defiant defensiveness" yet comments that this tone indicates
how important it was to establish evangelicalism as a viable alternative to
the liberalism that dominated British Christianity at the time.[50] Packer's goal
for the book was "to reassert biblical authority and the biblical method of
living under that authority," which also basically described his ministry at
Latimer House.[51]

By the late 1960s evangelicalism in Britain and the United States was much more established than it had been a decade earlier. Billy Graham's ministry continued to give the movement momentum through new converts, new unity, and new institutions. Christian colleges and seminaries were growing in the United States, and Anglican evangelicals were becoming a large and active body within the Church of England. Yet problems were already arising that threatened the foundations of the movement's theology and unity.

Perhaps chief among these issues was the nature of the Bible, which had been one of the movement's clear unifying beliefs. Fuller Seminary had adopted a statement of faith that did not include the term *inerrancy*, and some of its faculty members questioned openly the usefulness and accuracy of the term, which led to concerns in some circles about this key evangelical seminary's direction. Furthermore, there was no one predominant definition of inerrancy, despite the fact that the term had been used in popular and academic circles for several decades. Packer was drawn into discussions of inerrancy and the future of evangelicalism as early as 1966, when he was invited to participate in the Wenham (Massachusetts) Conference, a meeting held to arrive at an agreeable definition of inerrancy and thus help preserve evangelical unity. This conference failed to produce unanimity on a definition for inerrancy, though it did produce agreement on calling the Bible completely truthful.[52]

In 1976 the issue was raised in a much more public and polemical way when Harold Lindsell published *The Battle for the Bible*.[53] This volume asserted that evangelicalism ought to be defined in large part by adherence to inerrancy, and it named particular persons and seminaries Lindsell believed fell short of this ideal. Meanwhile Southern Baptists, the United States' largest Protestant denomination, had been embroiled in controversy over the nature of Scripture since at least 1962, and the issue spilled over in earnest beginning in 1979. American Lutherans and Presbyterians experienced similar titanic struggles, which led to various fractures in these communions. Meanwhile, some denominations continued to affirm views antithetical to evangelical belief. In short, it seemed that evangelicalism's coherence and unity could be eroding at a very inopportune moment.

By the end of this era Packer had crystallized his theological method for examining the doctrine of Scripture. He had arrived at a set of principles that guided his future research, teaching, and preaching on the subject. For him, the fact that God has spoken in written form means the Bible is a unified, redemptive, and practical book that carries the character of God. Since Jesus believed these things about the Bible and based his teaching on them, those who follow Jesus ought to do the same. These principles served him well when theological discussions shifted from revelation and inspiration to hermeneutics.

God Has Spoken a Unitary and Inerrant Word (1977–96)

As was noted above, Packer had already stated his belief in biblical inerrancy and its connection to Christian scholarship and obedience in his earlier writings.[54] Like many other evangelicals, however, he had previously preferred to use more positive terms. Indeed, he wrote in a reflective piece in 1988 that "inerrancy" was just another way of saying "totally true and entirely trustworthy."[55] He noted in this article, as he had written earlier, that many people used inerrancy in inaccurate and unproductive ways.[56] Yet he came to think that positive statements alone were not sufficient to safeguard an evangelical doctrine of Scripture. He had seen "older standard words like *revelation, inspiration, authority,* and even *infallibility* . . . expounded by some in a way that explicitly allows, and indeed insists, that there are matters on which the Bible ought not to have the last word because what it says is wrong."[57] He had experienced firsthand the problems evangelical scholars were having with the doctrine of Scripture.

For these and other reasons Packer became concerned that evangelicals secure their theological foundations. He believed they needed to do so by affirming their belief in a fully truthful and trustworthy Bible.[58] He also believed that at this point in time part of that affirmation required affirming the Bible's inerrancy. In light of the confusion in evangelical life he (and others) needed "a word which nails my colours to the mast as one who holds that there is no point at which the Bible ought to be denied the last word. That is why I personally embrace the word inerrancy and make much of it these days."[59] Therefore he accepted an invitation to join the International Council on Biblical Inerrancy in 1977 and was an active member until it closed its work in 1987. In this decade Packer moved to North America (1979) to join the faculty at Regent College, Vancouver, where he has taught ever since. He participated in each of the council's summits and shared in drafting the council's final statements on Scripture (1978) and hermeneutics (1982).[60]

In an effort to be as clear as possible, the council included definitions, affirmations, and denials in these summary statements. The council's finest achievement may well be its concise five-point "short statement" on inerrancy (1978). This summary begins with the fully truthful nature of God, moves to God overseeing the writing process of the Bible, continues with an assertion of the Holy Spirit's work in authenticating and teaching Scripture, proceeds to assert the Bible's truthfulness in every area it addresses, and concludes with the warning that any diminution of these previous points causes individual and congregational loss. This brief summary also encompasses crucial matters such as the Bible's redemptive message and sufficiency for Christian growth. It mentions, though could make clearer, the fact that accepting inerrancy is what the Bible teaches about itself and is in itself an act of faith. It is understandable that Packer affirmed this summary and its supporting affirmations and denials, for they in effect summarize his earlier writings on revelation and inspiration.

The council's statements on biblical inerrancy and biblical hermeneutics gave many evangelical colleges, seminaries, and organizations a way to express their views of inerrancy for colleagues and constituents in largely unambiguous ways without becoming overly strict on certain disputed matters, such as the age of the earth and the exact means God used to create the world. The books and articles that came as a result of the meetings gave renewed academic support to claims for inerrancy. As could be expected, however, some evangelicals concluded that the documents were too restrictive, too tied to rationalistic argumentation, and too closed to new scholarship. As was true of the Wenham Conference, the International Council on Biblical Inerrancy council did not produce complete unity among evangelicals. Nonetheless, while knowing that inerrancy was controversial, Packer still contended for the term's usefulness because it speaks to disciples' faith commitment to believe and obey God's Word as they interpret the Bible as a harmonious whole.[61] He concludes:

> What is gained by asserting the inerrancy of Scripture? The assertion of inerrancy primarily safeguards the Christian approach to Scripture as God's Word. Second, the assertion of inerrancy articulates the proper receptivity of faith, conscious of its own emptiness and ignorance and seeking to be taught by God. Further, the assertion of inerrancy establishes the Christian commitment to biblical authority in a clear way. It proclaims that the Bible is always going to have the last word. And, finally, the inerrancy commitment brings the church's handling of Scripture under critical control, at least in principle.[62]

Packer did more than serve on this council and help write its documents in these difficult years. He wrote several books and articles devoted to making inerrancy a term that avoided the pitfalls he identified with its least able practitioners and that addressed the era's most pressing questions about the Bible. The academic scene had shifted from revelation and inspiration to hermeneutics, as the council's agenda recognized. Thus, using his earlier affirmations about the Bible as a base, in a 1982 article Packer restated what he considered evangelicalism's basic hermeneutical principles: (1) "biblical passages must be taken to mean *what their human writers were consciously expressing*"; (2) "the *coherence, harmony, and veracity* of all biblical teaching must be taken as our working hypothesis in interpretation"; (3) "interpretation involves *synthesizing* what the various biblical passages teach, so that each item taught finds its proper place and significance in the *organism* of revelation as a whole"; and (4) "*the response for which the text calls* must be made explicit."[63] Thus he reaffirmed his commitment to historical-grammatical exegesis, the unity of the Bible, a synthetic approach to theology, and the necessity of a Bible-formed church.

He illustrated his beliefs about the Bible and synthetic theology in articles on the unity of the Bible (1982) and canonical interpretation (1985);[64] in two weighty, popular books, *Knowing God* (1973) and *God's Words: Studies of Key Biblical Themes* (1981); and in the reissued and expanded edition of *God Has Spoken* (1979, 1993). He underscored his commitment to responding to the Bible in all these works but perhaps most explicitly in "Inerrancy and the Divinity and Humanity of the Bible" (1988) where he asserts the necessity of believers letting Scripture shape them and responding to all of Scripture as coming from God and thus deserving of obedience.[65] He emphasized exegesis in treatments of subjects such as creation, women in ministry, and eschatology.[66] Of course, he also did so while preaching on a regular basis.[67]

In these and subsequent writings Packer uses these principles as a base from which to critique hermeneutical views he found incompatible with, or inadequate when compared to, evangelical thought. For example, in a 1990 article he asserted that evangelical hermeneutics are grounded in exegesis that reveals a truthful God who offers redemption to sinful humanity, reveals the coherence and veracity of the canon as evidenced in informed exegetical work using the analogy of faith as a guiding principle, reveals the organic nature of biblical truth, and reveals the necessity of obedience to God. He notes that evangelicals recognize diversity in the Bible, but they believe this diversity testifies to a plurality of voices claiming the same vital core truths.[68] These are not competing voices, then, but rather a cloud of witnesses akin to the people described in Hebrews 11.

Earlier, in a 1978 article, he had asserted that, in contrast, liberal hermeneutical approaches emphasize biblical interpretation as recapturing human insights helpful for today's evolving world, neoorthodox hermeneutical approaches offer assertions about revelation and the coherence of the overall biblical message without refuting liberalism's rejection of the Bible's full historical accuracy, and official Roman Catholic hermeneutical approaches emphasize infallible church teaching.[69] The first approach treats the Bible as a valuable compendium of human insights, not an authoritative Word from God. The second reaches several orthodox conclusions without building those conclusions on historical-contextual exegesis. The third places an authorized human interpreter between the text and the reader. These assertions do not lead Packer to conclude that nothing can be learned from these perspectives, but he does not believe they have the staying power that complete trust in the Bible's origins in God, unity of message in canonical context, and call to absolute obedience offers the church.

His comments on neoorthodoxy in this 1978 piece are important, for they address Karl Barth's interpretive methods, a subject that seems to have growing appeal for evangelicals today.[70] Packer appreciates Barth's rejection of liberalism's conclusions about God, humanity, and redemption. He is grateful for Barth's persistent focus on Christology, and he notes that Barth professes many results of inerrancy without claiming the Bible is inerrant. Yet Packer is troubled by Barth's refusal to equate the Bible and God's Word in favor of affirming the Bible as an instrument by which God reveals his Word. He is also concerned that Barth's rejection of the full truthfulness and trustworthiness of Scripture on historical matters leaves Barth making exegetical conclusions his method cannot sustain. This sort of exegesis bypasses the historical meaning of individual texts and their place in the canon in a way that sometimes produces right doctrine from wrong analysis and at other times models an interpretational method that "turns God's gift of insight into Scripture into uncheckable private revelations."[71]

Writing in 1996, Packer observed that Barth's exegetical method is indeed his most troubling legacy because its subjectivity allows interpretations that Barth himself would not have affirmed. In fact, Barth's method has helped produce "an uncontrolled and currently uncontrollable theological pluralism based on selective and fanciful use of biblical material by each thinker."[72] This, Packer fears, may well be "Barth's actual legacy to us."[73] Placed over against liberalism, the neoorthodox method of interpretation recaptured core truths. But when placed over against the evangelical views, Packer concludes, it lacks enduring foundations for accurate theological conclusions. It also has the potential to strip evangelicalism of its basis for reaching its core convictions.

It is important to note that Packer developed his views of inerrancy from his exegetical conclusions about God, the canon, and the Holy Spirit's work in believers' lives. This realization helps one avoid thinking that Packer reached his conclusions on inerrancy on solely rationalistic grounds. Packer rightly claims that the apostles, the early church, and the reformers also held these foundational principles on exegetical grounds. In Packer's case, beliefs about revelation, inspiration, hermeneutics, and authority did not flow from being taught inerrancy in a classroom. Rather, inerrancy became the way he expressed a view that he had first believed came from the Bible itself. Unlike Don Payne, I do not believe that inerrancy has been a philosophical a priori that means that in Packer's methodology "certain philosophical assumptions may be as important to the Christian life as Scripture itself."[74] Of course, exegesis has philosophical underpinnings. Nonetheless, most exegetes conclude that passages like Psalm 19:1–14, 2 Timothy 3:16, and 2 Peter 1:20–21 claim perfection for the Bible because it comes from God. One does not have to bring a precondition of inerrancy to these texts to reach this conclusion. One has to work out the name to call that conclusion and the implications of that conclusion, but the a priori belief Payne mentions is not the necessary first step in reaching the conclusion. I believe that the body of Packer's work, of which the inerrancy pieces are a part, indicates that Packer's commitment to the term *inerrancy* came as a matter of faith seeking reason, a goal Packer had been pursuing for some time.[75]

In both *Truth and Power* (1996) and the fifth edition of *God Has Spoken* (2005) Packer has continued to stand by the conclusions reached by the International Council on Biblical Inerrancy. Furthermore, Packer answered "no" when Bruce Hindmarsh asked him during the 2006 Beeson conference if he thought the council's conclusions ought to be revised. Having arrived at what he considered enduring foundational principles on revelation, inspiration, and interpretation in his early works, Packer has stood his ground. He has explained his viewpoints and grown in his presentation of them, but he has trusted these conclusions enough to continue to work out their implications.

Besides his insistence on a biblical definition of revelation and inspiration that uses God's character as a base, Packer's most enduring contribution to evangelical hermeneutics from this era is his resolve in asserting the unity of Scripture. He rightly argued that the Bible's unity safeguards the church from one-sided emphases and at the same time gives interpreters plenty of room to develop relevant biblically grounded applications of Scripture. This unity also gives evangelical interpreters sufficient grounds for challenging pluralistic readings that treat the Bible as a collection of competing voices or for disputing theological views based on a selective reading of parts of the Bible. The manner in which evangelicals explicate the implications of this unity will in large part determine the future of evangelical biblical and theological scholarship.

God Has Spoken a Unifying Word (1997–2006)

I will not use much space describing this era, particularly since many of the contributors to this volume address Packer's ecumenical spirit, especially as it has been exhibited in the Evangelicals and Catholics Together dialogue. Participation in this process, which began in 1994, has been Packer's most-discussed venture of the past several years. This interaction with Catholics has not been his only attempt at seeking unity among believers in this period, however, for he has also continued to work for Anglican unity and served as chairman of the English Standard Version (ESV) Translation Oversight Committee beginning in 1999.[76] He has engaged in the former task because of his ongoing commitment to evangelical renewal of Anglicanism. He took up this latter task in part because he desired an essentially literal Bible that could serve as a common text for Christians who speak English as the King James Version once had.

It is important to note why Packer has been involved in these and earlier efforts at Christian unity. Stated quite simply, he has done so because he believes the Bible indicates he should. As he wrote in 1995, the main reason he engaged in dialogue with Roman Catholics is that Jesus's prayer in John 17:20–23 that his people be one is definitive. He explains, "This prayer clearly entails the thought that God's one international family should seek to look and sound like one family by speaking and acting as such, and that means aiming at togetherness wherever togetherness can be achieved. The alternative is to grieve the Lord."[77] Similarly, Packer has not given up on true Anglican unity despite the recent seismic changes in the communion. He does not wish unity to come at any price but rather to emerge from a renewed commitment to the centrality of the Bible in ideal Anglicanism.[78] Only time will tell if the evangelical/Catholic dialogue will produce a biblically ordered union, if the Anglican Communion will return to its scriptural roots, or if the ESV or any translation can aid a united Christianity. The results belong to God, but Packer's efforts in these ventures speak of his own shaping by Scripture, for they reflect his answer to Jesus's call to unity.

J. I. Packer and the Evangelical Future

Like other pioneering giants such as Billy Graham, John Stott, Carl Henry, and Ken Kantzer, J. I. Packer has left a significant legacy that should be embraced by current and subsequent generations of evangelicals. Much will be written about this legacy in years to come. When these histories are written they should take into consideration the fact that these giants were first and foremost persons shaped by the Bible and persons who believed that the Bible is God's perfect Word to imperfect people. They were truly like the church's Catholic and Protestant Reformers in this sense. Though a longer list could be offered, I believe that five key points from Packer's work deserve emphasis.

First, Packer's claims about the internal witness of the Holy Spirit should fuel scholarly efforts based on the principle of faith seeking understanding. Packer has made it clear that those who accept the Bible for what it is and claims to be do so as an act of faith as a result of the Holy Spirit's work. Because of the Holy Spirit they have a personal, relational trust in God, and they accept the Bible as his words because their master, Jesus, teaches them to do so. Part of the Holy Spirit's work is "a healing of spiritual faculties, a restoring . . . of a permanent receptiveness towards divine things"[79] that helps believers affirm what the Bible says about itself. Therefore Christians seek a reasoning faith, not a faithless reasoning, and they cannot do otherwise unless "they go against their own deepest spiritual instincts."[80] This reasoning faith requires of a Christian scholar great mental exertion and deserves "the highest level of scholarly attainment in the fulfillment of his exegetical vocation."[81] Yet it means this scholarship is subject to the Holy Spirit in practice no less than in intent. This means the Christian scholar's task is to "present the Christian faith clothed in modern terms, not to propagate modern thought clothed in Christian terms. Our business is to interpret and criticize modern thought by the gospel, not *vice versa*. Confusion here is fatal."[82] Christians must perform this ministry with humility, kindness, precision, and competence. Yet those who adopt this view of scholarship and present the Bible as it presents itself know they must be "reforming biblical criticism according to his word."[83] Partial adherence to this principle will lead to partial freedom in a healed mind.[84]

These reminders should help evangelical scholars avoid pitting faith against reason and separating their faith from their academic disciplines. Our job is to determine *how* to integrate faith and learning by putting faith first, not *if* we will attempt this task. Putting faith first is not a hindrance unless we believe the Holy Spirit's view of Scripture is a hindrance. Christian scholars are committed to the faith-then-reason ordering, but they are not less objective than other scholars who have put reason or an interpretative method ahead of faith. Both have to set priorities. They are also in no better position hermeneutically, for the Holy Spirit requires mental labor; he does not give Christians automatic understanding or install exegetical brilliance. But Christians are in a position to have their minds free to follow the One who made minds.

Second, evangelicals need to maintain Packer's insistence that the heart of historic Christian belief is the conviction that a perfect and honest God has spoken perfectly and honestly in his written Word. Our doctrine of Scripture develops from what we think about God, whether we are discussing what we think about God's character or what we think about God's ability to safeguard his word from falsehood. Thus, views that treat the Bible as an instrument through which God works may produce results with which we agree, but they will not produce a foundation that will in the long run do full justice to biblical theology.

Third, evangelicals need to develop all the implications of Packer's claim that God speaks in a unified manner through a unitary canon of Scripture. This claim must be at the heart of evangelical hermeneutics in a pluralistic age. To connect the preceding point to this one, today there are many biblical interpreters who use parts of Scripture to claim that God is unreliable, abusive, and unable to control world events. Thus, evangelical interpreters need to find an increasing number of ways to connect the Bible's claims for unity and the wholeness of the divine redemptive revelation. As they do so they will present the God of the Bible as the whole Bible presents him: full of grace and full of moral excellence backed up by action. Careful exegesis of the Bible's parts while keeping in mind the Bible's overarching theology as found in the Bible's many lengthy summative statements must aid this process. Biblical and theological experts need to work together on this project, for the task is complicated in current resource-laden scholarly discourse. Such partnerships will produce fruitful results.

Fourth, evangelicals must retain and expound Packer's belief that only a clear commitment to obeying the Bible will lead to helpful discipleship and the healing of the divisions in the church. Without total commitment to obeying the Bible because it is God's written Word it simply makes no sense to love one's enemies in a dangerous world. Without this commitment it makes little sense to exert one's self to help heal centuries' old divisions in a busy and needy world. Without this commitment there is a great temptation to settle for the sort of "unity" that leaves us tolerating one another rather than having fellowship with one another. With this commitment, however, progress can be made even in a fallen world. We can have a biblical view of "neighbor" and of "brothers and sisters in Christ" that will lead to real change in a dangerous and busy and compromising world.

Fifth, evangelicals need to share Packer's desire to speak positively about the Bible but also be willing to use controversial words meant to protect the faith. We cannot be hoping for a theological fight and be obedient Christians, but we cannot avoid such battles due to weariness or wariness or winsomeness either. Sometimes using positive words like *true* and *trustworthy* convey what we need to assert. Yet experience proves that even using positive words requires one to answer questions about exactly how the Bible is "true" and in what manner it is "trustworthy." We will never avoid the need to have both affirmations and denials that express the doctrine of Scripture. Thus, inerrancy or some word like it will always be as necessary as less controversial words. We must never forget that words that "nail our colors to the mast,"[85] as Packer put it, become important because for a variety of reasons we are always tempted to back away from the full implications of the faith we profess.

The future of evangelicalism depends on its faithfulness to God, who has spoken a redeeming and shaping Word to us. Packer is correct when he writes that God's church will always have "two constant needs: instruction in the truths by which it must live, and correction of the shortcomings by which it is marred." Thankfully, the Bible "is designed to meet this twofold need," so we must be about the business of exegesis, synthesis, and proclamation.[86] As we go about this we will not only honor the legacy of J. I. Packer and secure whatever future God intends for evangelicalism, we will please our Savior, and that has been Packer's goal all along.

6

J. I. Packer and Pastoral Wisdom from the Puritans

Mark E. Dever

Introduction: Puritanism

There are some people for whom it is an honor to be asked to honor, and J. I. Packer is certainly one of them. And this is a surprising honor, considering that I disagree with him on baptism, church, and the resources of and prospects for rapprochement between Protestants and Roman Catholics. After all, I am a fundamentalist, Calvinistic, separatist Baptist—I barely believe in rapprochement with Presbyterians!

We begin our consideration of "J. I. Packer and the Evangelical Future" by considering where much seemed to begin for Packer, with that theological band that became his conversation partner during his Oxford years, and that has continued to inform much of his ministry—the Puritans. We could spend much time recalling caricatures of Puritans. Macaulay, in his *History of England*, wrote that "the Puritan hated bear-baiting, not because it gave pain to the bear, but because it gave pleasure to the spectators."[1] I believe it was the famous newspaperman H. L. Mencken who said that a Puritan was one who feared that someone, somewhere, somehow, might be having fun. Even Garrison Keillor has tried his hand at representing the Puritans. He said that "the Puritans came to America in the hopes of discovering greater restrictions than were permissible under English law."[2]

In fact the Puritans were not fundamentally characterized by restrictions, fear, or hatred. They were instead—as J. I. Packer has taught us in that wonderful collection of writings published in America as *A Quest for Godliness*—characterized by the joy of finding liberty in the gospel, assurance of their acceptance by God through Christ, and a renewed understanding of the church as the people of God.[3]

The Christians in England in the sixteenth and seventeenth centuries began to be more self-consciously shaped by Scripture in their understanding of the gospel and of the church. Five of the so-called sacraments were found to be without sufficient scriptural warrant. The right preaching of the Word of God and the right administration of baptism and the Lord's Supper were widely understood to be the essential marks of a true Christian church.

I should note that occasionally people will use the word *Puritan* interchangeably with the word *Presbyterian*. This is understandable for a few reasons that we will not take time to go into now, but it is not accurate. So, for instance, some of the most famous Puritans were not Presbyterian: John Bunyan was a Baptist and John Owen a Congregationalist—and J. I. Packer is an Anglican.

Since his own discovery of the Puritans when he was an undergraduate, Packer has been a potent popularizer of the Puritans. From talking with his undergraduate friends, to writing in Inter-Varsity's *Christian Graduate* and running The Puritan and Reformed Studies Conference in London for ministers, to teaching about the Puritans in seminaries around the world, the Puritans have been a platform for Packer to introduce modern-day myopic Christians into something of the wideness and the richness of the Reformed tradition. It was in this latter role as a professor of Puritanism that I first met him. Twenty-two years ago he taught a class (Introduction to the Study of English Puritan Theology) at Gordon-Conwell Theological Seminary. I had the good fortune—or providence—to be among the students in that class.

From the Puritans' written remains, he has taught us of God and his love, of salvation and the experience of spiritual conflict, of God's protection, and, supremely, of God's glory. Now let us consider together a few of the ways that this vigorous theological tradition has been handed down to us through the teaching and writing of J. I. Packer.

The Bible

The place to begin is the Bible. J. I. Packer was not only studying and reading in the late 1950s about the Puritans as interpreters of Scripture but also reading current writings. One that caught his attention and called for a response was

exhorts his readers about the privilege of adoption and the trustworthiness of God through all our trials.

Knowing God may have become a seminary text, but it was written more as an extended evangelistic tract. Consider the way the book concludes:

> "Thou hast said, 'Seek ye my face.' My heart says to Thee, 'Thy face, LORD, do I seek'" (Ps. 27:8, RSV). If this book moves any of its readers to identify more closely with the psalmist at this point, it will not have been written in vain.[10]

Packer has passed on Puritan wisdom about God.

Gospel

Packer has also passed on Puritan wisdom about the cross. I remember reading a booklet many years ago that became one of my favorite things to read to excite me about the gospel. It was a reprint of J. I. Packer's introduction to John Owen's treatise *The Death of Death in the Death of Christ*. Packer's introduction was not a part of Owen's first edition, but it had been joined to it by Banner of Truth before I was born, and it seemed to enshrine Packer there with Owen and Bunyan and Sibbes as one of the broadly Puritan authors published by Banner. I was so taken with it that phrases from it still ring in my mind. I remember being at a Christian camp while still a college student and ordering twenty copies of the booklet from a publisher in Montana so that I could give it out to the other students at the camp.

Later reprinted as "Saved by His Precious Blood" in *A Quest for Godliness*, this introduction certainly galvanized many young ministers and sent us off to the Synod of Dort to learn the gospel. We agreed with him as he contrasted the "old" and the "new" gospels. We were enlightened by his exposing that the gospel centered on man and the help God gives him was a different gospel than the one centered on the glory of God. "To recover the old, authentic, biblical gospel, and to bring our preaching and practice back into line with it, is perhaps our most pressing present need."[11] In this essay Packer quoted approvingly Spurgeon's remark in his *Autobiography* that "I have my own private opinion that there is no such thing as preaching Christ and him crucified, unless we preach what is nowadays called Calvinism. It is a nickname to call it Calvinism; Calvinism is the gospel, and nothing else. I do not believe we can preach the gospel . . . unless we base it upon the special and particular redemption of His elect and chosen people which Christ wrought out upon the Cross; nor can I comprehend a gospel which lets saints fall away after they are called."[12]

On July 17, 1973, J. I. Packer gave the annual Tyndale Biblical Theology Lecture in Cambridge. It was published the next year in the *Tyndale Bulletin*

as "What Did the Cross Achieve? The Logic of Penal Substitution."[13] In this
lecture, Packer sought to address objections to penal substitution and to re-
juvenate understanding of and appreciation for this central pillar of the New
Testament's presentation of Christ's death. Among other books that had
undermined faith in a penal substitutionary understanding of Christ's death,
Gustaf Aulen's *Christus Victor* had for decades been attracting admirers and
convincing scholars in the mid-twentieth century to replace the centrality of
penal substitution with the more ambiguous though no less biblical motif
of "victory." Packer drew on the old Reformed thinkers to reassert the biblical picture of Christ's death on the cross as both penal and substitutionary.
Retribution, solidarity, mystery, salvation, and divine love were all presented
in their relationship to Christ's substitutionary death. John Owen was cited
at length, as were Luther, Calvin, Cranmer, Edwards, and various Hodgeses.
Packer left the reader with the typically English Socratic question: "Can we
then justify ourselves in holding a view of the atonement into which penal
substitution does not enter? Ought we not to reconsider whether penal substitution is not, after all, the heart of the matter?"[14]

In these articles, Packer faithfully passed on Puritan wisdom about the
nature of Christ's gospel and especially of his work on the cross.

Christian Life

Another Puritan-like trait that has marked J. I. Packer's preaching, teaching,
and ministry of writing has been his emphasis on living the Christian life.
Packer has the very Puritan tendency to trace lines of thought backward to
their source and forward to their implications. During my years in England, I
had opportunity to get to know Packer's doctoral supervisor—the inimitable
Geoffrey Nuttall. Though Nuttall did not share all of the Puritans' theology,
he certainly seemed to have acquired some of their manners and modes of
thinking. He told me about a game his family would play when he was a child.
They would, in mid-conversation, stop and ask Geoffrey to remember what
someone had just said, and then to try to recall what was said before that, and
so on, until they had, from memory, reconstructed the entire conversation.

Something of the fruit of that habit of mind is revealed in Nuttall's works.
For example, in his most well-known work, *The Holy Spirit in Puritan Faith
and Experience*, each chapter begins with an outline of what is going to be
said in the chapter. Packer's dissertation follows the same practice. Thinking
carefully about doctrine and tracing out its logical implications in our daily
lives is a Puritan practice par excellence, and Packer has introduced this wise
practice to many.

In his classroom teaching on the Puritans, Packer used Bunyan's *Pilgrim's
Progress*, and, I think to a lesser extent, William Gurnall's *Christian in Com-*

plete Armor to teach his students about the Christian life and its nature as a life of conflict. However much there may be blessings and even times of celebration, this life is not home. The Puritans were intensely aware of that and spoke of it often.

Richard Baxter wrote that he

> oft heard his late wife [Margaret] speak of her hopeful persuasions that we should live together in heaven; it being my judgment and constant practice to make those that I teach understand that the gospel is glad tidings of great joy; and that holiness lies especially in delighting in God, his Word and works, and in his joyful praise and hopes of glory, and in longing for and seeking the heavenly Jerusalem, and in living as fruitfully to the church and others as we can do in the world; and that this must be wrought by the most believing apprehensions of God's goodness as equal to his greatness, and of his great love to mankind manifested in our redemption, and by believing the graces and riches of Christ and the comforting office of the Holy Ghost, and studying daily God's promises and mercies and our everlasting joys; and that religion consists in doing God's commanding will and quietly and joyfully trusting in his promising and disposing will; and that fear and sorrow are but to remove impediments and further all this.[15]

Even in his dissertation, Packer's divinity was practical. He had a section on Baxter's use of thoughts of the afterlife to affect this life. Packer's theologizing, too, has been put to useful purposes; his *Evangelism and the Sovereignty of God* is the work of a careful theologian dealing with one of the most common and important questions that Christians ask—If God is sovereign, why should I do anything at all? Especially, why should I evangelize? Packer's answer is careful and considered, biblical and helpful. In this concern to not only understand God's sovereignty but also consider how that will impact the young Christian in his life, Packer is clearly an heir of the Puritans.

Puritans on the Definition of Justification and Questions of Church Cooperation

Where Packer's acceptance and transmission of the wisdom of the Puritans is most in question is in the relationship between evangelical Protestants and Roman Catholics. Here is how Packer, in 1958, described the Puritans and other Reformed Christians in their understanding of the Roman Catholic Church: "Numerically, the unreformed Church of Rome is the biggest party; but many anti-fundamentalists would no doubt agree with four centuries of Protestant theology that the self-styled 'Catholic Church' is in fact the biggest schismatic group in Christendom. It is often said that one with God is a majority, however many stand against him; and it is no less true that one

with Christ is a catholic Christian, however many deny his right to the title."[16]
Packer understood himself to be standing with the Puritans on the questions
of church and salvation. "Historic Protestantism looks on preaching as the
supreme means of grace and of communion with God."[17] And so did Packer.
He would distinguish himself from Roman Catholics but also from theological
liberals. "The more one probes the differences between Roman and Protestant,
Liberal and Evangelical, the deeper they prove to be; beneath the cracks on
the surface lie fissures which run down to the very foundations, broadening
as they go."[18]

At the same time, Packer did not see the growth of a seventeenth-century
Tridentine Romanism as the biggest threat facing the church in Britain. Instead,
he saw the growth of theological liberalism, and its near-cousin secularism, as
the coming crisis. Packer wrote in *Christianity Today* in 1958, "In the writer's
judgment, the reinvigorating of the local church as an aggressive witnessing
community is strategic priority number one in the present British situation,
and evangelicals will fail miserably if they do not direct their chief efforts to
this end."[19] Packer acknowledged the changing threat in an article he wrote
in 1994, explaining why he signed the Evangelicals and Catholics Together
(ECT) document.

> In the days when Rome seemed to aim at political control of all Christendom
> and the death of Protestant churches, such partnership was not possible. But
> those days are past and after Vatican II can hardly return. Whatever God's
> future may be for the official Roman Catholic system, present evangelical part-
> nership with spiritually alive Roman Catholics in communicating Christ to
> unbelievers and upholding Christian order in a post-Christian world needs to
> grow everywhere.[20]

At this point, Packer would maintain that he is faithful to the same goals
as the Puritans had—forwarding the gospel and gospel work—but that he
does so by different methods. Where the Puritans opposed Roman Catholicism (as Packer still does) that meant largely opposing Roman Catholics,
particularly in any kind of Christian work. But because of changes in the
shape of Satan's work and changes in Roman Catholicism, Packer would say
that the Puritan purpose is now best executed by cooperation with those the
Puritans opposed.

This topic is large and thorny enough to be the subject of a paper by itself.
Let me simply say, as one who has Roman Catholic friends who I assume
are born again, but as one who also disagrees with what I understand of the
Evangelicals and Catholics Together process, that my concern is not with
some evangelicals and some Roman Catholics but with evangelicalism and
Roman Catholicism. While one cannot fail to appreciate commonalities that
cut across our differences (defenders of many aspects of orthodoxy may be

either Roman Catholic or Protestant), I see no official Roman Catholic retreat from the theological conclusions of Trent on justification, and where those positions may have been supplemented, I think that is more a part of the general theological loosening of Vatican II than anything approaching the biblical reform in understanding the gospel that the sixteenth- and seventeenth-century Puritans stood for.[21] Of course two people, regardless of the church they attend, can believe that we are saved only by trusting in Christ, but a suggestion that the Roman Catholic Church has changed its teaching on salvation is at best only a half truth, and a half truth masquerading as a whole truth . . . well, you know the rest.

Packer clearly appreciates that there are continuing differences. He said so in his 1994 article "Why I Signed It."[22] He writes a very full paragraph in explanation of his "Yes and No" answer to the question "May Evangelicals and Catholics Together realistically claim, as in effect it does, that its evangelical and Catholic drafters agree on the gospel of salvation?" Time and space forbid us here to explore this more fully. Let me simply publicly regret his choice of words when he wrote "If you mean, could they all be relied on to attach the same small print to their statement, 'we are justified by grace through faith because of Christ,' no." While the statement is beyond doubt true, to describe every disagreement that was left unresolved by the Evangelicals and Catholics Together expression on justification as "small print" was at least ill-advised and has proved inflammatory and confusing. If new unities have been brought about by Packer's involvement in Evangelicals and Catholics Together they have been purchased with the price of new divisions.

Here's my understanding of Packer and justification: he believes the same thing he believed fifty years ago when he penned that introduction to Owen's *Death of Death*. He does not think anyone will be saved by trusting in anything other than Christ alone. He assumes many Roman Catholics who may even articulate something else could, by God's grace, be trusting in Christ alone. This construction seems to me both most accurate and most charitable.

And it sounds a bit like Jonathan Edwards on justification. Edwards wrote that

> how far a wonderful and mysterious agency of God's Spirit may so influence some men's hearts, that their practice in this regard may be contrary to their own principles, so that they shall not trust in their own righteousness, though they profess that men are justified by their own righteousness—or how far they may believe the doctrine of justification by men's own righteousness in general, and yet not believe it in a particular application of it to themselves—or how far that error which they may have been led into by education, or cunning sophistry of others, may yet be indeed contrary to the prevailing disposition of their hearts, and contrary to their practice—or how far some may seem to maintain a doctrine contrary to this gospel-doctrine of justification, that really do not, but only express themselves differently from others; or seem to

oppose it through their misunderstanding of our expressions, or we of theirs, when indeed our real sentiments are the same in the main—or may seem to differ more than they do, by using terms that are without a precisely fixed and determinate meaning—or to be wide in their sentiments from this doctrine, for want of a distinct understanding of it; whose hearts, at the same time, entirely agree with it, and if once it was clearly explained to their understandings, would immediately close with it, and embrace it:—how far these things may be, I will not determine; but am fully persuaded that great allowances are to be made on these and such like accounts, in innumerable instances; though it is manifest, from what has been said, that the teaching and propagating contrary doctrines and schemes, is of a pernicious and fatal tendency.[23]

To this writer, anyway, these considerations are more humble than they are confusing.

In the preface to a volume of essays celebrating Oak Hill Theological College's fiftieth anniversary, Packer wrote of the doctrine of justification that "no other biblical doctrine holds together so much that is precious and enlivening."[24] Later in the volume he writes that "first, the foundation of the Reformed doctrine is belief in the total inability of fallen man . . . , particularity of Christ's redemption . . . , and the sovereign mercy of God in effectual calling . . . , and it cannot be stated in any other context or frame of reference. . . . It is greatly to be hoped that the Reformed doctrine will reassert itself."[25] Such clarity was wisely advocated by the Puritans. In matters of church cooperation despite differences about justification, Packer makes the disputed claim that he carries on the same goals and says openly that he advocates positions different from those that the Puritans deemed wise.

Conclusion: Personal Appreciation and the Future

Referring, I take it, to the martyrologist John Foxe, Richard Sibbes once said "It helps us also in taking benefit by the example of other men. . . . The very sight often, nay, the very thought of a good man doth good, as representing to our souls some good thing which we affect . . . which makes histories and the lively characters and expressions of virtues and vices useful to us."[26]

Great men and women of faith are an encouragement to us. I've heard J. I. Packer say several times that Martyn Lloyd-Jones was "the greatest man I ever knew." Earlier this year, I had the privilege of giving two talks in England at a small gathering to consider God's blessing in the ministry of Martyn Lloyd-Jones, who departed this life twenty-five years ago. Even as I differed somewhat with Lloyd-Jones when it comes to church matters and separation— and said so at the conference—so do I also differ with Packer. But even these disagreements that I have laid out with J. I. Packer—disagreements that are both significant and baffling to me—cannot obscure the true benefits that I and so many others have derived from his faithful handing on of the great Puritan tradition of Reformed theology and revived life. Packer himself concluded about the Puritan Richard Baxter, "He was a gifted theologian, more stimulating in his mistakes than many lesser men in their orthodoxy; and he was a great Christian."[27]

And what of J. I. Packer and the evangelical future? As I was interviewing Thabiti Anyabwile, a pastor of our congregation who was about to leave and pastor a Baptist church in the Caribbean, he recounted the story of his first days as a Christian. Anyabwile was brought up in North Carolina and converted to Islam in college. After a few years he drifted into agnosticism, and by God's grace was, after a few more years, converted. In this interview, he recounted his first trip into a Christian bookstore after his conversion. He knew nothing about Christian books and authors. Two books drew his attention, and he bought them: Martyn Lloyd-Jones's *Great Doctrines of the Bible* and J. I. Packer's *Knowing God*. And as I consider Anyabwile's hand reaching to take that volume of Packer, I can't help but think of Packer's hand, half a century earlier, reaching out to pick up his first volume of Owen.

The future is, of course, in the hands of God. But surely our brother Anyabwile is not the only one to be so blessed by Packer's faithful recounting of God's truth. Nor, I trust, will he be the last. Would not we all join together in our desire for our errors to perish with us but for the good we have done to live on to others' good and God's glory? So may it be with the Puritans, and with J. I. Packer, and with us all.

7

Retrieval and Renewal

A Model for Evangelical Spiritual Vitality

D. BRUCE HINDMARSH

This book celebrates J. I. Packer's ministry and reflects on his contribution to the evangelical movement over the past half century or so and seeks to use this as a springboard for considering the future of evangelicalism. Of the many aspects of Packer's work that we could focus on in this way, I would like to single out just one, and take as my starting point the Robin Hood character of his public ministry.

Why We Need Church History

By training and by dint of his own disciplined study, Packer acquired early in his career a deep knowledge of church history and the classic works of Christian theology. Popular evangelicalism, though, has often been profoundly ahistorical and anti-intellectual in outlook. Modernity has left the church in chaos, just as the absence of good King Richard had left England in chaos during the time of Robin Hood. Packer has therefore, like Robin Hood, contrived to "take from the rich and give to the poor." He has been able to *retrieve* riches from the past and employ them for the purpose of *renewing* the life of Christians in the present. This model of "retrieval and renewal" is, I think, an excellent model for evangelical spiritual vitality, and it is a model I would like to focus on as holding great promise for the future of evangelicalism.

An interesting contemporary parallel in the mid-twentieth century to J. I. Packer's evangelical exercise of historical retrieval for the sake of present renewal was a movement among certain European Catholic theologians in the decades leading up to Vatican II. Henri de Lubac, Jean Danièlou, Hans Urs von Balthasar, Louis Bouyer, and others participated in this movement that was labeled derisively *la nouvelle thèologie*, or *the new theology*, by its opponents. "What united this diverse group," says one critic, "were the convictions that (1) theology had to speak to the Church's present situation and that (2) the key to theology's relevance to the present lay in the creative recovery of its past." In the language that came to be used later, the key to *aggiornamento* (renewal or adaptation) was to be found in *ressourcement*—"a rediscovery of the riches of the Church's two-thousand-year treasury, a return to the very headwaters of the Christian tradition."[1] The cry of *ad fontes* that we associate with the Protestant Reformers was sounding from the lips of these twentieth-century Catholic theologians. "In their writings," claims Marcellino D'Ambrosio, "the word 'source' only secondarily refers to a historical document; the primary meaning they assign to the term is a fountain-head of dynamic spiritual life which never runs dry."[2] By immersing themselves in the Bible, the liturgy, the creeds and councils, the teachings of the fathers and doctors, and the saints and mystics, these Catholics were seeking not principally a more accurate historical understanding but rather a renewal in the same Holy Spirit that was the common inspiration of these writers and the common source of their wisdom. Out of this movement came the whole patristic revival in France, with its renewed scholarship, translation efforts, and focus on spirituality. I think this is parallel to the Puritan revival in the same years among evangelicals, which was likewise expressed in a renewed scholarship, fresh editions, and the stress on spirituality. In both cases there was a hermeneutic of retrieval and renewal that was seen as critical to addressing the condition of a church that was cut off from its own sources by the caustic ahistorical and pragmatic culture of modernity.

There were, of course, differences between Catholics and evangelicals at mid-century in terms of the understanding of tradition, the magisterium, and the role of Scripture in this double movement of retrieval and renewal. And there is a big difference between Jean Danièlou republishing the mystical writings of Gregory of Nyssa and J. I. Packer encouraging the reprinting of John Owen on the atonement or on the mortification of sin in believers. And Packer has been concerned to appraise tradition critically in the light of Scripture. He writes, for example, "Scripture must have the last word on all human attempts to state its meaning, and tradition, viewed as a series of such human attempts, has a ministerial rather than a magisterial role."[3] Tradition is a guide and it has great sapiential value, but it does not have canonical status; it is not a separate source of revelation apart from Holy Scripture. But the differences here with Catholics also ought not to be overstated or caricatured. Note how similarly the Lyon Jesuits described their own use of the church fathers in the mid-twentieth century:

> The Fathers clearly do not have the same authority [as Scripture]; they are sources which are secondary, derived, never sufficient of themselves; yet this does not prevent them from playing a capital role. And they play this role not only in the past, but they continue to play it in the present. They are sources, not in the restricted sense in which literary history understands the term, but in the sense of wellsprings which are always springing up to overflowing.[4]

Samuel Taylor Coleridge referred to Scripture in this sense as the "living educts of the imagination" so that a mind that has learned to discern meaning in biblical history is able to draw up nourishment from all of history in this life-giving way. I think that is the sense of tradition here for these mid-twentieth-century theologians, Catholic and Protestant, where going back is a way of going forward and retrieval is a step toward renewal. For both Packer and like-minded evangelicals, as for the *ressourcement* theologians, this was a critical strategy for renewal. It was a way of throwing a lifeline to a church sinking beneath the toxic waves of modernity.

C. S. Lewis was yet another Christian writer from the mid-twentieth century who adopted this strategy of retrieval for the sake of renewal, as a response to modernity, especially to that aspect of modernity that produced what he called "chronological snobbery," where it is assumed that what is new and recent must of necessity be better. In 1944, when J. I. Packer was in his late teens, Lewis wrote an introduction to a new translation of Athanasius's classic work *On the Incarnation.* Lewis wrote that he did not wish the ordinary reader to read no modern books at all but that if it was a choice between only the new or only the old, he would advise reading the old books. Why? "A new book is still on its trial," he said, "and the amateur is not in a position to judge it. It has to be tested against the great body of Christian thought down through the ages, and all its hidden implications (often unsuspected by the author himself) have to be brought to light. . . . The only safety is to have a standard of plain, central Christianity ('mere Christianity' as Baxter called it) which puts the controversies of the moment in their proper perspective." And then Lewis lapses into his teacher's voice and looks over his eyeglasses, as it were, to lecture his pupils: "It is a good rule, after reading a new book, never to allow yourself another new one till you have read an old one in between. If that is too much for you, you should at least read one old one to every three new ones."

Lewis argued that the characteristic blindness of a given age can only be discerned by reading the old books. What is necessary, he says, is to keep the "clean sea breeze of the centuries blowing through our minds." Lewis stumbled into reading the Christian classics almost accidentally through his studies as a literary critic. But what he found there is what J. I. Packer and others have called the "Great Tradition." Lewis said that when one has once found this, one has got on to "the great level viaduct which crosses the ages and which looks so high from the valleys, so low from the mountains, so narrow compared with the swamps, and so broad compared with the sheeptracks."[5] For Packer and Lewis in England, as for de Lubac and Danièlou in France, it was important to recall the church in the modern world to this level viaduct, this Great Tradition. This was a place to stand in the midst of modernity.

This hermeneutic of retrieval for the sake of renewal has been applied not only to the great consensual tradition of the church (singular) but also to the traditions (plural). By the great consensual tradition I mean Nicene and Chalcedonian Orthodoxy, the Vincentian canon, or what C. S. Lewis and Richard Baxter both called "mere Christianity." J. I. Packer once summarized his understanding of this Great Tradition in an address he gave to a conference of Protestant, Roman Catholic, and Eastern Orthodox theologians in 1995.[6] But, within this Great Tradition, there are the traditions (plural), in different times and places, culturally specific movements of renewal in the history of the church. These more narrow traditions are also sources and resources, founts of wisdom that can put us in touch with the work of the Holy Spirit over time. At Vatican II the council called for a renewal of religious life, that is, the life of the religious orders. How, it asked, would the religious orders be renewed? The council answered by calling on the religious "to be faithful to the spirit of their founders, to the intentions and the example of their sanctity. In this it finds one of the principles for the present renewal and one of the most secure criteria for judging what each institute should undertake."[7] In other words, Jesuits ought to recover something of the charism of Ignatius, Dominicans something of the spirit of Dominic, Franciscans something of the original vision of Francis, and so on. And indeed the mid-twentieth-century monastic revival among Catholics owed much to this sort of renewal through retrieval, such as, for example, through the influential scholarship of Jean Leclercq on early Cistercian spirituality. The council recognized that in "the charism of our founders" was a deeper charism, a gift of the Holy Spirit to the whole church itself. To the extent that a movement in church history was inspired by the Spirit of God, to that same extent this movement remains a witness and a resource to the church in later generations.

In dialogue with nonevangelicals J. I. Packer has sought to lay his stress on mainstream "Great Tradition" Christianity, but he has of course been especially influenced by one particular tradition within this mainstream, namely, the English Puritans.[8] Indeed, he was one of the key catalysts in the postwar revival of Puritan or neo-Calvinist theology among evangelicals on both sides of the Atlantic. This was the renewal of a *particular* tradition, a culturally specific

have Packer's gift of concision ("Packer by name, Packer by nature"), so I'll give just five reasons why I think we need the early evangelicals. This is at least a beginning.

The Early Evangelicals Modeled a Balanced Appreciation for the Individual and the Community

Some people today think of evangelicalism as unduly individualistic, focusing on "me" and "my experience" in an almost consumerist way. Evangelicals can seem preoccupied with private religious experience. Critics rightly ask, "What about incorporation in the church?" "What about the sacraments?" Evangelicalism seems a religion of "you in your small corner, and me in mine." In various ways the individualism of evangelical popular piety has been brought into question today: through the more relational insights of trinitarian theology, through the more corporate sense of salvation in the "new perspective" on Paul scholarship, through the more communitarian readings of Scripture in narrative theology, through the critique of Enlightenment autonomy in postmodernism, and so on.

Walter Truett Anderson argues that the social conditions of late modernism have changed the way we go about being religious: "Never before," he says, "has a society allowed its people to become consumers of belief, and allowed belief—all beliefs—to become merchandise."[12] One need not look far today to find examples of this consumer-driven, market-oriented, technique-infatuated individualism among evangelicals. For some younger intellectuals a reaction has set in, and this has been reason enough to reject evangelicalism altogether. Although the concerns here are to be taken seriously, I think this rejection of evangelicalism in toto is hasty and based on a thin and provincial reading of the tradition. Wherever valorized as such, individual autonomy must be critiqued. But I think the resources for evangelical reformation and renewal are right there within the tradition itself.

The early evangelicals were not rank individualists. The story is complex, but the followers of Wesley, Whitefield, and Edwards were far more communitarian than we might assume. They were on the cusp of the modern period and certainly adapted well to the new free market that was emerging in religion. All the developments in communications, transportation, capitalism, science, the media, and the bureaucratic state—all the developments that will constitute the modern period are there in embryo in the eighteenth century. Turnpike roads, canals, the merchant marine, an efficient postal system—all of these practical developments contributed to a greater mobility and heralded a greater decision-making power on the part of individuals, a greater voluntarism. In one sense, the evangelicals took advantage of this. When Whitefield stood up and preached in theatrical idiom in the marketplace, he was competing with the other popular entertainments of the city, not presuming on a state-supported monopoly over his hearers. So at one level one could say, "Aha! There is the beginning of our unhealthy individualism." Perhaps. But remember, they were on the verge, the edge, of the modern period. Just as we are *post*modern, they were *early* modern.

One of the virtues we need to recover from the early evangelicals is their capacity to affirm the uniqueness of the individual while emphasizing the necessity of belonging to a close-knit, disciplined Christian community. Many of the early women and men of Methodism had never found anything worthy of the name ecclesia in their experience of official religion, until they were incorporated into John Wesley's class meetings, or the cottage prayer meetings of an evangelical clergyman, or the Moravian bands. It should be remembered how central to evangelicalism the small, intimate group meetings were. With the help of the Pietists and the Moravians, the early evangelicals almost invented the small group meeting/care group/Bible study group/Alpha course—whatever one wants to call it. They called them bands, societies, and class meetings. Within these eighteenth-century cell groups the fellowship was close and men and women could unburden their souls to each other. Thomas Olivers was one who had heard some Methodist preaching at Bristol, and he was soon in deep spiritual concern for his soul. He used to stalk the Methodists, secretly following them to their meetings and eavesdropping on them. As they would sing their hymns, he would be outside crying. When they came out, he would follow them at a distance, still listening, sometimes following them for over two miles. He knew they had something he wanted.[13]

Again, when the laywoman Margaret Austin was abused and abandoned by her husband and left with two small children, she happened to go and hear George Whitefield preach. In all her days at church, she said she had never heard anything like it. She found herself in all the stories he told and her conscience was pricked. She wanted desperately to join one of the bands, and it was there she unburdened her soul and found relief under the guidance of one "Sister Robinson," who sang with her, counseled her, and like a midwife saw her through her spiritual travail.[14]

John Newton wrote a hymn to dedicate a new meeting place for his religious society, and it includes the stanza,

> Within these walls let holy peace,
> And love, and concord dwell;
> Here give the troubled conscience ease,
> The wounded spirit heal.[15]

It was within precisely this kind of close fellowship that women and men experienced the touch of God. Indeed the genre of the hymn itself, a kind of "folksong for Christian folk," was inseparable from the evangelical revival, and this communal genre points to the importance of such a fellowship.[16] We ought to think of these evangelicals more in terms of the individual-in-the-community than solely in terms of private religious experience. Salvation included the whole people of God, whom God was calling out, and whose spiritual solidarity in Christ was recognized in a new sense of community that could only adequately be expressed in terms of kinship. It wasn't simply sectarian cant when the early Methodists called one another brother and sister. They were "born again" not only in Christ as solitary individuals; they were also "born again" into new family relationships, into the community of Christ's people. For many, this was the family they never had.

But at the same time, the sense of individuation within this communal context was profound. As George Whitefield exhorted his hearers in eighteenth-century Glasgow, when preaching on Saul's Damascus Road experience, "Ah my dear Friends, this must be done to you as well as to *Saul.* . . . God must speak to you by Name, God must reach your Heart in particular."[17] And, so it seems, God did. Time and again, men and women who thought the whole of religion consisted in public religious observance and public rectitude—time and again, these people literally appear in history with a name and a unique story, as they narrated their discovery that the gospel message had to do with them personally and related to their own experience. Margaret Austin wrote to Charles Wesley not about just her new sense of community but also her new sense of identity: "The Lord saw fit," she wrote, "to Let me See my Self."[18] And the fact that she emerged at all from the mists of history with a name and a story is only because the gospel message preached by Whitefield seemed to uniquely apply to her and call forth her individual voice.

The sense of early evangelicals such as Wesley, Whitefield, and Edwards that the salvation construed in these terms had to do with individuals must however be seen in context. It must be seen in the context of an ancien régime society with an established church that had still had the overwhelming support of the population, a context in which most people were baptized and regarded themselves as Christian in the way that I regard myself as Canadian: I emerged into a consciousness of my citizenship without ever thinking about it as a conscious choice. Christendom still cast its shadow over eighteenth-century society in such a way that most women and men regarded it as their duty (whether they fulfilled this duty or not) to "go to church and sacrament" and to "do no harm." Evangelicalism represented a protest against the idea that adhering to Christian civil society as a nominal Christian was sufficient for salvation.[19] Evangelicalism emerged precisely on the trailing edge of Christendom and the leading edge of modernity. Enough scope had opened for individual agency that an appeal could be made to men and women to respond knowingly and personally to the gospel message. No wonder so many regarded it as a message not heard before. But their protest is not ours. Whereas we now protest against an excessive individualism in the old age of modernism, they were protesting against an excessively corporate but nominal view of salvation in the old age of Christendom. We worry that our typical understanding of salvation is deeply individual but not broad; they worried the typical understanding of salvation was broad but not deeply individual.

Just think for a moment of all the personal pronouns in Charles Wesley's hymns, pronouns that the printer often set in italic type: "Died he for *me* who caused his sin? For *me*, who him, to death pursued? Amazing love, how can it be, that Thou, my God, should die for *me*?" But note that this would be sung by a whole group of believers together. This was not an experience of individuation that pushed toward autonomy and privacy; this was an experience of being named and specified by divine love in such a way that people felt they could open their soul transparently to others who shared this same experience. And these men and women submitted themselves to demanding disciplines in small group fellowships that really were accountable. Every now and again Wesley would go through and purge the societies, such as at Newcastle in 1743 when two were expelled for habitual Sabbath breaking, seventeen for drunkenness, twenty-nine for lightness and carelessness, one for beating his wife, and nine because they were unwilling to be laughed at. These small groups were *not* lifestyle enclaves. There was a balanced appreciation among the early evangelicals for the individual and the Christian community, and this is a model that could well help renew and reform our churches today. Rank individualism is *not* an essential mark of an evangelical. Quite the contrary. To fail to enter deeply into mutual self-giving with other believers—into accountable relationships with the people of God—is to be not evangelical enough.

I have spent some time on this issue of the alleged individualism of evangelicalism because this is a concern I hear voiced often these days by those within and without the movement. More briefly, now, let's turn to consider four further reasons why we need the early evangelicals.

The Early Evangelicals Remind Us that to Be Evangelical Is to Be of the Gospel Rather Than to Form a Narrowly Partisan Identity

What is an evangelical anyway? A friend of mine says that it is easy to define the word *evangelical*—an evangelical is anyone who *really* likes Billy Graham. During the middle of the twentieth century, the term *evangelical* was being championed by a new generation of Americans to distinguish themselves from their allegedly more narrow fundamentalist forbears. In the midst of these debates, the renowned fundamentalist preacher Bob Jones Sr. was known to define an evangelical as "someone who says to a liberal, 'I'll call you a Christian if you'll call me a scholar.'" As a consequence of these sorts of debates, it is almost impossible for us to hear the term today without hearing in it a distinctively "partisan" ring. *Evangelical* as opposed to *fundamentalist* or *liberal* or *Catholic*. As an American evangelical friend enthusiastically asked me in Oxford, shortly after we had met, "So, what camp are you in?" As a Canadian evangelical, I asked for diplomatic immunity.

In contrast, the men and women we think of as the leaders of the early evangelical movement understood themselves less in partisan terms than in theological terms. It has, of course, also been a concern of J. I. Packer to help the evangelical movement become more deeply theological. The early evangelicals did not actually use the term *evangelical* often. Instead, they used terms like *gospel* as an adjective. There could be a gospel preacher, a gospel sermon, or even a gospel conversation. They also used the adjectives *serious*, *awakened*, or *spiritual* to describe clergymen, books, sermons, or ministries that they approved of. What they meant to recall by these labels—and by the term *evangelical* when they used it—was the scriptural message of salvation through Christ, taken as a matter of vital personal concern. That is a theological idea. They were not conjuring up a political alignment or institutional matrix within the broader church. That would come later, in the early nineteenth century when evangelicals in the Church of England had grown in numbers and developed more of the apparatus of party organization—magazines, clerical societies, patronage trusts, Bible and mission societies, and so on. And that sort of organizational sophistication has its place. But in the early days, evangelical leaders distinguished themselves not as a new religious phalanx but as Christian women and men seeking after real religion, as opposed to nominal, cultural Christian identity.

I do not want to overdraw this contrast, since the early evangelicals had their problems too. It is true that there were New Lights and Old Lights in New England, and that personal connections or alignments formed around strong figures such as Wesley, Lady Huntingdon, and others. Still, their ideals come through in their better moments: to be evangelical was to be of the gospel. They had a sense of shared identity that went beyond their parish or denomination and that was well and truly evangelical, but this was less a partisan mindset than a theological one. We would do well to retrieve their sense that evangelical identity has to do with something kerygmatic, a saving message about the Lord Jesus Christ. Even all the talk about the relationship between the individual and the community is only so much sociology if it is not about finding one's individuation and one's social connectedness through faith in Christ.

The Early Evangelicals Show Us What It Means to Be Missional without Becoming Narrowly Pragmatic Activists

There was no lack of energy and drive for mission among the early evangelicals. At twenty-two years of age George Whitefield preached about nine times a week in London. Charles Wesley wrote 8,989 hymns, which works out to be about ten lines of verse every day for fifty years. His brother John traveled a quarter of a million miles on horseback, preached forty-two thousand sermons, and published with his brother about five hundred titles. John Wesley's published journal alone was over a million words, and the critical edition just completed this year runs to 3,845 pages. George Whitefield made thirteen voyages across the Atlantic to preach the gospel in an international itinerancy. No, there was no lack of passion to preach the gospel for this early evangelical generation. But how did they understand their activism? How do we?

Popular evangelicalism today is in many cases preoccupied with an administrative approach to church life. It is written in letters almost too large to read. It is a technological mindset that approaches all problems in terms of the rational application of the most efficient means to achieve predetermined ends. This means/end rationality is really remarkably pervasive, and it rebounds on us in terms of program fatigue, and the ever-present fear of the ubiquitous Sunday school recruiter, who will ask us to join another committee or staff another program.

In contrast to the technological mindset of evangelicalism today, the mindset of the early evangelicals was more ecological. Ministry took place within an ecology of relationships without a great deal of bureaucratic apparatus. The eighteenth century was the great age of friendship, hospitality, and letter writing. Organizational initiatives were few and unsophisticated for the most part. Wesley was the best organizer and disciplinarian of the lot. But still, the early evangelicals had no strategic marketing plans, pyramidal discipleship schemes, or mission statements; no designated greeters at the door either. More often their networks were built up through the exchange of household hospitality, letters, and semiformal small group meetings. Rather than discussing strategy, they preferred to talk of a certain number of ordained means of grace, such as preaching, holy communion, the reading of Scripture, prayer, and Christian conversation and friendship. These are not made up in response to perceived needs or market trends. The phrase they used sounds remarkably passive to our ears: people "wait on God in the means of grace." This phrase appears in the Prayer Book in the Prayer of General Thanksgiving where the worshipers give thanks for "the means of grace and the hope of glory." But note that for the early evangelicals this was an intense on-the-tip-of-your-toes kind of waiting. When some of the Moravians in the 1740s were caught up in the "stillness" movement, claiming that people ought to be completely passive until God gives them faith—that they ought not to pray or receive the sacrament or do anything that might imply a false legal dependence on themselves for salvation—John Wesley dragged the Welsh preacher Howell Harris around London with him to tell his testimony. Howell Harris was awakened spiritually and then converted *during* the devout reception of Holy Communion. He waited on God in the means of grace. Catch the God-centered focus too— waiting on *God* in the means. And their waiting was indeed rewarded with countless examples of spiritual renewal at a personal and community level. So here too, as evangelicals today look for new ways to be efficacious communities without falling into the practical atheism of technique-driven church life, we have resources for renewal in early evangelical spirituality.

The Early Evangelicals Demonstrate for Us What It Means to Worship God Passionately with Mind and Heart United

Several years ago I was invited to Nashville to give a set of lectures on eighteenth-century hymnody to a group of about three hundred worship leaders who worked with college-age students. I was intrigued by the invitation and went. I was surprised and delighted by what I found. Here was a whole worship movement among Reformed University Fellowship students and other related groups that was predicated on a revival of classical hymns in new musical idioms. In the worship session before I got up to speak, I found myself sitting beside a twenty-year-old college student who came to faith in Christ only recently. We sang together Charles Wesley's "And Can It Be" to a tune I'd never heard before, with a folk rock mix of acoustic and electric instruments, thundering bass, and driving percussion. The musicianship was excellent. The college student beside me was clearly into the worship. When I chatted with him further I found out that he had no idea who Charles Wesley was or that "And Can It Be" had ever been sung any other way. But it was one of his favorite songs.

That, for me, is an example of retrieval and renewal in the area of worship. There are dozens of Christian session players and recording artists in Nashville who have been sitting around in their living rooms with a copy of Gadsby's hymnal open on the floor, plucking out new tunes to hymns that haven't seen the light of day for years. One of the hymn writers they have revived is Anne Steele, a little-known eighteenth-century Baptist poet whose religious verse poignantly expresses trust in Christ in the midst of all life's hardships. Her verse is a treasure from the evangelical attic well worth bringing back downstairs.

What is specifically being revived here is the desire to hold together robust theology, true poetry, and deep feeling—to draw the whole person into worship with both mind and heart. And this is what classical eighteenth-century hymnody did so well. It was one of the most remarkable revivals of song in the Christian church since the time of Ambrose. And it bore its own witness to the deep joy that was at the heart of this revival. Remarkably, this was a period in which, instead of the church dividing between elite and popular expressions of worship, evangelical hymnody held the two together. As I have read through hundreds of letters from ordinary laypeople in the evangelical revival, I have been impressed by how often these rank-and-file evangelicals quote lines from hymns or sang them on their own at night, in times of trouble, or informally with friends. Converted criminals sang hymns on the way to the gallows. Others reported how they were converted during the singing of a hymn. Perhaps the surest sign to me of the popularity of hymns was Elizabeth Halfpenny's letter, in which she mentioned two men visiting her for breakfast and how the three of them sang hymns together. I think that when laypeople are singing hymns at breakfast, you know you have a revival on your hands.

But hymns were not just popular; they were also elite. The combination of theological and poetic gifts that went into the hymns of Isaac Watts and Charles Wesley was truly remarkable. This was didactic verse, constrained by the needs of worship and the necessity of immediate congregational understanding and consent. And yet both these men, and countless others, perfected their art in such a way that they wrote dense theology in a poetry of worship. On this subject, let me quote one of the most insightful scholars of eighteenth-century hymnody, Donald Davie, himself a practicing poet. He says of Charles Wesley, and the same could be said about Watts and other contemporaries, "His hymns are not, like most later hymns, geysers of warm feeling. And yet, heaven knows, the feeling is there. We respect its integrity and we take its force just because it is not offered in isolation but together with its occasion, an occasion grasped and presented with keen and sinewy intelligence. Intelligence comes into the poetry of this period not as contraband, smuggled in . . . as 'ingenuity' . . . but straight forward and didactic. And the intellectual strength does not desiccate the emotions but gives them validity and force."[20] This evangelical aesthetic, this gospel poetics, is, I think, well worth retrieving for the sake of the reinvigoration and renewal of evangelical worship today. When we begin singing songs that are little more than "I love the way I feel when I love you," we have fallen far from the ideal set for us by the first generation of evangelicals.

The Early Evangelicals Can Inspire Us with a Vision Not Only for Conversion But Also for Transformation and Consummation

John Wesley was resolute that salvation was not from the punishment of sin but from sin. His doctrine of entire sanctification or perfection was controversial then, as now, but it leant to his whole order of salvation a strongly teleological sense of salvation. The hymn, "Love Divine, All Loves Excelling," that has been sung so politely at so many weddings by the well-meaning sister of the bride, was included in Wesley's hymnbook under the heading, "Seeking for Full Redemption," and it expresses the fervent longing of many Methodists to know here and now the fullness of salvation. When listening to the lyrics of this hymn, we must think of the perfectionist revivals of the mid-century in which some women and men were crying out that they had been sanctified and others were longing for the same experience in tears and groaning. The lines, "Fix in us thy humble dwelling" and "Visit us

with thy salvation" are cries of invocation, not words of decorative poetry.
Recall the last stanza:

> Finish then thy new creation,
> Pure and spotless let us be;
> Let us see thy great salvation,
> Perfectly restored in thee;
> Changed from glory into glory,
> Till in heaven we take our place,
> Till we cast our crowns before thee,
> Lost in wonder, love, and praise.[21]

The goal of salvation was nothing less than "that holiness without which
no one will see the Lord." Increasingly, Wesley came to emphasize faith as a
means to the end of holiness: *fides caritatem formata*, faith working by love,
became the center of his theology of salvation.[22] Perfection, though, was a
contested point even among his followers. William Grimshaw of Haworth
would have none of it. When some were claiming to be perfected, he said,
"I wish they knew their own hearts. My perfection is to see my own imper-
fection. . . . I know no other, expecting to lay down my Life and my Sword
together."[23] And yet other evangelicals picked up this teleological drive in
Wesley's understanding of salvation. Newton wrote to a friend in 1772 saying that he was far, very far, from maintaining this idea of sinless perfection,
"yet there is a liberty and privilege attainable by the Gospel, beyond what is
normally thought of."[24] In other words, there are undreamt of possibilities
in the spiritual life in terms of how God might indeed transform us before
death into holy persons. Newton said of Wesley's doctrine of perfection that
he would rather strive toward it than enter into dispute against it. To another
correspondent he laid out a series of typical stages in Christian experience
from the initiation of faith through conflict and testing to an experience of
contemplative union with Christ that comes about as close as possible to
Wesley without ceasing to be Calvinist.[25]

This sense of "a liberty and privilege attainable by the gospel" is the larger
sense of salvation I would like to stress, since it contrasts with predominant
images of evangelicalism today that focus on one-time decisions made in the
context, for example, of crusade evangelism. Often in the past, evangelicals
have understood salvation to include what Catholics call ascetical theology,
or what many of us today would describe as formative spirituality. Since the
late 1970s evangelicals seem to have discovered spiritual disciplines as though
these were something alien to their own tradition, as though Wesley and
Whitefield did not regularly fast, keep spiritual diaries, observe the Sabbath,
and seek to "live by rule." These were the means of grace, but their vision was
for something more than muscular self-discipline. Their hope was, by grace,
to move on toward their final salvation and the glory yet to be revealed. Salva-

tion has a past, a present, and a future tense. When we become too focused on one-time experiences in the Christian life, the early evangelicals can inspire us with this vivid awareness of the call to holiness and the hope of glory—the goal of our spiritual life.

Conclusion

We have explored together five possible sites for retrieval and renewal in the evangelical tradition: the relationship of the individual to the community, the priority of the gospel message for evangelical identity, the capacity for confident mission rather than programmatic activism, the ideal of heart and mind united in ardent worship, and a spiritual passion not only for initiation into the faith but also for the maturing and perfecting of that same faith. And so we could continue, like Robin Hood, stealing from the riches of one generation to supply our own needs where we have been cut off from our roots by modernity with its relentless focus on present concerns. We could explore early evangelical concern for the bodies as well as the souls of those they cared for. We could take note of the way in which they recognized the need to formulate principles of discernment to assess and pastor congregations caught up in revival. We could expound their appreciation for the radical, addictive, and disabling nature of sin, and their corresponding appreciation for the need for a divine Savior. But this is perhaps enough for one day. We can retreat to Sherwood Forest, empty our sacks, and return another day to scout out more riches yet. This task—*retrieving* theological insight from history for the sake of the *renewal* of the modern church—is one of the many theological tasks J. I. Packer has done well over the course of his lifetime. In this, he has provided a model for evangelical vitality for another generation. And we can all shout heartily, "Well done, good Robin!"

8

J. I. Packer

An English Nonconformist Perspective

CARL R. TRUEMAN

Introduction

J. I. Packer is, arguably, one of the great beneficiaries of the long-established North American tradition of granting almost guru-like status to British evangelicals. Stott, Packer, McGrath, Wright: the list is ever-expanding and, one might add, perennially perplexing to the British for whom such figures, while sometimes significant "back in Blighty," never seem to have quite the same authoritative mystique and uncritical adulation back in Britain as they do across the Atlantic.

In the case of Packer, the difference between his reception in America and that in Great Britain is, however, not simply because of the cultural phenomenon alluded to above but also because of key differences in the evangelical ecclesiastical politics of the last fifty years. With the exception of his involvement in Evangelicals and Catholics Together, Packer has by and large avoided serious ecclesiastical controversy during his time in North America; in Britain, however, his reputation has frequently been refracted through the events of the 1960s that proved so traumatic in the setting of evangelical ecclesiastical trajectories down to the present day. For many of the generation of British evangelicals who cut their theological teeth in the sixties and seventies, Packer is not the benign grand old statesman that he is for so many in North America. Rather, British evangelical opinions about Packer can be quite polarized and divided. Thus, it seems appropriate in a collection of essays such as this to offer an English perspective on his life and contribution, in order to bring into relief how he is not simply a significant figure for North America but was also central to the events which have shaped British evangelical identity over the last half-century.[1]

English Evangelical Nonconformity

Before addressing the issue of Packer directly, I need to qualify my analysis in one further way. Not only are my thoughts here offered as those of an Englishman; they are also those of an evangelical nonconformist that, for the sake of argument, I define here as evangelical Protestant non-Anglican. This is a key category, as the defining moment of Packer's career in English eyes occurred in 1966, when he and the influential evangelical leader Martyn Lloyd-Jones parted ways over precisely the issue of whether Anglicanism was a viable, legitimate option for British evangelicals. We shall discuss this in more detail below; but first it is necessary to indicate that the kind of what one might call cultural division between Anglicans and nonconformists is one that goes back a significant distance in English church history, and that provides the broader context for understanding the events of the 1960s.

The reformation of the English church took a fairly tortuous path in the sixteenth and seventeenth centuries but was finally settled in 1660 when the monarchy was restored, Charles II became king, and the House of Stuart effectively brought an end to the debates about what the Anglican Church should look like. The Book of Common Prayer became the prescribed form of worship and, by a series of parliamentary acts passed in 1662, conformity of both mind and practice was imposed on the clergy. Those who could not acquiesce were forced to leave the established church, and so English nonconformity was born. The privileged legal status that the Church of England then enjoyed (and, in a much more muted way, still enjoys) had profound social and political significance. It is sometimes remarked that Catholics were subject to legal discrimination in England until the nineteenth century; but such was also the case for Baptists and Congregationalists, who also lacked the vote and could not attend either of the two universities then in existence or hold jobs in Parliament or the civil service. Nonconformists were every bit as marginal as the Catholics, and the cultural divide this established remained long after the legal codes enforcing this had been removed. With the changes of the nineteenth century—the enfranchising of non-Anglican males and the rise of industrial production and commerce—nonconformists began to grow

tangible, and, in my experience as a young Christian, pervasive in churches led by men who looked to Lloyd-Jones as their mentor and 1966 as the defining moment in recent British evangelical history. At a more verifiable level, it is arguable that the intellectual and theological revival among British nonconformist evangelicals stalled as the more intelligent conservative thinkers were discouraged from pursuing higher degrees and really engaging theologically with the Christian tradition and the wider world. In England, independency carried the day among nonconformists, and so the result was an ecclesiologically weakened tradition that was vulnerable both to personality cults (not least that of Lloyd-Jones himself, though there are far more sinister examples) and to theological excesses, whether charismatic, secondary separatist, or whatever. As for paedobaptism, traditional forms of worship, creedal self-consciousness, and so on—all of these things were always going to be far more difficult to maintain within independency, and so it has proved. The spirit of 1966 left English nonconformity in particular in a highly weakened, fissiparous, intellectually impoverished, and increasingly fragmented condition.

Throughout these groups, the followers of Lloyd-Jones exerted considerable influence and ensured that the marginalization of Packer within British nonconformist ranks was maintained. He was seen as a compromiser who had ultimately not had the courage to stand with Lloyd-Jones against the inroads of ecumenism and liberalism. On the other side, however, the kind of Anglican evangelicalism that emerged in the 1970s and '80s was no more conducive to Packer, no more sympathetic to systematic theology, and no more connected to historic creedal and confessional trajectories than its nonconformist counterpart. Packer stood for rigorous, Reformed, systematic, and comprehensive theological thinking. The Anglican charismatics, and then groups such as the Proclamation Trust, did not represent that kind of thinking at all. And the kind of evangelicalism in the Anglican theological colleges of the time, such as Wycliffe at Oxford, Trinity in Bristol, Ridley at Cambridge, St. John's in Nottingham, and Oak Hill in London, was far removed from Packer's vision (though recent years have given much cause for hope that several of these institutions are moving in a more theologically astute direction). In short, he had nowhere to call home: the nonconformists despised him as a traitor; the Anglicans distrusted him. The result: his move to Canada must surely be seen as much as indicating the theological and ecclesiastical poverty of Britain as any positive commentary on North America. Sadly, this antiecclesiastical and antitheological culture remains strong in today's Anglican evangelicalism: that a leading institute for the training of preachers uses Bruce Milne's *Know the Truth* as its only systematic theology textbook is an eloquent testimony to the fact that *systematics*, if not theology, is a dirty word in many Anglican circles. And the impact of the biblical theological approach of Moore College, excellent as it is in many ways as a tool, is yet problematic in the way that it seems to have gained a virtual pedagogical monopoly in many Anglican circles and thus helped to marginalize historic systematic, creedal, and ecclesiological categories within Anglican evangelicalism. To give a personal example, I gave a paper at an Anglican gathering some years ago on the importance of the Lord's Supper in worship, using as my sources the Thirty-Nine Articles, the Homilies, the Book of Common Prayer, and the writings of Thomas Cranmer. The strong negative passions that the paper generated among the audience reminded me of how far typical Anglican evangelicalism is, not simply from my own Presbyterian tradition but also from its own historical roots and doctrinal standards. If Bishop David Jenkins was out of step with the Thirty-Nine Articles, then there is a whole Anglican evangelical culture out there that is subject to precisely the same criticism. And that is neither the culture nor the theology of J. I. Packer. No wonder he had to leave for Canada.

An Exercise in Virtual History

Given the sad tale outlined above, one way to bring out the importance of Packer's role is perhaps to engage for a few moments in an experiment in virtual history by asking the questions: What would have happened if Packer had followed Lloyd-Jones in 1966? If he had "come out" what would British evangelicalism now look like?

Had Packer left the Church of England, it is ironic that Anglican evangelicalism would probably not have been much affected. It would have lost its single sharpest theological mind, but, as argued above, that is precisely what made Packer a marginal figure within Anglican evangelicalism even as he decided to stay in the church. A working-class systematician was functionally irrelevant to the culture of a Bash Camp evangelicalism. Packer teaching at, say, London Theological Seminary would not have made him any more marginal to Anglican evangelicalism in Britain than his occupying an academic chair at a college in the far west of Canada. Perhaps the biography would have been written by Iain Murray rather than Alister McGrath, but that is surely a minor point.

On the other side, however, the impact on English evangelical nonconformity could have been immense. It would not have found that it had only one leader but would have perhaps enjoyed something of a healthy balance of power that might well have emerged at the top, so to speak. Lloyd-Jones met his intellectual and theological match in Packer, and he appears to have known it; if Gaius Davies's analysis is to be believed, that is one of the nontheological reasons that it was always inevitable the two would fall out. But if Packer had nonetheless come out, the iconic guru status accorded to "the Doctor" by a whole generation of English and Welsh church leaders would not have gone unchallenged and several positive outcomes may have flowed from this.

First, the Reformed theology of the Lloyd-Jones constituency may have ended up being really Reformed. *Reformed* in Lloyd-Jones circles tends to mean the five points of Calvinism, frequently bound to a strong interest in revival and, at times, an almost mystical concern for Christian experience. As noted above, Lloyd-Jones read the Reformed tradition through the grid of eighteenth-century revivalism; and so the ideal of a learned ministry and the importance of ecclesiology, sacraments, creeds, confessions, and liturgy all tended to be marginalized in his thinking and critiqued through the lens of his pneumatology. Thus he generally saw them as potentially hindering revival. This is not Reformed theology in the historic sense of the term. For a Presbyterian, for example, the catholic creedal tradition, the confessions and catechisms of the Westminster Assembly, the need for a learned ministry, and the centrality of the sacraments are all part and parcel of what it is to be Reformed and, critically, what are needed to maintain precisely the kind of doctrinal purity and testimony that was so dear to Lloyd-Jones. For the Reformed, this purity can only be maintained within a proper ecclesiastical context. Loose, unconfessional, independent churches, no matter how committed they are in the first generation to the gospel, are inherently unstable as theological entities and ultimately dependent on the personality and theology of the pastor and the makeup and tastes of the congregation; Lloyd-Jones's vision was fatally flawed by its ecclesiology-free incoherence. Packer, however, could have brought his immense learning in history and theology to bear on these matters; he could have challenged Lloyd-Jones and no doubt frequently beaten him in arguments on these points; and maybe, just maybe, nonconformist evangelicals might have recovered something of a historic, churchly, confessional context in which the truth can not only be coherently defended but also from which it can be coherently articulated to the wider world.

Second, evangelical nonconformity may have retained a catholicity of spirit (and thus a unity of purpose) that it so signally lacked in the decades after 1966. Packer clearly had, and still has, a passionate love for the church and for its visible unity. Lloyd-Jones did too, though his vision of unity was really unity on his terms, as I argued above and to which effect I quoted from Packer's own writings. Particularly Anglo-Welsh evangelical nonconformity became highly fragmented and marginal after the split, and talk of church unity was rarely more than just talk, with the vision of some form of loose connectionalism being the height of ecumenical ambition. Indeed, the fear of an unbiblical ecumenism created a culture where all who were not one hundred percent with us were against us and where even the reading of a book by someone from outside the accepted canon could create suspicion of one's orthodoxy. I well remember the unease with which my own decision to pursue a PhD was greeted in some such circles; and yet I was also stunned on reading John Owen, the great Puritan, to find that he read with appreciation writers from all periods of church history as he strove to articulate a fully-rounded and truly catholic theology. Such a reading of the Puritans was not made available through the work of Lloyd-Jones and his immediate successors, and this was a function of the picture of the church and Christianity that was driving the project. Packer knew the Puritans better, and he could have drawn from their catholicity to help nonconformists recover the real riches of the whole Christian tradition.

Third, the kind of rapprochement between Anglican evangelicals and their nonconformist brethren that has slowly but surely started to take place over recent years (symbolized, for example, by Anglicans such as Dick Lucas and Garry Williams speaking at the Banner of Truth Conference and by Oak Hill Theological College attracting many students from independent churches) might have happened much earlier. The net result of 1966 was that everyone lost: in British evangelicalism, the whole was always greater than the sum of the parts. Of course, this last point is perhaps the most debatable. Perhaps if Packer had left, the bitterness felt by those who stayed may well have prevented him from ever brokering an ecumenical agreement between the two parties, but he would surely have worked hard behind the scenes to make such a thing happen if at all possible.

But Packer remained an Anglican. That was, I believe, a mistake and greatly impoverished the British evangelical scene. He failed to be the leader that he should have been because he simply refused Lloyd-Jones's call rather than building on it. He was the one man who had the theology and, more importantly, the ecclesiology to have potentially offered some positive church vision to which others might come out even as they heeded Lloyd-Jones's call. But nonconformity failed badly too, not least because Lloyd-Jones's call to agree with him on the nonimportance of so many critical ecclesiological points did not really give Packer a viable alternative to staying in, nor give those who left much to build on.[16]

Conclusion

I probably owe more to J. I. Packer in terms of theology and life than to anybody else. Thus, when I write about him, I am inevitably biased. His writings are among the clearest and most lucid statements of orthodoxy available, lacking both pomposity and that dusty piety that so often weighs down other writers of the neo-Puritan revival. Yet my admiration is not uncritical. There are two points where Packer has failed. As should be clear from the above, for me he is the lost leader of English nonconformity, the man who failed to come out in 1966 and provide us with an ecclesiological nonconformity and a counterbalance to the ultimately unchallenged leadership of Martyn Lloyd-Jones. The disaster of 1966, from which British evangelicalism is only just emerging, could have been so much less damaging if Packer had listened to Lloyd-Jones's negative call to come out and supplemented it with that which Lloyd-Jones failed to do: a proper ecclesiological, doctrinal, confessional alternative to remaining in a mixed denomination.

Further, it is surely disappointing that he has never produced a full systematic theology. *Knowing God* is a great book, as are his other volumes such as *God's Words*, but like Bruce Milne's *Know the Truth*, they are really where Christian learning starts, not where it ends. Packer has a brilliant mind, full of theological footnotes; indeed, only a brilliant mind could write deep theology in such a profoundly simple way; yet he should have given us more. All those footnotes that he holds in his head—would that he had written them down somewhere! Those who have great learning have an obligation to the church to make sure that it is appropriately imparted.

Yet, as a final point, it is Packer's failure in these two areas that, perhaps perversely, leads to his greatest success. He is surely the classic example of a modest, Christian gentleman. As he was reviled by those who felt he failed them in 1966, he reviled not in return; and he has never used his learning as an excuse to exempt himself from serving even the most humble of God's servants. His writings and his willingness to speak to the least in the kingdom have surely helped countless Christians. Setting aside the disaster of 1966, which really brought credit to no one on either side, it is in these areas, in some ways intangible as they are, that he leaves his greatest legacy to the evangelical church, that of the example of a humble servant of Jesus Christ and his people, one who loves his Lord and all those for whom he died.

9

Packer, Puritans, and Postmoderns

CHARLES W. COLSON

It is a thrill to help honor J. I. Packer. Very few people in my Christian life have had the impact on me that he has. A number of years ago, there was a dispute between two Christian leaders over a certain book that had come out. There were charges of heresy, and it was a roaring controversy. A number of Christian leaders called me and said, "Can you figure out one person who would be our 'bishop' who could mediate our dispute?" In the course of conversation, we immediately agreed on J. I. Packer. We decided that he was the bishop of evangelicalism, at least in North America. He handled the situation in very irenic fashion and brought together those angry parties. That is just one little anecdote, one insight into the character of this extraordinary man who has defended the gospel and taught us all in his classic book *Knowing God*. It was a very influential book for me right after my conversion.

I think what I have always appreciated most about Packer, however, is his courage. As a former Marine, I admire courage. I got into something a few years ago called Evangelicals and Catholics Together. That created quite a dustup at the time. I was taking a great deal of heat from people who did not quite understand what we were doing. I think now most people applaud it. But in those days Packer was one of the men who stood with me and mediated that dispute as he has mediated so many other disputes of evangelicalism. He always had that gift of being able to write exactly the right word at exactly the right time and just settle the problem among the people. I have admired and appreciated this man whom I am proud to call my friend.

The title of my essay is "Packer, Puritans, and Postmodernism." What theme would throw those three together? I think the central theme that draws them together best for me is *truth*. Packer has been one of the great defenders of truth. His great legacy to evangelicalism, I think, will be not only his sterling preaching, biblical exegesis, and books but also the defense of orthodoxy all these years, orthodoxy that was represented by the preaching of the Puritans and orthodoxy that is today in grave jeopardy among evangelicals. It is in great jeopardy because truth is in great jeopardy. The very existence of truth is being debated today. Yet we follow the One who says, "I am the truth." I love Colossians 1:16–17: "All things have been created through him and for him. He is before all things, and in him all things hold together" (TNIV). The truth is the ultimate logos, the plan of creation. We sometimes minimize Jesus. We make him just the redeemer. But he is also the Creator; he is everything.

Many evangelicals say there is no such thing as truth. I don't know how one puts together "the truth, Jesus, whom we worship" and "there's no such thing as truth." What is truth? A very bright and genial seminary student greeted me at the airport, and we got started talking about this in the car. I said, "What is truth?" He remembered that it was Pilate's question. He ended up coming up with a pretty good answer. Truth, very simply friends, is that which corresponds to reality. Truth is the way things are. When we say "the truth," we are saying "the ultimate reality," the way things are and how they came to be this way.

What is our culture saying today, what does our postmodern culture say? The postmodern culture says that there is basically no such thing as truth. Stanley Fish is a leading academic and one of the leaders in what is known as deconstruction—taking literature and then law and every other area of life and saying that what people wrote cannot be trusted because it was simply the prejudice of that particular cultural construction. Therefore, we can't take anything that was written seriously. He did as much as anybody else to diminish our understanding of truth or belief in truth. After the terrorist attacks of 9/11/2001, Fish said, let us not be too hasty in judging their motives; we do not know why they did what they did. Of course, everybody jumped on him, and most of us were saying "that is it, that is the end of postmodernism," because it was such a ridiculous statement. So he came back and wrote an op-ed piece in the *New York Times*.[1] He is a very clever man. In the piece he argues for agnostic epistemology with respect to any universal truth standard. However, if there is truth but we cannot know it, then that truth has no meaning. This is basically what the American academic and the Western academic establishment is saying today. This is postmodernism in a nutshell. It is saying there is no truth and if there were truth we would not be able to know it; therefore, we are living in this great age of relativism where my truth is my truth and your truth is your truth, and we can have it any way we fashion it.

This tension is rooted in the story of Jesus himself, in the great dramatic confrontation between Jesus and Pilate. Remember how that confrontation took place? It took place when Jesus was brought before Pilate. Pilate asks him questions. Jesus finally says, "My kingdom is not of this world. If it were, my servants would fight to prevent my arrest by the Jewish leaders. But my kingdom is from another place" (John 18:36 TNIV). "You are a king then!" says Pilate. Jesus answers, "You are right that I am a king. In fact, the reason I was born and came into the world is to testify to the truth. Everyone on the side of truth listens to me" (John 18:37 TNIV). At which point, Pilate said, "What is truth?"

Every translation that I have read has a question mark after "What is truth?" Mel Gibson got it right in *The Passion of the Christ*.[2] When translating from the Aramaic (which was the language spoken in the movie) in the subtitles he used an exclamation point: What is truth! There is nothing new about post-modernism. Pilate was sneering dismissively then, "What is truth!" Precisely what our culture is doing today.

The most scandalous thing that one can do today is make a truth claim. There is a story I tell in a book I wrote called *In Search of the Good Life*.[3] I was out in Silicon Valley with a lot of the leaders of the high-tech industries there and was seated next to a futurologist. He writes a newsletter that people spend hundreds of dollars per year to get. I was brought to this luncheon by Christians, and they said, "Witness to him because he is not a believer." So I was trying to do it as gently as I could. He was sitting immediately to my left and I thought that I made a couple of good points. He turned to me and said, "You know, that is what I resent about you Christians. You think that you have the truth. All religions have the truth. All religions are going to the same place."

I said, "You are a very intelligent man, you write some very interesting things. I have read your newsletters. You cannot believe that. Truth is truth." I took out my pen and dropped it several times. "Is it fair to say that when I drop the pen, it drops?" He referred to the quantum theory. "No, it is just molecules; it is just particles passing through particles." I said, "Come on, what did you see when you saw the pen drop? Mass will hit mass. There are truth claims. The law of gravity is a truth claim. Every religion makes a truth claim: no man comes to the father but through me. Everybody has a truth claim. They may all be wrong, but they cannot all be right. So, it is not a very intelligent statement to say, 'All religions lead to the same place.' It is not a respectful statement either." Red was coming up from the back of his neck at this point, and I said, "You would not suspend the law of noncontradiction, would you?" He said, "Let us just say it is extra-natural." I love it. They cannot get off that hook.

There is only one thing more scandalous than making a truth claim: making it and proving it. That is really an offense in today's culture. Prison Fellowship launched the Inner-Change Freedom Initiative (IFI), which is now operating in seven prisons. The first one opened in Texas in 1997 when then-governor George Bush gave us permission to start it. These programs have been hugely successful in prisons located in Iowa, Kansas, Minnesota, Missouri, and Arkansas. The prisoners are in there twenty-four hours a day. There is no television. They are in Bible study, they are working, they go to classes, and they do jobs. They have vocational training. They have worship in the evening. They are there for eighteen months, and a mentor is matched up with them when they get out. A study was done by the University of Pennsylvania to determine the results of our Texas program, our first one. The study found only 8 percent recidivism among the inmates who completed all phases of the program. We are making a truth claim: The gospel is true and it changes lives; it conforms to reality. It is what is, and we see it because these lives are changed and then we proved it with a peer-reviewed study by Princeton and Harvard and published by the University of Pennsylvania.

Barry Lynn went right out to Iowa, found a sympathetic judge, sued us, and we were told that we had to shut down our IFI program in Iowa—the only program that was working in the prison.[4] Not only that, but the judge wrote up a 147-page decision in which he takes twenty pages to describe evangelicals and says that we are basically a cult because we believe in such legalistic doctrines as the substitutionary, atoning death of Christ on the cross and even in the resurrection of Jesus.[5] That judge's opinion shows how confused people are about religion. This culture gets incredibly angry about a truth claim. Truth claims get in our way because we cannot make up our own truth.

Why does all this matter? If we do not take truth seriously, we will not take God seriously. The crisis we face in this country, unless we find a way to winsomely engage the postmodern culture, is that people will not take our God seriously. They may like having our God as an experience. They may want something from it. But they are not going to take it seriously. The problem, however, is not just in our culture today. The problem is also in our church, where we have stopped taking truth seriously. In 1997, the Barna Research Group reported results of a survey showing fifty percent of Christians who said they believe in moral absolute truth.[6] In August 2005, an updated survey by the Barna Group reported that among American adults of various worldviews, seventy percent of evangelicals believe that moral truth is absolute. It was somewhat like this in the 1960s during what was then called the "back to Jesus" movement, when people said that all we need is Jesus. Similar things are happening now in the emerging church movement and in the wider evangelical fellowship.[7]

Let me provide some quotes from a pastor in a large postmodern church. Here is what he said: "We are rediscovering Christianity as an eastern religion, as a way of life. Legal metaphors for faith don't deliver a way of life."[8] Yet the

Apostle Paul had recourse to legal forensic language in describing the central doctrine of justification by faith (see Rom. 3:19–48 ESV).

He went on to say that he is now questioning assumptions about the Bible itself and discovering the Bible as a human product rather than a product of divine fiat. The Bible is still the center for us, he says, but it is a different kind of center. "We want to embrace mystery rather than conquer it." One emerging church leader's wife, Kristen Bell, who shares in the ministry of Mars Hill Bible Church in Grand Rapids, Michigan, with her husband, Rob, says that she grew up thinking that "we've figured out the Bible, that we knew what it means. Now I have no idea what most of it means. And yet I feel like life is big again—like life used to be black and white, and now it's in color." And this comes from one of the most prominent spokesmen from the emergent church: "I don't think we've got the gospel right yet. What does it mean to be 'saved'? When I read the Bible, I don't see it meaning, 'I'm going to heaven after I die.' Before modern evangelicalism nobody accepted Jesus Christ as their personal Savior, or walked down an aisle, or said the sinner's prayer."[9] This statement confuses the style of modern revivalism with the historic Christian belief that personal commitment to Jesus Christ is the only way of salvation for all persons everywhere.

There was a front page article in the *New York Times* which quoted megachurch pastor Gregory Boyd. Reverend Boyd stated in one of his sermons, "The church should steer clear of politics and give up moralizing on sexual issues."[10] He argues, as do many younger leaders, that we should go back to the original first-century church. However, in the early church, one of the first big issues they had to deal with was the practice of infanticide and abortion, which they called murder (*Didache* II.2).[11]

We are not talking here about technique. We are not talking here about church growth. We are talking about the heart of the gospel. Because what folks are saying now is that we cannot know truth unless we can experience it. While there is a valid experiential aspect of truth, the reality of truth itself does not depend on an experience of it. When we experience truth, we are simply discovering what is already true; we did not make it truth.

Why is this so important? Because the Bible was revealed to us; nobody made it up. It is propositional; that is, it is expressed in language that is to be understood. It is truth, it is reality.

Once we say we can know truth just through the relationship with Jesus—get rid of all the dry, dusty doctrine—we are going back to liberalism in the church. Liberalism is not another form of Christianity; it is a different religion. It is liberalism. This is exactly the point made by J. Gresham Machen nearly a century ago in his classic book *Christianity and Liberalism*.

What must we do? The number one task is to understand, as Francis Schaeffer was wont to say, that even before we can deal with the question of God, we have to deal with the concept of truth. We have to arrive at the point where we can say there is something called truth that is knowable. What are we talking about here? We are talking about whether we are really here in this room tonight and able to know one another. René Descartes said, "I think, therefore I am."[12] He put it all on himself, but he was struggling with this question: "How can we know reality?" We have only two choices. Either what we are part of and experiencing is real and we can know it or, as the Hindus say, we are a dream in the mind of God. The greatest intellectual search of all time is for reality. A Christian believes that truth is knowable. The truth is found in the One who says, "I am."

There are three basic presuppositions that Christians begin all thought with. One, God is. Two, he has spoken. Three, God's speech is not nonsense; it means something. If "God is" is correct and he is an intelligent God, when he chooses to reveal something about himself to us, then it is logical that his self-revelation is not irrational. As Schaeffer often opined, if we are simply a product of impersonal matter times chance times a random process, then there is no intelligence to be spoken to us. But if a Creator has spoken to us—a knowing, loving Creator—then he is going to tell us about ourselves. I would say the two presuppositions—"God is" and "God has spoken"—are the foundation of all clear thinking. They are also the foundation of the beginning of understanding what Christianity means.

Alvin Plantinga, professor of philosophy at the University of Notre Dame, starts all his talks by saying, "God is." Many listeners would think that this is an irrational statement. But he has argued many times that this is the only rational statement we could make. He sometimes asks, "You're thinking it is irrational to simply say, 'God is.' But would you believe the statement that other people have minds? And many philosophers and debaters say that they believe other people have minds." Then Plantinga replies, "Why is that not irrational?" The listeners usually answer, "Because we know all people have a mind." I can almost hear Plantinga respond: "I know there is a God who created us. To believe this requires no more faith than to say other people have minds." But he continues—"When you stop and think about the possibility of 'God isn't' and the possibility of 'God is,' and you weigh all the rational arguments, it is far more rational to start with 'God is.'"[13]

We Christians start with our presuppositions, and it gives us the right to then say "the God that is and has spoken has revealed himself in this revealed propositional truth." The test for the Christian is to say, yes this is truth: God is. He has spoken. And I can understand that truth.

We can take every single view of life—every philosophy, ideology, religion—and work them out as to how they respond to four great questions: Where did I come from? Why is there suffering? Is there an answer to the meaning of life? What is my purpose?[14] Cornelius Van Til claims that these basic questions can only be answered by the presupposition that God is.[15] This is a very rational approach to reality. Postmodernism is, above anything else, totally irrational, a flight from reason. In my book *How Now Shall We Live?* I used an example of Maxine Waters, who was a young congresswoman from California. Maxine Waters marched in a prochoice parade in Washington, and a female reporter came up to her and said, "You have had abortion rights all your life. What are you protesting for?" She said, "I am protesting because my mother did not have the right to an abortion."

I had an editorial meeting one day with newspaper reporters. The publisher was bragging about how he had run the campaign to take the Ten Commandments off the classroom walls in his city. I was talking about criminal justice, especially what was going on in the juvenile prisons. Later on, he talked about all the stealing going on in the classrooms. "Isn't there something that we can do about stealing in the classrooms?" I said, "A sign, maybe, that says, 'Thou shalt not steal'?" It does not take long to figure out that this system does not work. Lee Strobel is a journalist and former skeptic who reports in his well-known book *The Case for Christ* that he came to Chrsitianity not in a rush of emotions but in a rush of reason. He examined the claims and evidence for Jesus and the Bible and found them true.[16]

When we as Christians argue for truth, the case is on our side as long as we know how to present it. This is the message that I want to leave with you— how important it is to present truth well. There is another way that we can present truth: *What We Can't Not Know*, as my friend J. Budziszewski titled his book.[17] It is written on our heart. We know it is true. I love to ask student groups I talk to, "Do you think there is any objective truth?" Very often, even with a Christian group, hands will not go up because it takes a lot of courage to respond. That is a tough deal today; believers in objective truth are really looked down on. Then I give the students the example that Francis Schaeffer used through the years: You are on the street corner, and there's an old lady with shopping bags. You come up to the street corner and the traffic is whizzing by in both directions. You have three choices with that old lady. You can help her across the street, you can look the other way and ignore her, or you can push her into the traffic. Which one is right? Kids laugh. Light bulbs go on instantly. I ask them again, "How many of you believe in objective truth?" The hands all go up. We know it.

In his book *Moral Minds*, Marc Hauser, a professor of psychology, evolutionary biology, and biological anthropology at Harvard, details how biologists have now discovered evidence of a "moral organism in the mind," or what he calls a "moral grammar."[18] I wonder if he has read the apostle Paul. The law is written on our hearts, and now we are even beginning to discover it biologically. The brain is wired to connect, we know that.

Finally, there is the book of nature. The first chapter of Romans is one of the most powerful chapters of one of the most powerful books in Scripture. I love it because what we are being told by Paul is "since the creation of the world God's invisible qualities—his eternal power and divine nature—have been clearly seen, being understood from what has been made, so that people are without excuse" (Rom. 1:20 TNIV). We see the Creator's work in beauty and in the Creator's gifts that he gives us. We see the Creator's work in nature. Even people who are illiterate and cannot read the Bible can know God because they can see the reality of God in nature.

I had a bad year in 2005 because two of my three children had cancer. One had a very severe case of cancer of the spine and had to go through ten hours of surgery and months of chemo. He is doing fine now. We then found out that my daughter had melanoma. Both had cancer at the same time. There were a lot of other complications in my life at the time. It was one of the dark nights of the soul, and I was feeling really low and depressed. I had my moments of doubt, moments of waking up in the night, walking in the darkness and saying, "God, where are you? I have been serving you for thirty years now. I have given you everything that I have. Why would this happen to my kids?" I went through pity parties. Then, one day that summer I was at a friend's home in western North Carolina. I woke up in the morning and went out on the deck that looks out over the Smoky Mountains. There, rising out of the mist, were gorgeous mountains. I stood there for a long time and realized that most of the ways in which I thought I knew God were probably wrong and unreliable because they were based on subjective feelings. He answered my prayer, and I said, "Thank You, God. I know you are God!"

What happens when he does not answer our prayers? What happens when we do not feel close to him? What happens in the midst of worship like that when we feel nothing? What I realized that day standing out on that porch is that *God is*. That is all that I need to know. I came through that whole period with a much deeper faith because it rested not on my experiences or what I could apprehend of God but on the reality that *God is God*. If we fail to see he has given us the works of his creation, we have no excuse.

This is a bit of a side note, but it is really important because I think a lot of people miss this. Evangelical Christians are accused of being homophobic. We are not, but one of the reasons we care about this issue is that in this first chapter of Romans, Paul talks about people giving in to depraved lust because they rebelled against what was known to them. Their thinking became futile and foolish, and men began to lie with men and women with women. It is the ultimate debauchery. Every time that I have been on a talk show, the talk show host has said, "Why are you all hung up on abortion and gay rights? Why are you homophobic?" I take personal offense at that because I have been going into prisons for thirty years; I have held men and women in my arms who were dying of AIDS. I led a woman to Christ in the early 1980s before we knew how AIDS was contracted. She was an African American woman on death row in North Carolina, in segregation because she had AIDS. I held her hands and said, "Bessie, I want you to know Jesus today." She came to Christ and died nineteen days later. I get mad when people call me homophobic. I should not, but I do.

But why did Paul single out homosexuality in Romans 1? Because he is basically saying that we have no excuse; there is a created physical order and we can see it. What is the ultimate rebellion against the physical created order? "God, I do not like the way that you made me." Romans 1 is the clearest expression of two things: First, there is an accompanying moral order that goes with the physical order. Second, that is where moral law comes from; it is what fits the physical order. There is a physical order that applies not only to the mountains, the beauty of the oceans, the majesty of the skies, and everything that God made but also to the way that men and women are made.

In Romans 1:19, we go from the mountains that make God known—because what was made is plain to them—all the way to physical relationships and the way we are made as human beings. We do not consider homosexuality wrong because we are homophobic but because it is the ultimate sense of "I do not want to be what you made me, God." It is the ultimate rebellion.

I will say this in conclusion: our challenge, our job, is to defend truth. Much of the legacy of evangelicalism is going to be the Packer Legacy—this will be known as the Packer Era because J. I. Packer has been the towering figure of this era—defending truth, defending orthodoxy (I love that word), and defending great preaching. If we are going to line up to continue the legacy, we have got to do a few things. Pastors, especially, have got to go back and educate their flocks in the concept of truth and the rebuttal to the postmodern nihilism, which says there is no such thing as truth. The church needs to understand this issue. The church needs to understand that we cannot let this notion of the subjectivity of truth invade us doctrinally. We have got to understand that if we do not take truth seriously, we will not take God seriously. If we do not understand that, we are never going to be able to preach it or teach it. We have to equip our people on how to defend it. Go through these four or five arguments I have raised here. They are fairly simple. It does not take a sophisticated person or a special course on apologetics. These arguments are self-evident from Scripture.

The empirical method of comparing worldviews is very easy to do. When we do this, we will get people's attention. They will quickly see the postmodern impasse, that this view of life does not work.

The church has a critical role to play particularly because we are in a time of a great clash of civilizations. We are not going to talk about it this evening because we do not have time and it is not the purpose of my talk. To learn more about the differences between the two, go to Timothy George's book *Is the Father of Jesus the God of Muhammad?*—which is to me a classic.[19] I love the title. It spurs thought, doesn't it? I got the wrong answer the first time that I responded to that question. One has to think it through a little bit. But he lays out the two worldviews. They are utterly different, particularly Islamic fascism.

This is a sobering note to end this essay on, but I've got to say this. In 1997 a book was published called *The Clash of Civilizations and the Remaking of World Order* by Samuel Huntington, a professor emeritus at Harvard.[20] These writings were dismissed at the time because we were in the era when Western liberal democracy had "won" the great ideological contest of the West. Francis Fukuyama wrote a book to that effect, *The End of History and the Last Man.*[21] But Huntington predicted that there was to be a great clash of civilizations. Three great civilizations, three great religious blocks exist in the world: Eastern religion, Islam (thirty-eight nations stretching in an arc from Indonesia to Nigeria), and Western liberal democracy informed by Judeo-Christian tradition. The battle of the twenty-first century would be between Islam and the West, Huntington predicted.

That was in the 1990s. He also predicted that Islam, because it is monolithic, aggressive, and warlike, would win. If anyone has the idea in mind that we are going to see the end of this war against terrorism and struggle in the Middle East—just bring all of our troops home and it will be over—get real! That is not going to happen.

When I was in the White House during the height of the Cold War, I would go to briefings. The generals and admirals would come in and brief the president and all of the senior staff. They would talk about megatonnage, throw weight, mutually assured destruction, second strike capabilities, and first strike. We would go through all this stuff until my head was spinning, and I would go home to my wife, Patty, at night and I would actually be ill because I would think to myself, *Decisions that we made today could lead to Armageddon, could lead to a nuclear holocaust.* That is scary stuff. But we were dealing with rational men. We were not dealing with people who were disciples of an Egyptian radical known as Sayyid Qutb who wanted to see the Western world destroyed. This is a more dangerous situation than we have ever faced. It is exactly why Pope Benedict is talking about secularism being no match for aggressive Islam and why Christians have to reenergize and revitalize our societies in order to be a defense against an aggressive, hostile, angry movement that wants to destroy us.

The life-affirming, culture-building aspects of the gospel that preserved reason and civilization in Europe and America are threatened. We are the heirs to that influence, which built this civilization. But if we are to be that constructive influence, the church has to live out its faith. The church not only has to make these kinds of arguments but it also has to incarnate them. Calvin and the Reformed tradition have stressed that the church's role is making the invisible kingdom visible in the world. Live it out in such a way that people see the realities and the excellence of the gospel. And do all that we do winsomely.

A famous quote about loving your enemy from Martin Luther King Jr. reads, "Whom you would change, you must first love."[22] We have to lovingly present what our great friend Father Richard Neuhaus often refers to as "a great proposal of the Gospel—truth." I call it a wonderful proposal: There is truth. It is knowable. It can order our lives. We can see it before our eyes. We know it in our heart when we compare worldviews. It is true and we can live it out. It offers us a wonderful, rational, loving way to live. That is a great proposal!

10

Christ without Culture

RICHARD JOHN NEUHAUS

It is an honor for me to be included in the celebration of J. I. Packer. I count it one of the signal blessings of my life to know him as a coworker and a friend. More specifically, the importance of his contribution to the ongoing project known as Evangelicals and Catholics Together is beyond estimation.

Packer's learning is profound but displayed with modesty. His devotion to the faith is as earnest as his witness to the faith is winsome. As it is said of the angels, so may it be said of J. I. Packer: he can fly because he takes himself so lightly.

Over many years he has been engaged in many arguments, always demonstrating a gift in achieving both disagreement and agreement. Disagreement, too, is a rare achievement. As Father John Courtney Murray observed, most of what we call disagreement is just confusion. And J. I. Packer is relentless in insisting that the only agreement with which we can be satisfied and God can be pleased is agreement in the truth.

In his biography of Packer, Alister McGrath says that he learned his "churchly identity" from the Puritan divines.[1] Over time, the Puritan was joined to the patristic as Packer more emphatically insisted that evangelicalism should understand itself not as a break from but as an expression of the Great Tradition of Christian faith, life, and intellectual reflection. Saint Augustine said that not all who think believe, since many think in order not to believe, but all who believe think.[2]

J. I. Packer thinks, and teaches others to think, with Christ and the church. To think with the church is to think with Christ, the *totus Christus*, both head and body. Packer is in mind and soul what I call an ecclesial Christian, one whose devotion to Christ is inseparable from his devotion to the body of Christ on its way through time toward the promised end time. While I am a Roman Catholic and he an evangelical Anglican, and therefore our ecclesial communion is not complete, I am pleased to join in paying tribute to one who is beyond dispute a brother in Christ and, despite our tragic divisions, a brother in the body of Christ, which is the Church.

The topic of this volume is "The Future of Evangelicalism." I propose to address the future of Christianity, including evangelicalism, with specific reference to the forming and reforming of culture. I suppose Packer's best-known book is *Knowing God*. Among the questions I propose to address is this: in what ways can "knowing God" count as public knowledge in our kind of world?

Our most immediate cultural world is chiefly Europe and the Americas. We do well to keep in mind, however, that the majority of Christians, and the most expansive growth of the Christian movement, is today in the Global South, led by Catholics and those who are described as evangelicals and Pentecostals, although many indigenous movements do not fit easily into our familiar categories. Only God knows what world Christianity will look like a hundred years from now, and that is perhaps just as well.

Speaking of Christ and culture will, for many, immediately bring to mind H. Richard Niebuhr's classic book of that title. Readers of that book will recall his typology of the ways in which the relationship between Christ and culture, meaning Christianity and culture, has been understood over the course of Christian history. Niebuhr suggests that there are essentially five ways to frame this relationship: Christ against culture, the Christ of culture, Christ above culture, Christ and culture in paradox, and Christ transforming culture. While Niebuhr's typology is suggestive and therefore useful, it is also seriously misleading on several scores. I confess that, after some years, I stopped using it in classroom teaching when I found that I was spending more time in arguing with Niebuhr than in being guided by him.

Nevertheless, Niebuhr is certainly right that the questions of Christ and culture have been a constant in Christian history from the apostolic era to the present, and will be until our Lord's promised return in glory. Barrels of ink have been spilled trying to define what is meant by *culture*, and I do not presume to have the final word on the subject. By *culture* I mean the historical ambiance, the social context of ideas and habits, within which the church proclaims and lives the gospel of Christ. This includes the dominant moral assumptions, the widely held aspirations, and the beliefs and behaviors that characterize economic, political, religious, and educational life, along with the institutions that reflect and support those habits, beliefs, and behaviors. One might go so far as to say that culture is to us what water is to fish; it is more assumed than analyzed.

There is an American culture. Although the phrase is hotly contested, we speak of "the American way of life." In a society so vast and various as ours, there are many subcultures and even countercultures. Indeed, the proponents of unbounded pluralism would persuade us that there is no longer an American culture; that what was American culture has been displaced by a maddening mix of subcultures and each of us lives in one subculture or another. Those who feel constrained by the prevalent patterns of life in America tend to think this is a very good thing.

People who have a more comprehensive appreciation of world history, however, along with those who have the experience of living in other and very different societies, know that there is such a thing as American culture. Precisely in its being a capacious and hospitable culture with a marked respect for pluralism, it is American culture. Although it includes many non-Europeans, American culture is in the main an extension and reconfiguration of European culture, which is to say it is part of the culture of the West. And today it is the strongest and most vibrant part of the cultural tradition of the West. The challenge of Islam in its militant form of Jihadism powerfully reinforces our awareness that we are part of the West and, however ambiguously so, the Christian West.

In addition to the above-mentioned five ways of framing the Christianity and culture relationship suggested by H. Richard Niebuhr—Christ against culture, the Christ of culture, Christ above culture, Christ and culture in paradox, and Christ transforming culture—we might add a sixth way to his typology: Christ without culture. Now, as a matter of historical and sociological fact, Christianity is never to be found apart from a cultural matrix: Christianity in all its forms is, as it is said, "enculturated." In relation to a culture, the Church is both acting and being acted on, both shaping and being shaped. What then do I mean by suggesting this sixth type, namely, Christ without culture? I mean that the Church—and here *Church* is broadly defined as the Christian movement through time—can at times adopt a way of being in the world that is deliberately indifferent to the culture of which it is part. In the "Christ without culture" model, that indifference results in the church unconsciously adopting and thereby reinforcing, in the name of the gospel, patterns of culture that are incompatible with the gospel.

Saint Paul writes, "Do not be conformed to this world, but be transformed by the renewal of your mind" (Rom. 12:2 ESV). Worrying about the cultural conformity of Christianity is nothing new. Such worries are a staple in the history of Christian thought, from third-century Tertullian's defiant question, "What has Athens to do with Jerusalem?" to Kierkegaard's withering critique of culturally domesticated discipleship, to Karl Barth's emphatic *Nein!* thrown in the face of the *Kulturprotestantismus* that was the form taken by the "Christ of culture" model in Protestantism. And, of course, there are today in America forms of principled nonconformity, finding expression among both left-wing and right-wing Christians who would revive, at least in theological and moral rhetoric, a "Christ against culture" model, meaning most specifically Christ against *American* culture.

Our subject is the future of Christianity, including evangelicalism. If that is reformulated as the future of religion in this society and the world, there is, from a historical and sociological perspective, nothing to worry about. For as far as one can see into the future, religion is a bull market. In America, where more than 90 percent of the people say they believe in God and well over 80 percent claim to be Christians of one sort or another, Christianity is a bull market.[3] We can debate until the wee hours of the morning whether this is "authentic" or "biblical" or "orthodox" Christianity, but the fact is that this is the form—composed of myriad forms—of the Christian movement in our time and place.

Religion in general, and Christianity in particular, is a bull market because it is now evident that *homo religiosus*, the human need for transcendent meaning, is irrepressible. The secularization theories that held sway over our high culture for three hundred years, ever since the eighteenth-century Enlightenment, have been falsified by the very history to which they so confidently appealed. Or at least it would seem so. That form of Enlightenment rationalism confidently assumed the unstoppable progress of modernity. As people became more enlightened—meaning more educated and skeptical—religion would gradually wither away, or at least be confined to the sphere of privacy where it is hermetically sealed off and prevented from exercising cultural influence. In important respects, history is not turning out that way. I have already mentioned the explosive growth of Christianity in the Global South. When China really opens up, it may seem that we are witnessing the fulfillment of Pope John Paul II's vision of the twenty-first century as "the springtime of world evangelization." And then there are other forms of religious resurgence, such as the newly assertive Islam mentioned earlier.

If one is inclined to put it in vulgar terms, one might say that this is a good time to be in the religion business. And yet the Enlightenment prognosis of secularization may not be falsified in its entirety. While religion is certainly not withering away, one may wonder whether, in its very flourishing, it is fulfilling the second part of the prognosis: namely, that the "Christ without culture" model is impotent, and quite prosperously happy in its impotence, when it comes to exercising cultural influence. In our society there is a greater awareness of the public influence of religion than was the case more than twenty years ago when I published *The Naked Public Square*. But that awareness is almost entirely centered on the political influence of religious voters and activists, leading to alarmist cries of a threatening theocracy. At the risk of generalization, I think it is fair to say that Christianity in America is not challenging the "habits of the heart" and "habits of the mind" that dominate American culture, meaning both the so-called high culture and the popular culture.

On the contrary, some of the more flourishing forms of Christianity not only do not challenge those habits, but they also exhibit a wondrous capacity to exploit them, and thus to reinforce them. Preachers of self-esteem and the gospel of happiness and prosperity uncritically accept the debased and pervasive notion that unhappiness and discontent with one's circumstance in life is a disease; they would lead us to believe that self-criticism, along with its inevitably depressing discoveries, is a dangerous indulgence. The entrepreneurial spirit has built empires of Christian books, Christian music, and entertainment mislabeled as worship—all of which creates the delusion of living in a vibrant Christian subculture that is, in fact, a mirror of the habits of heart and mind that its participants think they are challenging, or at least escaping. As everything goes better with Coke, so everything goes better with Jesus, and, if that does not work, there is always Prozac.

The fact that such religious enterprise presents itself as "evangelization" should not mislead us. Despite all the talk about a religious resurgence or revival, the percentage of the population characterized by a disciplined commitment to Christ, however that might be described, and by active engagement in Christian service to the church and the world has not grown appreciably. Rather, religious entrepreneurs are increasingly competing for niche markets within a stable population that prefers religion to Prozac, or prefers their Prozac with the panache of religion.

I do not wish to paint too grim a picture. There is, to be sure, the undeniable reality of the culture wars. There are Christians not only voting their moral convictions but, especially with respect to the conflict between the culture of life and the culture of death, also making truth claims and advancing arguments in terms of public reason aimed at engaging the centers of cultural influence. For instance, there is the Evangelicals and Catholics Together statement issued September 2006—"That They May Have Life." That is a welcome exception, but it is an exception.

The centers of cultural influence in this country do not recognize that they are being challenged by Christians, except for the allegedly theocratic challenge in electoral politics. They do not recognize that they are being intellectually, conceptually, and culturally challenged, in largest part because Christians are not persuasively articulating such a challenge. Their complaint is that Christians are trying to "impose their values" on them. They do not understand that we want to engage them in a civil argument about the possibility of moral truth, about what kind of people we are and should aspire to be, and therefore about how we ought to order our life together. They do not understand because so few Christians understand and attempt to practice such engagement.

Engagement is very different from imposing one's understanding of the truth on others. In his encyclical *Redemptoris Missio* (The Mission of the Redeemer), John Paul II said, "The Church imposes nothing; she only proposes." But what she proposes she believes to be truth. She proposes as a lover to the beloved, reflecting as she does the words of John 3:16 that "God so loved the world." She proposes persistently, persuasively, and winsomely. Her proposal is not a conversation stopper but a conversation starter.

Of course it is true that many people will reject the proposal, and many will simply refuse to be engaged by it. They simply *know* that, no matter how winsomely proposed, the conversation with Christianity is but a cunningly disguised threat of imposition on their freedom. Their default position, so to speak, is one of methodological, if not metaphysical, atheism. Any reference to God or transcendent truth, any proposal associated with religion—and especially any proposal associated with Christianity—is a threat to the autonomous self and to the achievements of a rigorously secularist modernity. They live in what Max Weber called "a disenchanted world," and they are determined to keep it that way.

This is a mindset powerfully influential in our culture. Karl Marx spoke of those who control the commanding heights of economies, and so we may speak of those who control the commanding heights of culture. Even though they may be a minority of the population, they succeed in presenting themselves as "the mainstream" through their control of powerful institutions in the media, in entertainment, in the arbitration of literary tastes, in the great research universities and professional associations, and in the worlds of business and advertising that seek the approval of those who control the commanding heights of culture.

It is necessary but not sufficient to alert them to the fact that they are a minority by defeating them in electoral politics. Such alerts intensify their alarm that "the theocrats are coming!" They are thus reinforced in their determination to resist what they view as a populist uprising against the hegemony of their enlightened ways. On many questions pertinent to the right ordering of our public life, Christians view those who control the commanding heights of culture as political opponents, and they typically are that. While we view them as political opponents and engage them in fair battle, we must not view them personally as our enemies. Many of them may view us that way, because, for many of them, politics is the name of the game. But we know, or we should know, that politics is not enough.

The great contest is over the culture, the guiding ideas and habits of mind and heart that inform the way we understand the world and our place in it. Christians who, knowingly or unknowingly, embrace the model of "Christ without culture" are captive to the culture as defined by those who control its commanding heights. They are not only captive to it but also complicit in it. Their entrepreneurial success in building religious empires by exploiting the niche markets of the Christian subculture leaves the commanding heights untouched, unchallenged, and unengaged.

Christianity does indeed have its own culture, its own intellectual tradition, its own liturgy and songs, and its own moral teachings and distinctive ways of life, both personal and communal. The church must carefully cultivate that culture and, in times of severe persecution, cultivate it, if need be, in the catacombs. But that is not our time in America, although there are Christians who, embracing the model of "Christ against culture," invite us to take refuge in the catacombs of their own imagining.

A rich ecclesial culture, a distinctively Christian way of being in the world, sometimes finds itself positioned against the world as the world is defined by those who are hostile to the influence of the church. But even when the church is against the world, she is against the world for the world. "The Church imposes nothing; she only proposes." In season and out, whether the response is sympathetic or hostile, she proposes what Saint Paul at the end of 1 Corinthians 12 calls a "more excellent way." The way proposed is not so much a message as a person, the One who is the way, the truth, and the life. The Second Vatican Council says that Jesus Christ is not only the revelation of God to man but the revelation of man to himself. Those words of *Gaudium et Spes* were insistently repeated in the pontificate of John Paul the Great and have a premier place in the teaching of Benedict XVI.

The Christian proposal of a more excellent way is not just one option among others, although it must be freely chosen. Some years ago, in conversation with a prominent Anglican bishop in Britain, I asked how he would define the mission of the Church of England. After a pause for thought, he said, "I suppose I would say that the mission, so to speak, is to maintain the religious option for those who might be interested." Needless to say, those who control the commanding heights of British culture do not feel threatened by that understanding of the Christian mission.

While religion flourishes here in America, it is largely of the "Christ without culture" variety. What have been the distinctively Christian contributions in recent decades that deserve to command the attention of the cultural gatekeepers of America? In literature and the arts, in music and entertainment, in political philosophy and the humanities, such contributions are few and far between. Distinctively Christian cultural products typically cater to the Christian market. They are not proposals of a more excellent way for American culture. Recently the Fox movie studio announced that it was inaugurating a new series of films under the label of Fox Faith. Does this indicate a growing Christian influence in our public culture? Perhaps so, but it is much more obviously a commonsensical capitalist decision to take advantage of the niche market that is the Christian subculture.

The "Christ without culture" model induces contentment with being a subculture. But, as I have suggested, Christianity that is indifferent to its cultural context is captive to its cultural context. Indeed, it reinforces the cultural definitions to which it is captive. Nowhere is this as evident as in the ready Christian acceptance of the cultural dogma that religion is essentially a private matter of spiritual experience. Against that assumption, we must insist that Christian faith is intensely personal but never private. The Christian gospel is an emphatically public proposal about the nature of the world and our place in it.

Many Christians, possibly most Christians, have uncritically accepted the dichotomy between public and private, between fact and value, between knowledge and meaning. These dichotomies are deeply entrenched in American religion and culture and are closely associated with what is often described, and frequently decried, as American individualism. In what is called our high culture, this understanding of religion as private and intensely subjective was influentially depicted a hundred years ago in William James's classic work *The Varieties of Religious Experience*.[4] Early on in that work, James defines religion as "the feelings, acts, and experiences of individual men in their solitude, so far as they apprehend themselves to stand in relation to whatever they may consider the divine." Church, community, doctrine, tradition, morality—all of these are secondary and, as often as not, hindrances to genuine religion. Genuine religion is subjective *experience*, and subjective experience in *solitude*.

Many years later, in 1992, the influential literary critic Harold Bloom published *The American Religion: The Emergence of the Post-Christian Nation*. The post-Christian nation, says Bloom, emerged a long time ago and is exemplified in Ralph Waldo Emerson who declared, "It is by yourself without *ambassador* that God speaks to you. . . . It is God in you that responds to God without." Bloom, rather loosely, calls the American religion "Gnosticism," the belief that each individual possesses a divine spark and salvation consists in the liberation of that divine spark from the body and from the particularities of its constraints in history and cultural space. Bloom writes:

> Unlike most countries, we have no overt national religion; but a partly concealed one has been developing among us for two centuries now. It is almost purely experiential, and despite its insistences [to the contrary], it is scarcely Christian in any traditional way. A religion of the self burgeons, under many names, and seeks to know its own inwardness, in isolation. What the American self has found, since about 1800, is its own freedom—from the world, from time, from other selves.[5]

Of course, Harold Bloom overstates his case. It is not sufficient, however, to point out that there are innumerable ministries in the several Christian communities that insist on the objectivity of truth, the authority of Scripture and Spirit-guided interpretation, the ecclesial means of grace, and the reality of moral good and evil. But in preferring such religion, Bloom might respond, one is still exercising a private preference. One's preferred religion may be conservative or liberal, orthodox or foggy, but the point is that it is my religion, certified and secured by the fact that it is mine. By the privilege of privacy, it cannot be publicly questioned, and it is forbidden to publicly question the preferred beliefs of others.

Gnosticism may not be the right word for it, but it is what Bloom calls a religion of the self. It is a seductive way of accommodating differences by declaring a truce in contentions over truth. The "Christ without culture" model would seem to produce a circumstance in which religion is impervious to culture and culture is impervious to religion. But in fact it results in religion's acquiescing in the culture's demand that it confine itself to the sphere of privacy. Thus William James's radically individualistic solitude remains intact even if that solitude is celebrated in a five-thousand-seat auditorium of a megachurch.

It was not so in the apostolic period, as witnessed by Saint Paul's opening hymn in the letter to the Ephesians, his depiction of cosmic transformation in Romans 8, and his anticipation in Philippians 2 of every knee bowed and every tongue confessing Jesus Christ as Lord. It was not so in the patristic era when Justin Martyr proposed Christianity not as a more satisfying religion among other religions but as "the true philosophy." It was not true with Saint Augustine who proposed in *City of God* that the story of the gospel is nothing less than the story of the world.[6] Were Christianity what a man does with his solitude, there would be no martyrs. In every vibrant period of the Church's life it has been understood that her message and mission are based on public events, are advanced by public argument, and invite public response.

"The Church imposes nothing; she only proposes." For the past three hundred years, that public proposal has been inhibited and stifled by Christians who acquiesced in the Enlightenment demand that religion, if it is to survive at all, confine itself to the closet of privacy. In America, that acquiescence was embraced as a virtue. The freedom of religion was purchased at the price of agreeing to the public irrelevance of religion. Religious empires were constructed and flourish today by catering to private salvation and the "spiritualities" of solitude.

Today the Enlightenment settlement that imposed a public truce with respect to the truths that really matter, and bifurcated fact from value, knowledge from meaning, and faith from reason, is being boldly challenged. Whatever one may think of papal authority, on the world-historical stage that challenge is being pressed most boldly, even audaciously, by the bishop of Rome. That was the real significance of Pope Benedict's lecture at Regensburg University on September 12, 2006. The media excitement focused on a few words about Islam. And he did say that the use of violence to impose religion is to act against reason, and to act against reason is to act against the nature of God, for God has revealed himself as logos—the Word and the reason by which all came to be and in which all coheres.

But the bulk of the Regensburg address was directed to Christian intellectuals who, in the name of "de-Hellenizing" Christianity, pit biblical faith against the great synthesis of faith and reason achieved over the centuries of the Christian intellectual tradition. At Regensburg and elsewhere, Benedict has challenged also non-Christian intellectuals to free themselves from the truncated and stifling definition of rationality imposed by the Enlightenment. It is not reasonable, he argues with great intellectual sophistication, to hold that atheism or agnosticism is the default position of rationality. Nor, he insists, can the undoubted achievements of modernity be sustained without reference to transcendent truth.

Since we cannot prove beyond all reasonable doubt that God exists, the rational position is not to live as though God does not exist but to live as though God does exist. Here Benedict is urging a form of Pascal's wager. The seventeenth-century genius Blaise Pascal proposed that it is more rational, in view of the benefits to be gained, to believe that God exists than to believe that he does not exist. If the believer turns out to be wrong, he has lost what he had hoped for; if the nonbeliever turns out to be wrong, he has lost, quite simply, everything, including eternal life. C. S. Lewis rephrased Pascal's wager this way: "Christianity, if false, is of no importance, and, if true, is of infinite importance. The one thing it cannot be is moderately important."[7]

In these and many other ways, the case is advanced that Christianity is a public proposal within the realm of authentically public discourse and requires decisions of immeasurable consequences, both personal and cultural. In different times and in different places, the church has understood its relationship to culture in different ways. There is Christ against culture, the Christ of culture, Christ above culture, Christ and culture in paradox, and Christ transforming culture. As I said, H. Richard Niebuhr's useful taxonomy can be expanded and modified. The one model that is not possible, except by deluding ourselves and betraying the church's proposal to the world, is Christ without culture.

J. I. Packer has blessed millions with his profound reflection titled *Knowing God*. Our debt to him is beyond estimation. Our great task now, in the twilight of the long hegemony of Enlightenment rationality, is to convincingly make the case that knowing God is indeed *knowledge*. It is a public knowledge that the Church does not impose but proposes to the world that God so loved and continues to so love until the end of time.

Sadly, Father Richard John Neuhaus, a priest of the Archdiocese of New York, died on January 8, 2009. Father Neuhaus was the editor-in-chief of First Things, *a journal he founded in 1990, and director of the Institute for Religion and Public Life, an influential think tank that addresses issues of moral and social concern. The author of numerous essays and books, including his 1984 bestseller,* The Naked Public Square, *Father Neuhaus was the most consequential public theologian in America since Reinhold Niebuhr. Together with Chuck Colson he founded Evangelicals and Catholics Together, in which J. I. Packer was involved from the beginning. We have dedicated this volume to Richard John Neuhaus, our beloved friend and colleague, in* piam memoriam.

11

On Knowing God

James Earl Massey

And this is eternal life,
that they know you
the only true God,
and Jesus Christ whom you have sent.

John 17:3 (ESV)

Righteous Father, even though the world does not
know you, I know you,
and these know that you have sent me.

John 17:25 (ESV)

Growing up in a home where both my father and my mother were ardent Christians, I often saw and heard them pray. This taught me much about their faith. Sometimes my parents prayed openly in our presence about my brothers and me—making some request concerning us—and I got the distinct impression that they wanted us to overhear their petitions. This helped us know their concern for our future. Those prayer times now lie far in the past, but overhearing my parents talk to God about us as their children remains indelibly in my memory.

I mention this because the disciples overheard the prayer of Jesus that is recorded in John 17, and they knew that several of his petitions were uttered out of concern for them. Jesus allowed those disciples to "listen in" as he talked to God, intent to help them know God more fully and to live more responsibly. Early in his ministry, the disciples had asked Jesus to teach them to pray (Luke 11:1); now, as he was ending his earthly ministry, Jesus was still teaching them. One of my teachers commented about this prayer of Jesus in John 17, "Because there is an audience, the prayer is as much revelation as it is intercession."[1] Let us "overhear" this prayer of Jesus again, and listen for its message about how we can know God, a subject about which J. I. Packer, our conference honoree, has long thought, taught, preached, and written so engagingly.[2]

God as Father

Let us notice, first of all, that Jesus addressed God in this prayer as "Father." The disciples had heard Jesus address God this way many times before, and according to Matthew 6:9 and Luke 11:2, he taught them to address God the same way. Six times during this prayer (John 17:1, 5, 11, 21, 24, 25), Jesus addressed God as "Father."

The word *father* is a descriptive, heartwarming term. It is a family word. The term bespeaks a relationship of intimacy, trust, and a responsible caring that reassures and steadies those who belong as family members. Rightly understood, and biblically intended, the word *father* reminds us of our source, our origin; God is the One who is responsible for us and the One to whom we are accountable.

Many treasured hymns highlight these understandings about God as father. How inwardly bracing it is to prayerfully sing "Father Almighty, Bless Us with Thy Blessing!" To speak personally, I have felt divinely embraced while singing "Eternal Father, Strong to Save," or when voicing that plea in Samuel Johnson's prayerful hymn,

> Father, in thy mysterious presence kneeling,
> Fain would our souls feel all thy kindling love;
> For we are weak, and need some deep revealing
> Of trust and strength and calmness from above.

Many worshipers have felt their spirit deepen in worship as they sang the stalwart lines of "Immortal, Invisible, God Only Wise," the last stanza of which states:

> Great Father of glory, pure Father of light
> Thine angels adore thee, all veiling their sight;

All praise we would render; O help us to see
'Tis only the splendor of light hideth thee.[3]

For many in the African American church tradition, nothing stirs to prayer
or undergirds trust like the sung plea,

Father, I stretch my hands to thee,
    no other help I know;
If thou withdraw thyself from me,
    Ah! Whither shall I go?
. . . .
Author of faith, to thee I lift
    My weary, longing eyes;
Oh, let me now receive that gift;
    My soul without [Thee] dies.[4]

Some years ago, I preached on the Lord's Prayer at an interchurch gathering
in one of the southeastern states. The sermon was planned around the theme
of the meeting, and I sought to center the hearers in the scope and meaning
of the biblical passage in which the Lord's Prayer appears. After preaching, I
spent some time greeting those who lingered to speak with me. Two persons
in the line objected to my having mentioned the word *father* in the sermon.
They thought mentioning that word only strengthens a gender bias in the
church, and they added that the word *father* offends persons who have suffered
paternal abuse. I certainly understand the need to be sensitive in preaching
to those who have been abused and exploited, and I said so. But I added that
preaching must always respect and treat Scripture as it stands written. The
two objectors then betrayed their deeper concern. They told me that I should
have amended the address to God in the Lord's Prayer to read "Our Father/
Mother who art in heaven." Then *I* objected! I informed the two of them that
I stand committed to believe, teach, preach, and follow what Jesus taught. My
statement did not please them, but I am confident it pleased my Lord.

God as Holy Father

Let us notice, second, that the disciples overheard Jesus address God also as
"Holy Father" (John 17:11). *Holy* was an adjective Jesus used to honor God's
character, but he went on and prayed for God to make the disciples holy in
their character.

Serious readers of Scripture know that the word *holy* is so frequently
associated with God that this aspect of the nature of God cannot be missed
or overlooked. Throughout the Old Testament, God is referred to as "the Holy
One" and "the Holy One of Israel." Being "holy," God is separated in nature

from what is ordinary, common, or human. God is so distinctive and unique in his perfection and purity that humans have generally recoiled in awe from his revealed presence.

But God is Holy Person, which means that God does not delight to be remote or to remain removed. This Holy God wants to relate to us as "Father" and to share himself in such a way that we take on his character. The accounts in the Gospels let us see the holy character of God revealed on our level in the person and work of Jesus.

Jesus made five requests in this prayer, and the first of four on behalf of the disciples was that God would make them holy: "Sanctify them in the truth; your word is truth" (John 17:17 ESV). Sanctity—holiness in character—is dependent on truth, the truth associated with God's Word. Truth is not something to be known only intellectually; it is something to be lived and obeyed. The truth associated with God's Word involves more than aspects of meaning; truth is the territory in which sanctified persons "live, move, and have being," and beyond which they refuse to go. Jesus prayed that his disciples be "sanctified," that is, made "holy." He was eager to see each one intentionally submissive to God, living by the truth, fully engaged in obeying God, and demonstrating God's character in their lives. Jesus wants his disciples to be sanctified, to be "holy," and his prayer to God reminds us about this privilege and need.

God as Righteous Father

Notice, yet again, the disciples overheard Jesus address God as "Righteous Father" (John 17:25). The disciples needed to know, as Jesus knew, that God always does what is right, what is wise, what is just. They would need to remember this when the skies above them would darken and when perils of many kinds would clutter the path they would be guided to take in doing ministry for Jesus.

Many Scriptures, particularly the psalms, describe God as righteous and hold God's wisdom and justice to our view: "God is a righteous judge" (Ps. 7:11 ESV); "For the Lord is righteous" (Ps. 11:7 ESV); "Gracious is the Lord, and righteous" (Ps. 116:5 ESV);

> Righteous are you, O Lord,
>   and right are your rules.
> You have appointed your testimonies
>   in righteousness,
>   and in all faithfulness. (Ps. 119:137–38 ESV)

Hymn writer Samuel Rodigast understood this about God, and he voiced his response in these lines:

Whate'er my God ordains is right;
His holy will abideth;
I will be still, whate'er he does,
And follow where he guideth.
He is my God; though dark my road,
He holds me that I shall not fall,
Wherefore to him I leave it all.[5]

It is because God is righteous that he sent Jesus to reveal himself more fully: "No one has ever seen God. It is God the only Son, who is close to the Father's heart, who has made him known" (John 1:18 NRSV). It is because God is righteous that he provided in Jesus our salvation from sin and its penalties: "For God so loved the world that he gave his only Son, so that everyone who believes in him may not perish but may have eternal life" (John 3:16 NRSV).

To Give Eternal Life

During his prayer, the disciples overheard Jesus talk to God about the authority he was granted "to give eternal life" (John 17:2 NRSV) and they heard his request to be "glorified" so that those who believe on him could have that life effected in them. Behind the coming of God's own Son to make that life available to us was the holy, righteous, and compassionate love of God. As D. O. Teasley expressed it:

See the depths of his compassion,
Giving heaven's best to prove,
By a life of pain and sorrow,
That the Lord our God is love.[6]

Love is the word "that Christians have cherished more than any other through the years as the measure of the meaning of God to the worshiping [person] . . . the climactic term by which we express the innermost reality of God."[7] God's love is that holy, righteous, understanding, sympathetic, unrelenting, and inexhaustible concern to save us from sin and restore us to favor and holy character as his children. Such love as this stirred Paul's declaration of praise in Romans 8:38–39 (NRSV):

For I am convinced that neither death, nor life,
nor angels, nor rulers, nor things present,
nor things to come, nor powers, nor height,
nor depth, nor anything else in all creation,
will be able to separate us from the love
of God in Christ Jesus our Lord.

To know God involves something more than a rational understanding that God exists; it involves an experience of accepting Jesus as the One who reveals God to the world. That acceptance puts us in a right relationship with God and it grants us what Jesus referred to as "eternal life."

Eternal life differs from physical life. It differs both in its nature and quality. Eternal life does not come as part of our natural birth; it is gained through a "new birth" that God grants in response to faith, and it is immediately possessed when someone accepts Jesus in his saving role. Eternal life blesses and enhances the chronological span of our years, and it has a guaranteed future beyond the death of the body. Eternal life is for a godly life and a life with God forever, and it is received and experienced when we accept Jesus as savior from our sins. There are those objectors who think it irrelevant and offensive to be told that all humans need a savior, but the biblical message is that we humans cannot free ourselves from an enslavement to sin and we cannot bring our own selves into right relation to a holy God. Jesus came to do both for us and to give us eternal life. That is the message of our text: "And this is eternal life, that they may know you, the only true God, and Jesus Christ whom you have sent" (John 17:3 NRSV).

Jesus as God's Son

While visiting Cairo, Egypt, some years ago I had the unforgettable experience of hearing, for the first time, an Islamic muezzin's piercing voice calling out from a minaret in that section of the city, summoning the people to prayer. I was familiar with the sound of church bells in the cities of America and Europe, and my spirit was in tune with the message and meaning that those church bells conveyed, but the summoning sound of that muezzin meant something different to me as a Christian. That call, and the beliefs that energized it, served a religious system whose teachings and purpose significantly differ from the concerns of the God whom Jesus addressed as Father. Aware that Islam does not honor Jesus as God's Son or the Savior God sent, I knew that no redeeming benefit could result from trusting its claims. I knew that Islam gives no true knowledge of God. The New Testament clearly teaches that there is no true knowledge of God apart from a relationship with Jesus Christ.

That clear New Testament message is being steadily challenged by other religious traditions, Islam among them, and Christians need to have a solid footing in the faith to move the necessary work of evangelism and mission forward in strength. Although the benefits of religious pluralism are commonly appreciated in our land, there is still the need for disciples of Jesus to "be ready to make [a] defense to anyone who demands from you an accounting for the hope that is in you" (1 Pet. 3:15 NRSV). It is essential for our witnessing that we increase our understanding of other religious traditions, but we must not be timid and quiet about the truth regarding Jesus. To know the God whom Jesus has revealed, and to witness in the spirit of his love, is to share that witness without condescension, without contempt, without cowardice, and without compromise. Faced as we are in the world by rabid tribalism, baseless nihilism, rigid secularism, selfish consumerism, and competing religious claims, we must be engaged in a loving, informed, courageous, and assertive evangelism. Jesus is not just another religious figure from the past whose teachings can be isolated and pigeonholed as nonapplicable for our time. Jesus is God's Son, the anointed one who has made God known in a fresh, fundamental, and revelatory fashion. The apostle Peter's inspired statement about Jesus remains as true in this postmodern year of 2009 as when he first declared it in his Pentecost Day sermon back in AD 33, "There is salvation in no one else, for there is no other name under heaven given among mortals by which we must be saved" (Acts 4:12 NRSV).

> We've a Savior to show to the nations
> Who the path of sorrow has trod,
> That all the world's great peoples
> Might come to the truth of God,
> Might come to the truth of God.
> For the darkness shall turn to dawning,
> And the dawning to noon-day bright,
> And Christ's great kingdom shall come on earth,
> The kingdom of love and light.[8]

12

Unde, Quonam, et Quemadmodum?

Learning Latin (and Other Things) from J. I. Packer

Timothy George

God speaks to us in mysterious and unexpected ways; he directs our paths and guides our lives in different and sometimes strange ways. How often do we find ourselves somewhere in the middle of Robert Frost's two roads that emerged in the snowy woods: one beaten and worn, the other less traveled. He took the latter, not the former, and he said "It made all the difference." But at the time, at the crossroads, who could have known that?

There is a rare Greek word in the fifteenth verse of Philemon, where Paul speaks of the return of the slave Onesimus to his master. He says, "Perhaps the reason he was separated from you in the first place was that you might receive him back, not as a slave anymore, but as a brother." *Tacha*, in Greek— "perhaps." At least that is how almost all of our modern English translations render that word. But some of the older translations, even earlier than the Authorized Version, even earlier than Tyndale, going back to John Wyclif and the Lollards, render *tacha* with an old-fashioned English word: "peradventure." Perhaps. It does not sound like a Puritan word, does it? Is it more Arminian than Calvinist? Is it more Roman Catholic than Protestant, this word? Perhaps? Peradventure? Yet here it is in the Bible, in a letter written by the beloved apostle Paul.

I once had a colleague, professor Dale Moody, who was quite well known for his debating abilities. Once he found himself embroiled in a theological controversy in the state of Arkansas with a number of Baptist pastors there. They were debating a certain theological point. As Dale Moody was wont to do, he took his Bible and went from Genesis to Revelation to show in comprehensive depth how what he believed was really and truly biblical, in contrast to his interlocutors. At the end of that long disquisition one of the Baptist pastors of Arkansas shouted out, "Well, Doctor, it may be Bible, but it sure ain't Baptist!" *Peradventure* is that kind of word, but maybe it brings us closer to the neighborhood of *antinomy*, a word that J. I. Packer used in his *Evangelism and the Sovereignty of God* to describe how the Lord's sovereign election and human responsibility belong inseparably together in the economy of grace. It is an antinomy.

Peradventure? What would have happened had that seven-year-old J. I. Packer not been hit by the bread truck in 1933? Would humanity have gained a champion cricket player and lost a world class theologian? Peradventure. What would have happened had Packer, as a young Christian at Oxford, still seeking his theological bearings, reached into that bin of dusty old books and pulled out not John Owen, but a volume, say, by Jeremy Taylor or Lancelot Andrewes? Would that have lit a fire in his soul for the things of God? Or what would have happened had a beautiful young nurse named Kit Mullet not seen the visiting bachelor curate sitting alone at the lunch table after his presentation at church? What if Mullet had not struck up a conversation with that lonely fellow, a relationship that has led now to more than fifty years of marriage and three children? Did God meet J. I. Packer at the crossroads and direct him in ways that he could not have foreseen at the time? Peradventure. For Philemon 15 must be matched with Proverbs 16:33, which in none of our modern translations quite matches the beauty of the Authorized Version, "The lot is cast into the lap; but the whole disposing thereof is of the Lord." Antinomies everywhere.

Now a word about the title of this essay: yes, it sounds pretty pompous and a little officious, more so than I trust my comments will actually be. "*Unde, Quonam, et Quemadmodum?* Learning Latin (and Other Things) from J. I. Packer." *Unde*: whence. *Quonam*: whither. *Quemadmodum*: howsoever. In other words, where have we come from, where are we going, and how are we going to get there? The essays in this volume have explored from various angles these very questions. Here is a summary of some of these themes, some of the major ideas that have surfaced in our conversation about "J. I. Packer and the Evangelical Future."

But why Latin? J. I. Packer was a student of classics, even before he went to Oxford. Indeed, that was one of the reasons he received a scholarship to Oxford to study what are called Greats: *litterae humaniores*. The first job that he had was as a teacher of Greek and Latin at Oak Hill Theological

College in London. Moreover, one of his first books, published in 1957, was a translation done with O. R. Johnston of the Latin text of Martin Luther's 1525 treatise *The Bondage of the Will*. It is still a fine translation. It also has a fifty-page introduction that itself is a minor masterpiece. Packer and Johnston wanted to translate Luther afresh, they said, in order to allow the impetuous flow and dialectical strength of Luther's powerful Latin to resound again in the English tongue.

Still, it is not really Latin that has characterized Packer's impact on us so much as it is his fresh, pungent, punchy Anglo-Saxon. While Packer may have learned a great deal of his theology from John Owen, he has not imitated Owen's obtuse, difficult style with its echoes of a lumbering Latin. Instead, Packer's writing stands much closer to Chaucer, Shakespeare, Bunyan, and Spurgeon. Packer's English is closer to Luther's German "*ein feste Burg*," than it is to Luther's Latin, despite his elegant translation of *The Bondage of the Will*. What John Wesley once confessed, Packer could say as well: "I could, even now, write floridly and rhetorically, but I dare not. I dare no more write in a fine style than wear a fine coat! Let who will admire the French frippery. I am still for plain, sound English." Packer has given us a lot of plain, sound English, and this has helped us see some of the deep truths of God's Word.

Let us look at these three Latin interrogatives. *Unde*: whence? When Packer entered Christian life and ministry, evangelicalism on both sides of the Atlantic was at a rather low ebb. In Great Britain, the Tractarian movement on the one hand, and Protestant liberalism on the other, had conspired to marginalize and isolate the evangelical wing of the Church of England. The Church Missionary Society was formed in 1799 and had pioneered a great missionary outreach around the globe. But by the time J. I. Packer came on the scene this movement had already split. There was a more explicitly evangelical BCMS, a Bible Church Missionary Society. A parallel development had taken place within the student Christian movement. There were stirrings of renewal, even before Packer began to make a distinctive contribution, through the founding of the Tyndale Fellowship and Tyndale House, through the Evangelical Alliance, and through gospel-based student ministries at Oxford and Cambridge. Still, little had been done of a substantive and enduring nature that did not need replenishment and support.

In North America the situation was no more sanguine. The malaise of the fundamentalist/modernist controversies and schisms still lingered. When Packer presented his first major lectureship in North America at Fuller Theological Seminary in the early 1960s, there was no Trinity Evangelical Divinity School nor a Trinity School for the Ministry, as such. There was no Gordon-Conwell Theological Seminary, no Regent College, and no Beeson Divinity School. *Christianity Today* had been founded by Billy Graham in 1956, but the great international gatherings Graham would convene were still in the future: the great Berlin Congress on Evangelism of 1966 to be followed by Lausanne in 1974, Manila in 1989, and Amsterdam in 2000.

Let me mention some of the things we have pondered about "whither." Bruce Hindmarsh has reminded us that Packer's ministry and his lifework has been a work of "retrieval for the sake of renewal." First, *ad fontes: back to the sources*. Packer's emphasis on biblical and historical theology has not been made out of any antiquarian interest but for the sake of the renewal of the people of God in our time. We see this above all perhaps in his love affair with the Puritans. There is an entire cottage industry on how to define Puritanism, but no one has given us a better definition than Packer. This is how he defined it in his study on Richard Baxter:

> Puritanism was a total view of Christianity: Bible-based, church-centered, God-honoring, literate, orthodox, pastoral, and reformational that saw personal, domestic, professional, political, churchly, and economic existence as aspects of a single whole, and that called on everybody to order every department and every relationship of their life according to the Word of God, so that it would all be sanctified and become holiness to the Lord. Puritanism's spearhead activity was pastoral evangelism and nurture through preaching, catechizing and counseling. And Puritan teaching harped constantly on the themes of self-knowledge, self-humbling, and repentance. Faith in and love for Jesus Christ the Savior. The necessity of regeneration and of sanctification as proof of it. The need of conscientious conformity to all God's law and for a disciplined use of the means of grace; and the blessedness of the assurance and joy from the Holy Spirit that all faithful believers under ordinary circumstances may know. The Puritans saw themselves as God's pilgrims traveling home; God's warriors battling against the world, the flesh, and the devil; and God's servants under orders to do all the good they could as they went along.[1]

That is a great definition of Puritanism, and one that is especially applicable to the life of the church today.

Second, *evangelicalism has functioned as a renewal movement within historic Christian orthodoxy*. This draws us to the issue of the Great Tradition, and how the Great Tradition relates to the Puritan, Protestant, and Reformational exclamation points in church history. Packer reminds us that the reformers did not intend to begin brand new churches from whole cloth but that they saw themselves as faithful and obedient servants of the one holy catholic and apostolic church, ever calling that church to be reformed on the basis of the Word of God. As a renewal movement *within* historic Christian orthodoxy, evangelism is about mere Christianity, but not "mere" in the way we often use that word today—in the weak, attenuated sense.

The difference can be understood in the contrast of two little Latin adverbs. *Vix*. This Latin word means "barely," "hardly," "scarcely," or "merely," in our weak sense of that word. The other Latin word, *vere*, means "really," "truly," "absolutely," "most essentially," or "indubitably." C. S. Lewis, and before him Richard Baxter, were both "mere" Christians in the latter sense, *vere* not *vix*. E. J. Carnell once described fundamentalism as "orthodoxy gone cultic."[2] There is a temptation for evangelicalism to become a form of Protestantism gone myopic, *incurvatus in se*, twisted in on itself, detached from the ongoing life of faith among the entire people of God. Reformational Christianity calls the church, in all of its dimensions, back to the one holy catholic and apostolic faith.

Third, *we have discussed the issue of truth understood in a twofold way: propositionally and incarnationally*. Truth is certainly propositional, for we do not back away from the claim that what the Bible says, God says, and what the Bible says happened really happened. In the Bible the miracles are miraculous and the history is historical. But truth biblically framed is also incarnational, for the Word did not become a text but tangible, vulnerable flesh. Packer has reminded us that the propositional truth we confess must be lived out, enfleshed, in the real world of space and time. This is the world that Calvin called "the theater of God's glory."[3]

Fourth, *we discussed the coinherence of vital spirituality and sound theology*. Edith Humphrey has well described J. I. Packer as a theologian who models both a cool head and a warm heart. For the past decade every seminary in the Association of Theological Schools (ATS) in the United States and Canada has been required to give an account of how they deal with spiritual formation in the fulfillment of their mission. This is one of the standards for which theological schools are now held accountable when they are reviewed for accreditation. When Packer began work in theological education, at least in North America, this was not anywhere on our radar screen. Perhaps Roman Catholics and some of our Orthodox friends were inculcating spiritual disciplines and teaching the importance of the interior life, but most Protestants did not consider spiritual formation to be a necessary part of our job. We assumed students came to us already spiritually formed. We should have known better. Long before ATS decided to incorporate spiritual formation in the standards for accreditation, we should have paid more attention to the pioneering work of J. I. Packer and his colleague Jim Houston, who called the evangelical church to make spiritual nurture a priority in its training and preparation of ministers.

Fifth, while J. I. Packer has given much of his life in the training of ministers of the gospel for the service of the church, the general burden of his whole lifework has been to develop *a useful catechesis for the whole people of God*. For this reason he has written not only for scholarly journals but also for popular readers. As the vast bibliography at the end of this book reveals, Packer has offered instruction to the church on nearly every theological issue in Christian dogmatics. His introduction to John Owen's *The Death of Death and the Death of Christ*, first published in 1959, remains a classic statement

of the redemptive work of Christ interpreted along Reformed lines. What
Packer wrote of Owen's treatise applies equally to his own introductory essay
to it: "The work must be read and re-read to be appreciated." Basic to the
historic understanding of the atonement is another teaching long neglected
in evangelical theology: the character and reality of God the Holy Trinity.
Packer has emphasized the trinitarian shape of Christian faith and life. The
fact that the one eternal God has forever known himself as the Father, Son,
and Holy Spirit, and that he has revealed himself to us in this three-personal
way throughout the history of salvation, is not a mere theoretical construct
but a truth that transforms and brings life. Evangelical theologians are now
contributing constructively to the renaissance of trinitarian thinking that began
nearly one hundred years ago with the work of Karl Barth. Here, as with the
doctrine of Scripture and the centrality of the cross, Packer has led the way.

Sixth, *let us recognize Christian unity as a gospel imperative.* Bruce Hindmarsh has reminded us that the early evangelicals preferred *gospel* to *evangelical*, another Anglo-Saxon word for a Latinate or Greek word. In the wonderful
priestly prayer Jesus offered to the heavenly Father, he prayed that his disciples
would all be one just as he and the Father are one. Why? Not so that they
could build an impeccable ecclesiastical organization or engage in ecumenical
theology as an intellectual exercise but for this reason only: so that the world
might believe. Christian unity is an imperative of the gospel, for the sake
of Jesus Christ and his mission in this world. Packer's commitment to this
principle is a consistent thread running throughout his long career. It is also
true that no one feature of his work as a theologian has been more criticized
by some of his fellow believers. Yet through all of the tempests Packer has
remained consistent in this commitment ever seeking to speak the truth in love
and to speak to his critics with both charity and clarity.

Seventh, *any discussion of "the evangelical future" must include the global
expansion of Bible-believing Christianity, particularly south of the equator.*
J. I. Packer is an important part of this story, even though he was born in
England and has spent most of his teaching career in North America. Along
with Billy Graham and John Stott, Packer has done more than any other
evangelical leader to forge a coalition and community among gospel-centered
Christ-followers around the world. He has done this through his many travels, lectureships, sermons and, even more so, through his remarkable literary
output—the "Packer books," translated into numerous languages.

In his book *The Next Christendom* Philip Jenkins pointed to the explosion
of sound, biblically based Christianity, often with charismatic and Pentecostal overtones, in places far beyond the North Atlantic axis.[4] The validation
of Jenkins's thesis is seen dramatically in the catalytic influence of Anglican
Christianity in Africa and the new situation it has brought about in the world
Anglican community. In another eighty years, if another conference is convened
on the future of evangelicalism, it will doubtless take place somewhere other

than in North America. Packer has been a bridging figure between the older North Atlantic–centered evangelical movement and an expanding future still to be defined.

Now, in sum, a brief word about the third interrogative, *Quemadmodum?* How do we get there? As we consider in particular what J. I. Packer has to offer to us, I want to mention just three words. The first word is *integrity.* He is a theologian of integrity. We have heard his admonishing word regarding sloth. That is still another old-fashioned word: *sloth.* I think we should outlaw sloth here at Beeson Divinity School in the future: no sloth among our students! But Packer is thinking not only about getting assignments done on time but also about living out the Christian life assiduously, energetically, and faithfully, with integrity. Whatever future God may have for us, it has to embody that kind of integrity in life and thought, in doctrine and practice, in theology and ethics.

The second word is *charity.* Several years ago my friend John Woodbridge and I published a little book called *The Mark of Jesus: Loving in a Way the World Can See.* We took Francis Schaeffer's wonderful idea in his little book *The Mark of the Christian* and gave it a new, fresh airing. Francis Schaeffer noted that when Jesus admonished his disciples that they were to love one another that he intended for their love to be seen in the world. And he said, "By this everyone will know that you are my disciples, if you love one another" (John 13:34 TNIV). J. I. Packer has exhibited that distinctive mark of true Christianity both in the way he has fulfilled his theological vocation and in the way he has conducted his life in the church.

There is still another word that comes to mind when I think about J. I. Packer and the "howsoever" of the evangelical future: *humility.* In 1966 a number of Karl Barth's former students, colleagues, and friends came together to celebrate his eightieth birthday. Those who gathered in Basel for that occasion said many great and wonderful things about the famous theologian. When it was over, they asked Karl Barth to respond. This is what Karl Barth said on that,

> If I have done anything in this life of mine, I have done it as a relative of the donkey that went its way, carrying an important burden. The disciples had to say to its owner, "The Lord has need of it," and so it seems to have pleased God to have used me at this time just as I was, in spite of all the things, the disagreeable things that quite rightly are and will be said about me. Thus, I was used. I just happened to be on the spot. A theology somewhat different from the current theology was apparently needed in our time, and I was permitted to be the donkey that carried this better theology for part of the way, or tried to carry it as best I could.[5]

So, indeed, are we a company of donkeys, you and I. What was important about the donkey, of course, was not its size or pedigree or personality but rather what it carried. Our job is to be such donkeys too and to carry "it," the message, him, the one on whom the message centers, Jesus Christ, to bear him and the Word he has entrusted to us faithfully, steadily, humbly, proudly, joyfully, unashamedly, along that treacherous path that leads, finally, to Calvary. We dare to do this work because the precious cargo we donkeys are carrying is nothing less than the hope of the world itself. J. I. Packer has shown us how to do this work well and we honor him, a faithful *minister divini verbi*.

13

Reflection and Response

J. I. PACKER

The foregoing collection of conference papers, like the conference for which they were written, celebrates the ministry that for more than half a century I have sought to fulfill, and does so in a fashion that pays me a huge and indeed almost overwhelming compliment. The overall warmth and kindness of what has been said about me seemed to me, I must confess, fitter for a eulogy at my funeral than for the critical process of an academic conclave, while the stress in the conference brochure that I was still going strong made me wonder whether, like the man who was described as famous for being well known, I was henceforth to be described as famous for being still alive. But be that as it may, I am more grateful than I can express to my friends the honor their contributions do me, and I cannot begin to put into words the pleasure (God forgive me) that their expressions of goodwill have generated. A man, they say, is known by his friends; how privileged I am to be able to count as friends this group of dear and distinguished folk who have given time and effort to be involved in this particular celebration. To all of them I offer heartfelt thanks, but most especially to dean Timothy George, mastermind and host of the conference, and to professor Alister McGrath, my biographer up to 1996, who should have been co-host but was at the last minute kept by an emergency from being with us. The gratitude that I feel toward each of these my friends who produced papers, and toward the more than two hundred people who have sent me letters of good wishes on this occasion, is truly boundless. Who am I, to be blessed in this breathtaking way?

Yes, who am I? The suggestion that I am a kind of Robin Hood, taking from the wealth of wisdom that learned professionals have amassed in order to relay it accessibly to a general Christian lay readership led me not only to smile at the essential correctness of the thought, but to fantasize hoodily about the Merry Men (with the Merry Woman) round about me. I thought of Little George, the dean of Beeson, whose bigness of heart is matched only by the breadth and depth of his learning, and whose ecumenical vision is so close to my own; I thought of Maid Marian Humphrey, who had discerned me as a doctrinal watchdog, much as elsewhere I have been tagged as an evangelical traffic cop and a theological border guard; I saw in my Baptist brother Mark Dever a latter-day Sheriff of Nottingham, giving me a passing grade in the doctrine of grace but a firm "F" in ecclesiology; I recalled masterful King Charles Colson and genial Friar Richard John Tuck seeing me as a last-ditch fighter for truth and rationality in theology, shrewd Will Scarlett Hindmarsh locating me in the life-giving process of renewal through retrieval, and veteran journalist David Neff picturing me as an engineer pumping the water of truth into parched land (my resources of Robin Hoodery had run out by now); and as I thus let whimsy lead my thoughts, my delight in the acumen and affection of these my friends was renewed. And what they had affirmed about me certainly tallies with what I have at least tried to do over the years. Yet, responding to them now with a focus that they themselves have helped to sharpen, I realize there is something more about myself that I need to lay on the table.

On the momentous day when Nathan brought to David God's promise of a dynasty, the king sat before the Lord (*coram Deo*, as the language of a later theology would put it) and began his prayer of grateful wonder with the words: "Who am I , O Lord GOD . . . that you have brought me thus far?" (2 Sam. 7:18 ESV). Let me speak to that question as it applies to myself, drawing on such self-perception as God has been pleased to give me.

First, I am the product of a fairly sudden conversion, a three-minute event of forthright commitment following three years of prideful and less-than-honest religiosity while God was softening me up. The event was in no way spectacular; we were singing the hymn that Charlotte Elliott wrote after Cesar Malan had dealt with her about her soul, "Just as I am," and I was meaning it. It is hard nowadays to conceive a more conventional frame for conversion than that. Coleridge characterized poetry as the best possible words in the best possible order, and by that criterion Elliott's familiar verses are real poetry. So too is Saul Cain's account of his conversion in John Masefield's poem *The Everlasting Mercy*, which resonates directly with my own experience, still vivid in memory after sixty-three years.

> I did not think, I did not strive,
> The deep peace burned my me alive;
> The bolted door had broken in,
> I knew that I had done with sin.
> I knew that Christ had given me birth
> To brother all the souls on earth . . .[1]

That is exactly how it was with me.

Second, I am the product of a fairly steady theological growth. Starting with the sovereign-grace, pastorally developed theology of Martin Luther, John Calvin, the English reformers, and the evangelical tradition from Puritans Owen and Baxter through Whitefield, Spurgeon, and J. C. Ryle to Pink and Lloyd-Jones, and holding to this as the Western Bible-believer's basic heritage, I have come within this frame increasingly to appreciate the patristic fathers, most of all Tertullian, the Cappadocians, and Augustine, and with them Anselm, Thomas Aquinas, and the Oxford Inklings. As a result, my discernment of orthodoxy and heresy, my insight into Christ-centered communion with God and obedience to God, and my understanding of transformation by God into the image and likeness of Christ, seem to me to have deepened. Twenty years after my conversion, I remember telling the man who at that time counseled me that honoring and magnifying Christ had become the central concern of my ministry, and forty years further on so it remains. My pneumatology, enriched to be sure by Edwards on revivals and by interaction with charismatics, is still essentially that of John Owen, and though current needs have led me to say much about the Holy Spirit, Jesus Christ—crucified and risen, who is my Lord and Savior, my life and my hope—still stands at the center of my horizon—which surely is how it should always be, for all of us. My overall theological outlook has seen small adjustments but no major changes, and I thank God for the gift of consistency in holding to the things I first embraced, and embrace today, as his revealed truth.

Third, I am the product of a strong and sustained sense of vocation, in which my awareness of living under Christ's authority finds its focus. The call to become a disciple and bondslave of Jesus involves a readiness for whatever form of service he shall indicate. Soon after my conversion I was made vividly aware that I would only ever get job satisfaction from a life of pastoral ministry, shepherding my Savior's sheep along their path of life, and that is still a fixed point. Before beginning my theological studies I was providentially pitchforked into a year in a seminary teaching Latin, Greek, and philosophy, the subjects in which I had just graduated, to ministerial students; I found that adult teaching was in my blood, and I became sure that my future pastoral ministry would involve much of it, both in congregational settings and in teaching and pastoring the teachers and pastors of tomorrow within a seminary or seminary-type community; which is how it has worked out. Early on, too, God's blessing on commissioned literary efforts indicated that pastoral writing, no less than pulpit and classroom work, belonged to my calling, and so I am sure it will continue to be for as long as I am able to make words flow on paper.

So how should I be described? Alister McGrath labeled me a theologizer, a communicator rather than a constructor of theology, and I can settle for that. But I have come to think that the best way to describe myself is as a latter-day catechist—not, indeed, a children's catechist (I am not good with children), but what may be called an adult or higher catechist, one who builds on what children are supposed to be taught in order to spell out at adult level the truths we must live by and how we are to live by them. Such catechists stand in the succession of Irenaeus, Cyril of Jerusalem, Augustine, and the Puritan pastors as ministers of the gospel for whom giving this instruction is the main and never-finished ministerial task.

Nowadays, the word *theologian* suggests academic professionalism, guild membership, a passion to push out the walls of knowledge, cutting-edge and growing-edge debate with other theologians and champions of other disciplines, and distance from the routines of regular pastoral care. This conception, however familiar to us moderns, is in fact little more than two centuries old; it sprang from the late-eighteenth-century division of theological studies into the biblical, the creedal, the historical, and the pastoral, a division that has led to narrow specializing in each department with relative unconcern about the others, and so made the organic unity of theology hard to imagine and harder still to achieve. But before this a theologian had been a scholarly generalist with wisdom and skill to guide Christians on questions of belief, morality, devotion (what we now call spirituality), and forming holy habits to please God (what we once called sanctification, and now refer to as spiritual formation). When Gregory of Nazianzus and then John Calvin of Geneva were honorifically described as, quite simply, "the theologian," this is what was meant. It is this model of ministry—didactic and down-to-earth, biblical, spiritual, and transformational—that I have set before myself over the years, and it is with reference to this that, with a glance back at the adult catechumenate of the early Christian centuries, I call myself a catechist today.

The catechist concept points with maximum clarity, I believe, to the intellectual resources that all of today's pastors need. Most serve small churches, where willy-nilly they must function as something of a one-man band, and those in ministerial teams where job descriptions limit their range of responsibility will still do more good if they can look at all questions in terms of the fullness of God's truth and wisdom, rather than in terms of a narrowly specialist, and so inevitably if unconsciously manipulative, mindset. This is why, in my privileged position as an educator preparing tomorrow's clergy and Christian workers to bring real truth to real people, I have constantly stressed that theology is an organism of ten disciplines, four of which (exegesis, biblical theology, historical/ecclesial theology, and systematic/dogmatic theology) together yield a full-scale account of Christian truth as a whole, thought through and ready for use, and six of which (ethics, apologetics, spirituality, missiology, liturgics, and pastoral care) draw specific truths from this stock to apply to the matter in hand; and it is why I go on to labor the thought that no one is adequately equipped for ministry without some competence in all ten.

I confess that as I do this I often feel that the cards are stacked against me. In an age of surface-level smatterings I sound to myself a lone voice (the Elijah complex, no doubt; I hope it is as illusory in my case as it was in his, but I cannot be sure). As I speak against attitudes and influences that keep theological students from getting on top of my higher-catechist syllabus, I have a sense of replaying Horatius on the bridge. My vision, the goal of all this striving, is of congregations well educated by well-educated pastors, but the credibility of this vision is undermined, it seems to me, by the church's lack of easy-to-read literature written in full faithfulness to the Bible and the gospel at higher catechism level. Once the churches of the Reformation had bigger catechisms alongside their children's catechisms, devised for adult instruction (Luther's in Germany, Calvin's in Geneva, Nowell's in England, the Heidelberg, John Owen's Greater Catechism, and the Westminster Larger, are examples), and the churches knew how to use them; but today these documents, with very few exceptions, are forgotten. Once whole families were regularly catechized, as we learn, for instance, from Richard Baxter's *Reformed Pastor* (1656), which quickly became a handbook for this practice all over England prior to the Restoration; but nowadays such things do not happen. Adult instruction in the faith for church members (not to be equated with Bible study, which flourishes widely, thank God) is at a discount almost everywhere, and we evangelicals are short of resources that might help to turn this situation around.

Consider: we have good small basic books for beginner Christians, and the Alpha course and its progeny to set them going; we have good big technical books for clergy and ministerial students and a fine crop of first-class evangelical seminaries; but we do not have much in between, whether literary or institutional, to give ordinary adult believers adult insight into the coherence, breadth, wisdom, beauty, and glory of their faith. Roman Catholics are far further forward in this than we evangelicals are. The writings of C. S. Lewis, Francis Schaeffer, John Stott, and myself, which are pitched at a higher catechism level, may indeed easily be overvalued, just because so few others are composing theological material on that wavelength. I was moved to read, in one of C. S. Lewis's letters: "People praise me as a 'translator' [meaning here, a presenter of historic Christianity at thoughtful modern adult level], but what I want is to be the founder of a school of 'translation.' . . . Where are my successors?"[2] Sixty years after Lewis wrote, where indeed? If anything, we seem to have gone backward at this point. In Lewis's youth and, later, in mine, Anglican clergy were exhorted regularly to preach "teaching sermons," and some did; but that also is now largely a thing of the past. So where, I wonder, are my successors as adult catechists? And so my jeremiad might continue, but I am going to move on.

To avoid misunderstanding, let me state that *catechist* in my usage denotes only the area and angle of the teaching, not a commitment to question-and-answer or any other particular method of doing the job. Irenaeus, Cyril, and Augustine, to name just three, seem to have been orators teaching basically by explanatory monologue rather than by question-and-answer in the manner of sixteenth- and seventeenth-century schoolmasters and writers of popular Puritan instructional dialogues like *The Plain Man's Pathway to Heaven*. (It should be noted here that Puritans preached with a distinctly catechetical strategy, deploying deep doctrine with wide-ranging applications, stressing their many heads and subheads for memorization, and establishing a cultural pattern of "repeating" the morning sermon *en famille* over Sunday lunch to make sure that everyone had learned all that had been taught.) For us, the rule must be: let each teach any way they wish, so long as real learning takes place. There are many ways nowadays of engaging adult minds, and all may properly be put to service in the task of leading the entire adult congregation to understand and appreciate their faith in appropriate adult ways.

Question: What kind of Christians will, with God's blessing, be formed by the kind of adult catechesis that I have in mind? Answer: Christians whose lives display the following features:

doxology, the habit taught and modeled by Paul of constantly praising God and giving him thanks;

humility, the downward growth that comes by dwelling on the free, boundless, almighty grace of God that achieves the salvation of sinners, including oneself, through the atoning death of the Lord Jesus Christ;

generosity, the whole-hearted giving of oneself and one's resources in order to show love and render service both to God and to others;

honesty, the refusal to cut moral corners, practice deception, or come to terms with injustice;

intensity, a spirit that rejects euphoric sloth and laziness in favor of maximum effort to further God's cause, extend Christ's kingdom, and make the Savior known, and that goes flat out with an eye on the goal as one does when running a race;

bravery, which, though sometimes trembling in its shoes, stands firm for Christ against all forms of opposition, belittling, and ridicule; and

solidarity with the church, both worldwide and local, the people of God who are the body and bride of Christ and one's own spiritual family, so that one never wanders off into any form of churchless individualism, as if one were the only pebble on God's beach.

This profile, formed partly from the New Testament and partly by the examples of John Calvin, Richard Baxter, George Whitefield, C. H. Spurgeon, J. C. Ryle, and D. Martyn Lloyd-Jones, will be recognized as decidedly Reformational. I do in fact believe that, other things being equal, Reformed theology, which seems to me the soundest and profoundest that the world has yet seen, will give the most Christlike shape to our Christian character. Yet I see all the above-listed qualities in some persons, past and present, whose theology has not wholly matched mine; this too brings joy (and only joy) as I discern the goodness of God in action. And I see in all Christ's mature disciples one further quality that impacts me more and more as I get older, and that is realism about death, leading to readiness to face it grace-fully, if I may put it so. Since this means much to me, as an eighty-year-old, it shall have a couple of paragraphs to itself.

"Our people die well," said John Wesley somewhere, commending Methodist Christianity. Dying well, as the final climactic step in living well, was a prominent theme in older Roman Catholic, Protestant, and Orthodox teaching on the Christian life and in some places may still be so. But in the West death has become the great unmentionable, like sex in Victorian times, and little is taught to Christians in these days about preparing for it. Instead, we live as if we shall be here forever, and very many churchpeople, one fears, have matched the self-protective young man in Charles Williams's *Many Dimensions* who "passed . . . a not unsuccessful life in his profession, and the only intruder he found himself unable to cope with was death."[3] This being so, and knowing as we do that life in this world is a terminal condition, it is surely most important that our catechesis should promote readiness for dying. When the late Dag Hammarskjold wrote that only one who knows how to die can know how to live, he was absolutely right, and our churches are much at fault in having forgotten it.

Here it is lyrics from the great age of evangelical hymnody that give me most help. This, for instance, from Charles Wesley's "Jesus! The Name High Over All," I find bracing:

> Happy, if with my latest breath
> I may but gasp his name;
> Preach him to all, and cry in death
> "Behold, behold the Lamb!"[4]

And I constantly return to this, by Isaac Watts, which John Wesley amazed his friends by singing with a strong voice from his chair the day before his death:

> I'll praise my Maker while I've breath,
> And when my voice is lost in death

> Praise shall employ my nobler powers;
> My days of praise shall ne'er be past,
> While life and thought and being last,
> Or immortality endures.[5]

I think of Wesley muttering through the night that followed "I'll praise—I'll praise—" which was all he could then do (he died at about ten the next morning), and I am sustained.

My final word about death shall be this, from Richard Baxter, versifying the covenant with God that his future wife made in her early twenties, when she thought she might be dying:

> Lord, it belongs not to my care
> Whether I die or live. . . .
>
> Christ leads me through no darker rooms
> Than he went through before. . . .
>
> Come, Lord, when grace has made me meet
> Thy blessed face to see;
> For if thy work of grace be sweet,
> What will thy glory be?
>
> My knowledge of that life is small,
> The eye of faith is dim;
> But it's enough that Christ knows all,
> And I shall be with him.[6]

The title of this conference is "J. I. Packer and the Evangelical Future." Early on I asked that it be redrafted as "The Future of Evangelicalism: The Contribution of J. I. Packer," but my request was denied. All the same, the evangelical future is undoubtedly the more important thing for us to think about, and the rest of these personal reflections will focus on it.

In addressing it, we need to realize that the word *evangelical* itself could be a hindrance to us, just because of its past. Inasmuch as memory loss about the past always begets shortsightedness about the future, we must come to terms with that past, but what we find as we seek to do so is distinctly discouraging. Since *evangelical* became a common label on both sides of the Atlantic, following the formation of the Evangelical Alliance (in Britain, 1846; in America, 1867), it has become for some a party-word, similar in significance to *fundamentalist*, creating expectations of rigidity and defensive battling, while for others it has become what Francis Schaeffer called a "connotation-word," still evoking favorable vibrations after it has lost whatever precise meaning it once had. Under these circumstances, the habit begun by Harold Ockenga and Carl Henry of generalizing about "the evangelical church" does not get us very far: it yields little ecclesiological light and all too easily arouses sectarian heat. How then should we characterize evangelicalism, so as to be sure we agree on what we are talking about? Three ways of doing this seem to me to be on offer, and I shall urge that we need them all for they are complementary to each other.

The first is the historian's way, the way of *generalized description*, whereby evangelicalism can be recognized as it were from the outside. Such description will be based on how people who have called themselves evangelicals, or been tagged as such, have actually declared their beliefs and lived them out. Familiar today is David Bebbington's typology of evangelicalism as a Bible-based, cross-centered, conversion-oriented, outreach-attuned Protestant Christian ethos that took dramatic, experiential, pietistic form in Britain's evangelical revival in the eighteenth century. Other historians might add holiness-seeking and family-focused to Bebbington's list of qualities, and might point out that all these characteristics have a prehistory running back through the Puritans and Reformers to much earlier times. But Bebbington is right as far as he goes, and historical description, which recognizes evangelicalism as a style of conscientious personal discipleship to the Lord Jesus Christ, our crucified, risen and reigning Savior, is the first step toward the understanding we need.

The second method of identifying evangelicalism may be called the way of the catechists, confessionalists, and controversialists. It is the way of *doctrinal enumeration*, which sees evangelicalism as essentially the holding of a particular set of convictions about God and man that can be formulated and taught with precision and clarity. Such beliefs are certainly integral to evangelicalism, as witnesses the firmness of evangelical adherence to the ecumenical creeds, doctrinal declarations from the Reformation, and latter-day bases of faith to which evangelicals regularly subscribe.[7] As I have already said, I see myself primarily as an adult catechist, and in pursuit of that calling I formulate, teach, and preach from an evangelical catechetical syllabus conceived as follows:

1. *The authority of the Bible.* Holy Scripture is God telling and showing us things via the human writers' witness. All the truths we need to know about God and ourselves are there. Internally coherent (canonical, analogy-of-Scripture) interpretation brings them out. Since God is transcultural, so are they. The Holy Spirit, who inspired the books and led the church to recognize their divine authority, and the church's heritage of faith and life (tradition), both help in interpretation. God's people must neither add to nor subtract from biblical teaching but believe, obey, and internalize it.

2. *The reality of the Trinity.* The one God is a triune society working as a team, and in all divine acts in creation, providence, and grace all three persons are involved, even where the Bible mentions only one. But God

in himself is always as truly and essentially three as he is one. The Son does the Father's will and the Holy Spirit does the will of both, and the three are in total consensus throughout. Trinitarian reality is in solution, so to speak, in all the New Testament books.

3. *The sovereignty of God.* God's will of events is all-inclusive and is always being fulfilled, even when his will of command is being defied. God, who is holy, faithful, just, and loving, overrules sin and evil so as to bring about long-term good for rational beings who trust him and endless praise for himself (the "him" who, as I have already said, is also "them").

4. *The tragedy of humankind.* The human race is currently, and without saving grace will ever be, ruined and lost through sin. All human beings, though designed to bear God's image, are now by nature, in spiritual terms, dignified wrecks, tragic instances of good gone wrong, monuments of egocentric perversity and pride.

5. *The majesty of Jesus Christ, Savior and Lord.* Co-creator and Son of the Father, the second person of the Trinity is now and forever our incarnate Savior, Jesus Christ the Lord. He is the Father's supreme grace-gift to us. He redeemed us by his priestly sacrifice of himself on the cross as our representative and substitute, tasting the fullness of death on our behalf. Raised from the dead, he was withdrawn from this earth to reign over his kingdom, which includes the church, mediating to us the blessing of justification and adoption, pardon and peace, and the prospect of sharing his glory as our eternal inheritance. He will reappear for final judgment, for the perfection of his own people, and for a renewing of the universe.

6. *The necessity of faith.* We sinners are saved through trustful belief in, and commitment to, God the Father, his promises, and his Son, the world's living Lord. Our exercise of faith, our union with the risen Christ, and our inward regeneration of heart (new birth), are inseparably linked, all three occurring through the agency of the Holy Spirit, who thereafter indwells us as a pledge of glory to come. Christ the Lord fills our horizon, and we consciously live through, in, for, unto, and under him.

7. *The necessity of holiness.* A life of repentance, good works, loyal obedience, and thankful praise God-ward is the true fruit and vital evidence of genuine faith. This is Christian holiness, without which, so we are told, none will see the Lord with joy and delight.

8. *The centrality of the church.* The worldwide community of believers, which becomes visible in the life of each Christian congregation, is the new humanity in Christ and the focus of God's economy of salvation. No individual may cut loose from the church and act as if he or she is, so to speak, the only pebble on God's beach. Contrariwise,

the church's unity, given in Christ, must be expressed by celebrating a shared orthodoxy, by practicing godly love, by mutual acceptance, and by congregations actively helping each other in appropriate ways. In the church's life of worship, witness, and beneficent work, Christians must see themselves as the body parts through which Christ, the body's head, expresses himself. Both sacraments are constant reminders that the distinctive life of God's people, first to last, is found in, drawn from, and bestowed by the Christ who once died for the church and now lives to nourish, cherish, and energize it.

9. *The circuitry of communion.* Through what are called the means of grace (Scripture, prayer, fellowship, and sacraments) responsive fellowship with our Lord, and with his and our Father in heaven, becomes a life-changing reality. The resultant blend within us of realization, rejoicing, praising, and praying is true spirituality.

10. *The ultimacy of doxology.* God's declared purpose of being glorified, and our own deep desire for full contentment and delight, coincide, now and forever, in our adoration of the Holy Three for all that they are and all that they have done and are doing now. Loving praise will be the continuing climactic activity of our unending future life.

> When we've been there [in glory] ten thousand years,
> Bright shining as the sun,
> We've no less days to sing God's praise
> Than when we first begun.[8]

This ten-point syllabus is the doctrinal substructure of evangelicalism as I know, teach, and seek to live and model it, and it would, I think, commend itself to all Protestants who have ever professed an evangelical identity. The first thing to say about it is that evangelicals as a body insist that every Christian should master as much of it as they are capable of receiving, since it is by these divine teachings—ingested, digested, and applied—that our faith and obedience must be shaped. Where other Christian systems are content to call for conformity to established behavior patterns, evangelicals demand knowledge, thought, exercise of conscience in relation to known truth and a style of life determined by it, for to their mind this and nothing less than this is what God requires of us all. Here is one reason why reading and studying the Bible and ongoing adult education have always bulked so large in evangelical discipleship and nurture. The educational ethos of historic evangelicalism, witnessed to for nearly half a millennium by the quantity of printed matter produced, has not been matched by other sections of the church.

The second thing to say about this syllabus is that, whatever hostility to the Roman Catholic and Orthodox systems evangelicals may have shown in the past and may show in the future, most if not quite all of these doctrinal fundamentals would pass muster in Roman Catholic and Orthodox circles no less than they do on evangelicals' home turf. Nor should this surprise us, for evangelicals have always claimed to be moving in the mainstream of what has been called the Great Tradition of light and wisdom in God's church from the apostolic age until now. Indeed, the further claim is made that evangelicals have distinguished themselves by maintaining faithfulness to the New Testament revelation of God's grace in Christ where others have in part lost touch with it, and evangelicalism has been diagnosed as a characteristic mode of retrieval, renewal, reform, repositioning, and return to righteousness within the *una sancta*, Christ's one holy catholic church here on earth. I resonate with this approach, as must already be obvious. It does in fact reflect from one standpoint the third way of characterizing evangelicalism, to which I now turn.

This third way may be called the way of *dynamic analysis*. If method one was historical and method two intellectual, method three is pneumatological and views evangelicalism concretely as a particular divine operation: namely, an animating and revitalizing activity whereby through truth brought home with power the Holy Spirit impacts individuals and groups to reconfigure and direct their lives toward the mature fullness of Christ. From this standpoint evangelicalism appears not just as a doctrinal position with a pietistic life-style attached (which is how most nonevangelicals seem to see it), but rather as an organic reinvigoration of life in Christ from within, with everything that belongs to that life maintained in intensity. Already in the book of Acts Luke shows us some of this happening. He makes vivid to us the shattering sense of guilt people come to feel before the awesome God whom their sins have offended (see Acts 2:37, the effect of Peter's preaching; Acts 5:11, the impact of being detected on Ananias and Sapphira; and Acts 19:18–19, the public confessing and book-burning, an extreme expression of the felt need to repent thoroughly and put sin behind one forever). He highlights too the joy of the new Christians and their spontaneity in gossiping the gospel (see Acts 2:42–47; 8:4; 11:19–21). Christian vigor and enterprise overflow in the Acts story, and this temper is a mark of evangelicalism in all its forms. Despite disfiguring disorders due to lack of discernment, temperamental imbalance, and uncontrolled excitement, which regularly appear when the Spirit works in power, the end product of the Spirit's action is lively godliness (fidelity, morality, spirituality, liberality with one's possessions, and doxology), and this godliness, as we see most fully in Paul, is a radical personal convertedness within a large-hearted catholicity, a vivid sense of new identity in the body of Christ linked with an ecumenical concern for the purity, vitality, and welfare of all churches and Christians everywhere.

My point becomes clearer if we distinguish evangelicalism as a conceptual norm—an ideal standard of faith and life—from evangelicalism as a spiritual reality embodying the ideal. The words *revival* and *renewal* require a similar distinction. Without it, all three words will keep oscillating between signifying a concept and denoting an actuality, and confusion in applying each will result. The actuality is, as has just been said, the event of real people conforming to the doctrinal and behavioral ideal. Should persons who endorse this ideal notionally fail to pursue it practically, the right thing to say of them is that they are not real evangelicals.

Evangelicalism is thus a life-quality, personal and corporate, based on a biblical orthodoxy blessed by the Holy Spirit and centering on fellowship with the living Christ. It may become reality on a large or small scale at different times and in different circumstances, with different truths from within the evangelical cornucopia being highlighted and emphasized, against different cultural backgrounds and in different intra-church situational frames. Thus, for example, in the second half of the twentieth century the East African revival, the reordering of the Southern Baptist denomination, church growth in South Korea, and the charismatic renewal in North America and Britain displayed central aspects of the evangelical norm becoming realities in action. As movements they were quite different, yet they all sprang from the Holy Spirit taking God's people back to the Bible in order to advance the work of transforming grace in their lives. In other words, they were evangelical. Any movement in which the Holy Spirit works within a frame of Christ-centered biblical orthodoxy to lead God's people toward their predestined goal of full and mature Christlikeness is, so far, evangelical.

Thus the three ways of identifying evangelicalism come together, like three melodic lines in a Bach fugue, to form a harmonious full close chord, to which each separate note contributes in an integral way but which yet is more than any one of the notes on its own could ever be. The historical description on its own will seem eccentrically sectarian; the doctrinal formulation on its own will seem eccentrically rigid; the pneumatological account on its own will seem eccentrically romantic and sentimental; but put the three together, and what we have is the transcultural, transhistorical, transdenominational essence of mainstream biblical Christianity, arguably the central flow of life in the church: past, present, and future.

What now of evangelicalism's future? Not being any kind of futurologist, and being aware that guesswork is not knowledge, I shall be brief and tentative here, and perhaps disjointed. The most I can hope to do is offer realistic trajectories within which the path of evangelical faithfulness—faithfulness to Christ, Scripture, the gospel, the church, and the cause of God's kingdom—may be found as we travel forward.

First, we must remember that without God's blessing nothing good can be expected to happen either to evangelicalism or to the wider church or to the still-wider world. We observe that our planet is in increasing agony from global warming, global consumerism, global pollution, the population explosion, the AIDS explosion, freshwater shortages, wars, post-Christian materialism, Islamic aggression, and more. Short-term, Christianity advances in the Global

South while retreating in the north; long-term, however, the northern blight of post-Christian secularism is sure to spread south, and anti-Christianity will in time escalate there too, if indeed nuclear imprudence does not ruin the planet first. Evangelical triumphalism, fed by a spectacular increase in numbers, academic resources, and community influence in many places, is common today, but the factors listed, plus Bible teaching, make it obvious that it should not be. The future of the world church, and of evangelicalism within it, is in the hands of God, and all our concerns about the Christian future should drive us to prayer before anything else. As so many of the psalms actually say, only God can save us now.

Second, there are four specific interfaces involving antitheses that evangelicalism must continue to maintain. To start with, the post-Tillichian type of self-styled liberal theology, which posits a dumb God and relativizes all biblical instruction to community culture with its spontaneous religious feelings, so desupernaturalizing Christianity entirely, should be radically opposed wherever it appears; just as historic Gnosticism (to which this is really a throwback) had to be radically opposed in the early Christian centuries. Since this liberalism kills real Christianity, real Christianity must clearheadedly and uncompromisingly seek to kill it, and divert its devotees from poisoning themselves with so unwholesome a brew.

Next, the basic difference between biblical evangelicalism and both Roman Catholicism and Eastern Orthodoxy regarding the nature of the church must be kept in view while fellowship with these traditions develops at other points. Their conception, which grew with increasing clarity from the second century, is that Christ's one church is in essence a ministerial and sacramental network channeling grace, with its authenticity and authority guaranteed by, among other things, the apostolic succession of orders. John Wesley, high churchman though he was, spoke for evangelicals when he dismissed that succession as "a fable which no man ever did or could prove."[9] Evangelicals, by contrast, see the church as in essence the worldwide fellowship of the faithful, united to and in Christ, a fellowship that becomes visible wherever Christians associate to do together the things that the church does, and that appoints ministers from its own ranks as needed; and they explain apostolic succession, when asked about it, as faithfulness to the apostles' doctrine and mission, according to Scripture. However much joint pastoral work and witness with these older bodies we may see fit to practice (evangelicals differ here, as is well known), we must not lose sight of this basic divergence, which apart from all else makes anything like reunion impossible.

My third interface is with non-Christian religions. The authentic (though not, alas, invariable) evangelical approach to them has been, and should continue to be, to affirm all that is good in them, seeing it as the fruit of general revelation, while yet insisting on their need to know the redeeming love of God in our Lord Jesus Christ, without whom we are all lost. This stance, modeled on Paul's address to the Areopagus, should be seen as transcultural and nonnegotiable.

For the last interface, the necessary ongoing task of evangelistic engagement with adherents of post-Christian secularism in its many forms, we need, I would urge, to maintain the double-barreled holism of which Francis Schaeffer was such a master. Firing the first barrel means, in Schaeffer's phrase, "taking the roof off,"[10] showing analytically the incoherence, uncertainty, discomfort, and ultimate despair that all post-Christian worldviews and ideologies, when treated as homes for head and heart, prove to leave us with. Firing the second barrel means telling the full Christian story, from creation and fall through redemption and regeneration to consummation, the perfected life of love and joy in Christ that Christians will know hereafter. The call then is to allow the God of love to make the story of our own life and work part of the story of his own life and work by becoming disciples and followers of the Lord Jesus. This, I believe, will be the truly appropriate way to engage with the captives of Western secularism for as long as that secularism lasts.

Not long before his passion, Jesus, we are told, said aloud: "'Now is my soul troubled. And what shall I say? "Father, save me from this hour"? But for this purpose I have come to this hour. Father, glorify your name.' Then a voice came from heaven: 'I have glorified it, and I will glorify it again'" (John 12:27–28 ESV). Here I find encouragement for myself and for us evangelicals as a body. We have a great heritage, and at present, by God's mercy, we are enjoying fair health as a movement. But the pressure on us is great, and growing greater. What to do? The right move for us, I am sure, is to ask the God who has blessed the evangelical movement in the past to glorify his name in and through us once more. That will be the Christlike and apostolic response. So let us do that, again and again, and see how God answers our prayers.

Appendix A

Bibliography of the Works of J. I. Packer

July 1952–August 2008

J. I. Packer continues to write and publish prolifically. This is not a comprehensive bibliography of his works but does show the remarkable scope of his literary output. Audio recordings are not included here, but many are available through the theological institutions at which he has lectured, including Regent College, Westminster Theological Seminary, Beeson Divinity School, and Reformed Theological Seminary. Our thanks to the library staffs of Regent College in Vancouver, Canada, and Samford University in Birmingham, Alabama, for their assistance in compiling this bibliography.

1952

Articles, Essays, and Published Lectures

"The Puritan Treatment of Justification by Faith." *Evangelical Quarterly* 24, no. 3 (July 1952): 131–43.

"Sanctification—Puritan Teaching." *Christian Graduate* 5, no. 4 (December 1952): 125–28.

1953

Articles, Essays, and Published Lectures

"Great Pastors: Richard Baxter." *Theology* 56 (May 1953): 174–78.

1954

Theses

"The Redemption and Restoration of Man in the Thought of Richard Baxter: A Study in Puritan Theology." DPhil thesis, University of Oxford, 1954.

Articles, Essays, and Published Lectures

"Blind Spots." *Discipulus* (Advent 1954): 5–8.
"Revelation and Inspiration." In *The New Bible Commentary*, 2nd ed., edited by Francis Davidson, E. F. Kevan, and A. M. Stibbs. London: Inter-Varsity, 1954.

Reviews

Review of *The Christian Approach to Culture*, by Emile Cailliet. *Religion in Life* 23, no. 4 (1954): 618–20.

1955

Articles, Essays, and Published Lectures

"Baptism: Sacrament of the Covenant of Grace." *Churchman* 69, no. 2 (June 1955): 76–84.
"'Keswick' and the Reformed Doctrine of Sanctification." *Evangelical Quarterly* 27, no. 3 (July 1955): 153–67.

1956

Articles, Essays, and Published Lectures

"Some Thoughts on General Revelation." *Christian Graduate* 9, no. 3 (September 1956): 114–21.

Reviews

Review of *Apostolic Preaching of the Cross*, by Leon Morris. *Evangelical Quarterly* 28, no. 2 (April/June 1956): 113–14.

1957

Articles, Essays, and Published Lectures

"Puritan Evangelism." *Banner of Truth* 4 (February 1957): 4–13.

"Seventeenth-Century Teaching on The Christian Life: Part I." *Churchman* 71, no. 4 (1957): 166–73.

"With All Thy Mind." *Inter-Varsity* (1957): 4–8.

"The Witness of the Spirit: The Puritan Teaching." In *The Wisdom of Our Fathers: Puritan Conference, 1956*, 14–25. Privately printed, 1957.

Translations

Martin Luther on the Bondage of the Will: A New Translation of De servo arbitrio *(1525): Martin Luther's Reply to Erasmus of Rotterdam.* Translated by J. I. Packer and O. R. Johnston. London: J. Clarke; Westwood, NJ: Revell, 1957.

Forewords, Introductions, and Prefaces

Foreword to *Principles of Conduct: Aspects of Biblical Ethics*, by John Murray. Grand Rapids: Eerdmans; London: Tyndale, 1957.

1958

Books

"Fundamentalism" and the Word of God: Some Evangelical Principles. Grand Rapids: Eerdmans, 1958; London: Inter-Varsity, 1958. Published in Chinese, 1969; Korean, 1973, 1992; Dutch, 2000.

Articles, Essays, and Published Lectures

"Contemporary Views of Revelation (Part 1)." *Christianity Today*, November 24, 1958, 3–6.

"Contemporary Views of Revelation (Part 2)." *Christianity Today*, December 8, 1958, 15–17. These two articles were published as a single essay in *Revelation and the Bible*, ed. Carl F. H. Henry, 87–104. Grand Rapids: Baker Academic; London: Tyndale, 1959.

"Fundamentalism: The British Scene." *Christianity Today*, September 29, 1958, 3–6.

"The Fundamentalism Controversy: Retrospect and Prospect." *Faith and Thought* 90, no. 1 (August 1958): 35–45.

"The Puritans and the Lord's Day." In *Servants of the Word: Puritan Conference, 1957*, 1–24. London: Banner of Truth, 1958.

"Seventeenth-Century Teaching on the Christian Life: Part II." *Churchman* 72, no. 1 (1958): 23–29.

1959

Articles, Essays, and Published Lectures

"Calvinism in Britain." *Torch and Trumpet* 9, no. 7 (December 1959): 21–22.
"Christianity and Non-Christian Religions." *Christianity Today*, December 21, 1959, 3–5.
"God's Justification of Sinners." *Christianity Today*, March 16, 1959, 3–6.
Introduction and "Puritans as Interpreters of Scripture." In *A Goodly Heritage: The Puritan Conference, 1958*, 2–7, 18–26. London: Banner of Truth, 1959.

Editions

Ryle, J. C. *Practical Religion: Being Plain Papers on the Daily Duties, Experience, Dangers, and Privileges of Professing Christians*. Edited and foreword by J. I. Packer. Cambridge: Clarke; New York: Crowell, 1959.

Forewords, Introductions, and Prefaces

Introduction to *The Death of Death in the Death of Christ: A Treatise in which the Whole Controversy about Universal Redemption is Fully Discussed*, by John Owen. London: Banner of Truth, 1959.

Reviews

Review of *Revelation through Reason: Religion in the Light of Science and Philosophy*, by Errold E. Harris. *Churchman* 73, no. 3 (July/September 1959): 156–57.

1960

Books

The Plan of God. London: Evangelical, 1960.
Reservation: The Addresses Given at Church Society Annual Meeting, 14th June, 1960. Edited with J. A. Motyer. London: Church Book Room, 1960.

Articles, Essays, and Published Lectures

"The Bible in Modern Theology." *Bible League Quarterly* 240 (January/March, 1960): 129–32.

"Call," "Faith," "Freedom," "Ignorance," "Justification," "Orthodoxy," "Puritanism," and "Regeneration." In *Baker's Dictionary of Theology*, edited by Everett F. Harrison. Grand Rapids: Baker Academic; London: Pickering & Inglis, 1960. Later reprinted as *Wycliffe Dictionary of Theology*.

"Expository Preaching: Charles Simeon and Ourselves." *Churchman* 74, no. 2 (April/June, 1960): 94–100.

Introduction and "The Puritan View of Preaching the Gospel." In *How Shall They Hear? A Symposium of Papers Read at the Puritan and Reformed Studies Conference, December, 1959*, 11–21. London: The Evangelical Magazine, 1960.

"Puritan Preaching." *The Evangelical Christian* (October 1960): 18–21.

Reviews

Review of *Calvin's Doctrine of the Christian Life*, by Ronald S. Wallace. *Churchman* 74, no. 2 (April/June, 1960): 130–31.

Review of *Ideas of Revelation: An Historical Study, AD 1700–AD 1860*, by H. D. McDonald. *Churchman* 74, no. 1 (January/March, 1960): 42–43.

1961

Books

Evangelism and the Sovereignty of God. London: Inter-Varsity; Chicago: InterVarsity, 1961. Published in German, 1964; Portuguese, 1966; French, 1968; Chinese, 1968; Korean, 1977; Italian, 1978; Dutch, 1995; Czech, 2000; Ukrainian, 2001; Japanese, n.d.

The Thirty-Nine Articles. London: Falcon, 1961. This forty-six-page booklet is a revision of six articles first published in the Church of England Newspaper during October and November 1960.

Articles, Essays, and Published Lectures

"The Bible and the Authority of Reason." *Churchman* 75, no. 4 (October/December, 1961): 207–19.

"Jonathan Edwards and the Theology of Revival." In *Increasing in the Knowledge of God: Papers Read at the Puritan and Reformed Studies Conference, 20th and 21st December, 1960*, 13–28. London: The Evangelical Magazine, 1961.

"The Origin and History of Fundamentalism." In *The Word of God and Fundamentalism: Oxford Conference of Evangelical Churchmen, 19th to 21st September, 1960*, edited by T. Hewitt, 100–127. London: Church Book Room, 1961.

"The Revised Catechism." *Churchman* 75, no. 2 (April/June 1961): 107–18.

The Theological Challenge to Evangelicalism Today. Fellowship of Evangelical Churchmen, 1961.

"Training for Christian Service." *The Evangelical Christian* (September 1961): 10–15.

Forewords, Introductions, and Prefaces

Introduction to *The Doctrine of Justification*, by James Buchanan. London: Banner of Truth, 1961.

Reviews

Review of *Bread Which We Break*, by Greville Dennis Yarnold. *Churchman* 75, no. 2 (April/June 1961): 126–27.

Review of *Christopher Davenport, Friar and Diplomat*, by John Berchmans Dockery. *Churchman* 75, no. 1 (January/March 1961): 62.

Review of *The Doctrine of our Redemption*, by Nathaniel Micklem. *Churchman* 75, no. 1 (January/March 1961): 60–61.

Review of *Ethics and the Gospel*, by Thomas Walter Mason. *Churchman* 75, no. 2 (April/June 1961): 127.

1962

Books

Eucharistic Sacrifice: Addresses Given at the Oxford Conference of Evangelical Churchmen, September 1961. Edited by J. I. Packer. London: Church Book Room, 1962.

Articles, Essays, and Published Lectures

"Assurance," "Authority," "Conversion," "Earnest," "Election," "Good Inner Man," "Incarnation," "Inspiration," "Justification," "Liberty," "Obedience," "Perfection," "Piety," "Predestination," "Providence," "Revelation," and "Temptation." In *The New Bible Dictionary*, edited by J. D. Douglas, F. F. Bruce, and D. J. Wiseman. London: Inter-Varsity; Grand Rapids: Eerdmans, 1962.

"Basic Christian Doctrines: The Nature of the Church." *Christianity Today*, June 8, 1962, 22–23.

"The Holy Spirit—and Authority." *The Almond Branch* (1962): 9–12.

"Lambeth, 1958." In *Eucharistic Sacrifice: Addresses Given at the Oxford Conference of Evangelical Churchmen, September 1961*, edited by J. I. Packer, 1–21. London: Church Book Room, 1962.

"The Nature of the Church" in *Basic Christian Doctrines*, edited by C. F. H. Henry, 241–47. New York: Holt, Rinehart & Winston, 1962.

Our Lord's Understanding of the Law of God. Campbell Morgan Memorial Bible Lectureship, no. 14. Glasgow: Pickering & Inglis, 1962.

"The Puritan Idea of Communion with God." In *Press Toward the Mark: Papers Read at the Puritan and Reformed Studies Conference, 19th and 20th December, 1961,* 5–15. London: The Evangelical Magazine, 1962.

"Questions about Inter-Varsity Fellowship." *Break Through* 11 (May 1962): 13–19.

Reviews

Review of *Anglicanism in History and Today*, by John William Charles Wand. *Churchman* 76, no. 1 (March 1962): 48–49.

Review of *Concept of Holiness*, by Roger Jones Owen. *Churchman* 76, no. 3 (September 1962): 178–79.

Review of *Human Achievement and Divine Vocation in the Message of Paul*, by William A. Beardslee. *Churchman* 76, no. 2 (June 1962): 116–17.

Review of *The Theological Foundations of Ethics*, by William G. Maclagan. *Churchman* 76, no. 1 (March 1962): 59–60.

1963

Books

The Church of England and the Methodist Church: A Consideration of the Report, Conversations between the Church of England and the Methodist Church: Ten Essays. Edited by J. I. Packer. Marcham, England: Marcham Manor, 1963.

Keep Yourselves from Idols. Grand Rapids: Eerdmans; London: Church Book Room, 1963. This twenty-page booklet is a discussion of the book *Honest to God*, by John A. T. Robinson. Also published as "Episcopal Idol: A Consideration of *Honest to God*." *The Evangelical Christian* (October 1963): 4–5, 32–35.

Articles, Essays, and Published Lectures

"Approaching the Report," "Episcopacy," and "Where from Here?" In *The Church of England and the Methodist Church: A Consideration of the Report, Conversations between the Church of England and the Methodist Church: Ten Essays*, edited by J. I. Packer. 5–11, 23–30, 61–63. Marcham, England: Marcham Manor, 1963.

"Fellowship: The Theological Basis." *Christian Graduate* 16, no. 3 (September 1963): 7–11.

"Our Lord and the Old Testament." *Bible League Quarterly* 252 (January/March, 1963): 70–74.

"The Puritan Conscience." In *Faith and a Good Conscience: Papers Read at the Puritan and Reformed Studies Conference, 18th and 19th December, 1962,* 18–26. London: The Evangelical Magazine, 1963.

"What Is Revival?" In *The Best of "Crusade,"* edited by David B. Winter, 89–93. London: Victory, 1963.

Reviews

Review of *Divine Grace and Man*, by Piet F. Fransen. *Frontier* 6 (Summer 1963): 138–40.

Review of *Theories of Revelation: An Historical Study 1860–1960*, by H. D. McDonald. *Churchman* 77, no. 3 (September 1963): 202–3.

1964

Articles, Essays, and Published Lectures

"Atheism." *Inter-Varsity*, special introductory issue (1964): 4–6.

"The Bible, Yesterday, Today and Tomorrow." *The Gospel Magazine*, March 1964, 104–13.

"British Theology in the Twentieth Century." In *Christian Faith and Modern Theology*, edited by C. F. H. Henry, 23–41. New York: Channel, 1964.

"Broad Church Reformation." *London Quarterly and Holborn Review* 189 (October 1964): 270–75.

"The Devil." *Eternity* 15, no. 8 (August 1964): 7.

"The Holy Spirit and the Local Congregation." *Churchman* 78, no. 2 (June 1964): 98–108.

"The Puritan Approach to Worship." In *Diversity in Unity: Papers Read at the Puritan and Reformed Studies Conference, December, 1963*, 3–14. London: The Evangelical Magazine, 1964.

"The Status of the Articles." In *The Articles of the Church of England*, edited by H. E. W. Turner, 25–57. London: Mowbrays, 1964.

"Thomas Cranmer's Catholic Theology." In *The Work of Thomas Cranmer*, edited by G. E. Duffield, 10–37. Abingdon, UK: Sutton Courtenay, 1964; Philadelphia: Fortress, 1965.

"The Wretched Man in Romans 7." In *Studia Evangelica: Papers Presented to the Second International Congress on New Testament Studies held at Christ Church 1961*, vol. 2, edited by Frank Leslie Cross, 621–27. Berlin: Akademie-Verlag, 1964. Reprinted in *Keep in Step with the Spirit*, 1984.

1965

Books

All in Each Place: Towards Reunion in England; Ten Anglican Essays with Some Free Church Comments. Edited by J. I. Packer. Abingdon, UK: Marcham Manor, 1965.

God Has Spoken: Revelation and the Bible. London: Hodder and Stoughton, 1965. Revised and enlarged editions published in 1979, 1993, 1998, and 2005. Published in the United States as *God Speaks to Man: Revelation and the Bible.* Philadelphia: Westminster, 1965. Published in German, 1988; Spanish, 2007.

Articles, Essays, and Published Lectures

"All Men Won't Be Saved." *Banner of Truth* 41 (March 1965): and *Eternity* 16, no. 11 (November 1965): 15–17.

"Calvin: A Servant of the Word." In *Able Ministers of the New Testament: Papers Read at the Puritan and Reformed Studies Conference, December 1964*, 36–55. London: The Evangelical Magazine, 1965.

"Death: Life's One and Only Certainty." *Eternity* 16, no. 3 (March 1965): 22–26. Reprinted in *Death: Jesus Made It All Different*, edited by Miriam Moran, 13–21. New Canaan, CT: Keats, 1977.

"Ministry of the Word Today." *The Presbyterian Guardian* 34, no. 6 (July/August 1965): 87–90.

"Wanted: A Pattern for Union," and, with C. O. Buchanan, "Unification and Ordination." In *All in Each Place: Towards Reunion in England; Ten Anglican Essays With Some Free Church Comments*, edited by J. I. Packer, 17–40. Abingdon, UK: Marcham Manor, 1965.

Reviews

Review of *Hooker and the Anglican Tradition: An Historical and Theological Study of Hooker's Ecclesiastical Polity*, by John Sedberry Marshall. *Churchman* 79, no. 1 (March 1965): 76–78.

1966

Books

The Gospel in the Prayer Book. Appleford, UK: Marcham Manor; London: Church Book Room, 1966. This eight-page booklet is an expansion of a series of articles that appeared in *News Extra* parish magazine inset.

Tomorrow's Worship. Prayer Book Reform Series. London: Church Book Room, 1966. This is a thirty-one-page booklet.

Articles, Essays, and Published Lectures

"A Calvinist—and an Evangelist." *The Hour International* 31 (August 1966): 25–27.

"Calvin the Theologian." In *John Calvin*, edited by G. E. Duffield, 149–75. Appleford, UK: Sutton Courtenay, 1966.

"Gain and Loss." In *Towards a Modern Prayer Book,* edited by R. T. Beckwith, 74–94. Abingdon, UK: Marcham Manor, 1966.

"Led by the Spirit of God." *The Life of Faith* (May 1966): 499–500.

"Luther." In *Approaches to Reformation of the Church: Papers Read at the Puritan and Reformed Studies Conference, December 1965,* 25–33. London: The Evangelical Magazine, 1966.

"Luther against Erasmus." *Concordia Theological Monthly* 37, no. 4 (April 1966): 207–21.

"One Body in Christ: The Doctrine and Expression of Christian Unity." *Churchman* 80, no. 1 (March 1966): 16–26.

Forewords, Introductions, and Prefaces

Introduction to John Calvin, *Instruction in Christianity.* Translated by J. P. Wiles. Redhill, UK: Sovereign Grace Union, 1966.

1967

Books

Guidelines: Anglican Evangelicals Face the Future. Edited by J. I. Packer. London: Falcon, 1967.

The Spirit within You: The Church's Neglected Possession. With A. M. Stibbs. London: Hodder and Stoughton, 1967. Published in Korean, 2003.

Articles, Essays, and Published Lectures

"The Good Confession." In *Guidelines: Anglican Evangelicals Face the Future,* edited by J. I. Packer, 11–38. London: Falcon, 1967.

"Hermeneutics and Biblical Authority." *Churchman* 81, no. 1 (Spring 1967): 7–21.

"Isn't One Religion as Good as Another?" In *Hard Questions,* edited by Frank Colquhoun, 16–19. London: Falcon, 1967.

"John Owen on Communication from God." In *One Steadfast High Intent: Papers Read at the Puritan and Reformed Studies Conference, December 1966,* 17–30. Battersea, UK: The Evangelical Magazine, 1967.

"Reply to P. E. Hughes." *Churchman* 81, no. 3 (Autumn 1967): 209–10.

1968

Books

The Thirty-Nine Articles Today. London: Church Book Room, 1968.

Articles, Essays, and Published Lectures

"Anglican-Methodist Unity: Which Way Now?" In *Fellowship in the Gospel: Evangelical Comment on Anglican-Methodist Unity and Intercommunion Today.* Abingdon, UK: Marcham Manor, 1968.

"Church of South India and Reunion in England." *Churchman* 82, no. 4 (Winter 1968): 249–61.

"Must We Demythologize?" *Theological Students Fellowship Bulletin* 50 (Spring 1968): 1–5.

"The Necessity of the Revealed Word." In *The Bible: The Living Word of Revelation,* edited by Merrill C. Tenney, 31–52. Grand Rapids: Zondervan, 1968.

"The Puritans and Spiritual Gifts." In *Profitable for Doctrine and Reproof: Papers Read at the Puritan and Reformed Studies Conference, December 1967,* 15–27. London: The Evangelical Magazine, 1968.

"Relations between English Churchmen and Roman Catholics: Some Guiding Principles." London: Church Society, 1968. This is a five-page memorandum issued by the Church Society.

"Re-tooling the Clergy Factories." *Churchman* 82, no. 2 (Summer 1968): 120–24.

Reviews

Review of *The Authority of the Old Testament,* by John Bright. *Churchman* 82, no. 2 (Summer 1968): 138–39.

1969

Books

A Guide to the Thirty-Nine Articles Today. London: Church Book Room, 1969.

Articles, Essays, and Published Lectures

"Arminianisms." In *The Manifold Grace of God: Papers Read at the Puritan and Reformed Studies Conference, 1968,* 22–34. London: The Evangelical Magazine, 1969.

"The Inspiration and Infallibility of Holy Scripture." In *Symposium of Articles from the Theological Students Fellowship Bulletin* (TSFB), 16–18. London: Theological Students Fellowship, 1969.

"The Problem of Universalism Today." *Theology Review: Australian Journal of the Theological Students Fellowship* 5, no. 3 (1969): 16–24.

"The Way Forward in Church Union: A Paper Read at the Islington Clerical Conference." January, 1969. An unpublished eleven-page address.

Reviews

Review of *New Directions in Anglican Theology: A Survey from Temple to Robinson*, by Robert J. Page. *Churchman* 83, no. 1 (1969): 61.

1970

Books

Growing into Union: Proposals for Forming a United Church in England. With Colin O. Buchanan, E. L. Mascall, and Graham Leonard. London: SPCK, 1970.

Articles, Essays, and Published Lectures

"Doctrine of Justification in Development and Decline among the Puritans." In *By Schisms Rent Asunder: Papers Read at the Puritan and Reformed Studies Conference, 1969*, 18–30. London: The Evangelical Magazine, 1970.

"Training for the Ministry." In *Ministry in the Seventies*, edited by Clive Porthouse, 156–67. London: Falcon Books, 1970.

Reviews

Review of *Augustinianism and Modern Theology*, by Henri Cardinal de Lubac. *Church Quarterly* 2 (January 1970): 267–68.

1971

Articles, Essays, and Published Lectures

"Biblical Authority, Hermeneutics, and Inerrancy." In *Jerusalem and Athens: Critical Discussions on the Theology and Apologetics of Cornelius Van Til*, edited by E. R. Geehan, 141–53. Philadelphia: P&R, 1971.

"Groundwork for Unity." *Churchman* 85, no. 4 (Winter 1971): 214–16.

"Revival." *Christian Graduate* 24, no. 4 (December 1971): 97–100.

Reviews

Review of *Groundwork for Unity*, by R. P. C. Hanson. *Churchman* 85, no. 4 (Winter 1971): 214–16.

Review of *The Obedience of Faith: The Purposes of Paul in the Epistle to the Romans*, by Paul Sevier Minear. *Churchman* 85, no. 4 (Winter 1971): 301–2.

1972

Articles, Essays, and Published Lectures

"Representative Priesthood and the Ordination of Women." In *Why Not? Priesthood and the Ministry of Women: A Theological Study*, edited by G. E. Duffield and Michael Bruce, 78–80. Appleford, UK: Marcham Manor, 1972. Also published in *Churchman* 86, no. 2 (Summer 1972): 86–88.

"Reservation: Theological Issues." In *Reservation and Communion of the Sick*, edited by C. O. Buchanan, 15–21. Bramcote, UK: Grove, 1972.

"Towards a Corporate Presbyterate." In *Ministry in the Local Church: Problems and Pathways: The Islington Conference Papers of 1971*, edited by R. P. P. Johnston, 14–20. Bramcote, UK: Grove, 1972.

"The Way of Salvation, Part I: The Meaning of Salvation." *Bibliotheca Sacra* 129, no. 515 (July/September 1972): 195–205.

"The Way of Salvation, Part II: What Is Faith?" *Bibliotheca Sacra* 129, no. 516 (October/December 1972): 291–306.

1973

Books

Knowing God. Downers Grove, IL: InterVarsity; London: Hodder and Stoughton, 1973. Translations: German, 1977, 2005; Japanese, 1978; Norwegian, 1978; Chinese, 1979, 2004; Italian, 1979; Spanish, 1979; Korean, 1980, 1993, 1996; Finnish, 1981; Portuguese, 1981; French, 1983; Swedish, 1983, 1984, 1995; Spanish, 1985, 2006; Polish, 1989; Hebrew, 1990; Russian, 1990, 1992; Dutch, 1992; Bulgarian, 1994; Hungarian, 1994; Turkish, 1996; Greek, 1998; Indonesian, 2002; Estonian, 2004; Urdu, 2005. The twentieth-anniversary edition (InterVarsity, 1993) includes a new preface, as well as an "Americanization" of the text.

Knowing God: A Study Guide. London: Hodder and Stoughton, 1973. Translations: French, 1995; Dutch, 1995.

Articles, Essays, and Published Lectures

"Acquitted!" *Span* 1 (1973): 10–11.

"Myth," "Puritan Ethics," and "Revelation." In *Baker's Dictionary of Christian Ethics*, edited by Carl F. H. Henry. Grand Rapids: Baker Academic, 1973.

"Taking Stock in Theology." In *Evangelicals Today: Thirteen Stock-Taking Essays*, edited by John C. King, 15–30. London: Lutherworth, 1973.

"Thoughts on the Role and Function of Women in the Church." In *Evangelicals and the Ordination of Women*, edited by Colin Craston, 22–30. Bramcote, UK: Grove, 1973.

"Towards a Confession for Tomorrow's Church." *Churchman* 87, no. 4 (Winter 1973): 246–62.

"The Way of Salvation, Part III: The Problems of Universalism." *Bibliotheca Sacra* 130, no. 517 (January/March, 1973): 3–11.

"The Way of Salvation, Part IV: Are Non-Christian Faiths Ways of Salvation?" *Bibliotheca Sacra* 130, no. 518 (April/June, 1973): 110–16.

1974

Books

The New Man. London: Scripture Union; Grand Rapids: Eerdmans, 1974.

Articles, Essays, and Published Lectures

"Doctrinal Studies: Life in Christ" (a series of 51 short studies on the Christian life for laity). In *Bible Characters and Doctrines*, vol. 11. London: Scripture Union; Grand Rapids: Eerdmans, 1974.

"*Sola Scriptura* in History and Today" and "Calvin's View of Scripture." In *God's Inerrant Word: An International Symposium on the Trustworthiness of Scripture*, edited by John Warwick Montgomery, 43–62, 95–114. Minneapolis: Bethany, 1974.

"What Did the Cross Achieve? The Logic of Penal Substitution." The Tyndale Biblical Theology Lecture, 1973. *Tyndale Bulletin* 25 (1974): 3–45.

Forewords, Introductions, and Prefaces

Introduction to *The Reformed Pastor*, by Richard Baxter. London: Banner of Truth, 1974.

Reviews

Review of *Christ and the Hiddenness of God*, by Don Cupitt. *Churchman* 88, no. 1 (January/March, 1974): 59–60.

Review of *Crisis of Moral Authority: The Dethronement of Christianity*, by Don Cupitt. *Churchman* 88, no. 1 (January/March, 1974): 60–61.

Review of *The Openness of Being: Natural Theology Today*, by Eric Lionel Mascall. *Churchman* 88, no. 1 (January/March, 1974): 58–59.

Review of *The Spirit of the Reformed Tradition*, by M. Eugene Osterhaven. *Churchman* 88, no. 2 (April/June 1974): 146.

1975

Articles, Essays, and Published Lectures

"Abolish," "Accuse," "Arts," "Carpenter," "Defile," "Despise," "Dirt," "Firm," "Present," and "Ruin." In *New International Dictionary of New Testament Theology*, vol. 1., edited by Colin Brown, Exeter, UK: Paternoster; Grand Rapids: Zondervan, 1975.

"Hermeneutics and Biblical Authority." *Themelios* 1, no. 1 (1975): 3–12.

"On Knowing God." *Tenth: An Evangelical Quarterly* (July 1975): 11–25.

"Oxford Evangelicals in Theology." In *The Evangelicals at Oxford, 1735–1871: A Record of an Unchronicled Movement with the Record Extended to 1905*, by John Reynolds, 82–94. Abingdon, UK: Marcham Manor, 1975.

1976

Articles, Essays, and Published Lectures

"Representative Priesthood and the Ordination of Women" and "Postscript: I Believe in Women's Ministry." In *Why Not? Priesthood & the Ministry of Women: A Theological Study,* 2nd ed., edited by Michael Bruce and G. E. Duffield, 78–80, 164–74. Abingdon, UK: Marcham Manor, 1976. "Representative Priesthood" was reprinted from the 1972 edition, while the "Postscript" first appeared in this edition.

"Revival and Renewal." *Renewal* 62 (April 1976): 14–17.

"*Sola Fide*: The Reformed Doctrine of Justification." In *Soli Deo Gloria: Essays in Reformed Theology; Festschrift for John H. Gerstner,* edited by R. C. Sproul, 11–25. Nutley, NJ: P&R, 1976.

"What Is Evangelism?" In *Theological Perspectives on Church Growth*, edited by Harvie M. Conn, 91–105. Nutley, NJ: P&R, 1976.

Forewords, Introductions, and Prefaces

Foreword to *Introduction to Puritan Theology: A Reader*, edited by Edward E. Hindson. Grand Rapids: Baker Academic, 1976.

1977

Books

Across the Divide. With Roger T. Beckwith and G. E. Duffield. Basingstoke, UK: Lyttelton, 1977.

I Want to Be a Christian. Eastbourne, UK: Kingsway; Wheaton: Tyndale, 1977. Reissued as *Growing in Christ*. Wheaton: Crossway, 1994. Translations: Korean 1980, 2002; Chinese, 1981; German (3 vols.), 1982; Spanish, 1983; Japanese

("Lord's Prayer" only), 1990; Japanese ("Apostles' Creed" only), 1991; Dutch, 1995; Vietnamese 1996.

Articles, Essays, and Published Lectures

"Are Pain and Suffering Direct Results of Evil?" In *Moral Questions*, edited by Frank Colquhoun, 26–29. London: Falcon, 1977.

"Jesus Christ the Lord: The New Testament Doctrine of the Incarnation." In *Obeying Christ in a Changing World: The Lord Christ*, vol. 1, edited by J. R. W. Stott, 32–60. London: Collins, 1977.

"On Knowing God." In *Our Sovereign God: Addresses Presented to the Philadelphia Conference on Reformed Theology, 1974–1976*, edited by J. M. Boice, 61–76. Grand Rapids: Baker Academic, 1977.

"A Secular Way to Go." *Third Way* 1, no. 7 (April, 1977): 3–5.

"Theology of the Reformation" and "Ignatius Loyola." In *Lion Handbook of Church History*, edited by Timothy Dowley. Berkhamsted, UK: Lion, 1977. Published in the US as *Eerdmans' Handbook to the History of Christianity*. Grand Rapids: Eerdmans, 1977.

"Why Is Authority a Dirty Word?" *Spectrum* (May 1977): 4–6.

Forewords, Introductions, and Prefaces

Foreword to *Knowing God's Word*, by R. C. Sproul. Downers Grove, IL: InterVarsity; London: ARK, 1977.

1978

Books

The Evangelical Anglican Identity Problem: An Analysis. Oxford: Latimer House, 1978.

For Man's Sake! Exeter, UK: Paternoster, 1978. Published in the US as *Knowing Man*. Westchester, IL: Crossway, 1979.

Articles, Essays, and Published Lectures

"Encountering Present-Day Views of Scripture." In *Foundation of Biblical Authority*, edited by J. M. Boice, 61–84. Grand Rapids: Baker Academic, 1978.

"An Evangelical View of Progressive Revelation." In *Evangelical Roots: A Tribute to Wilbur Smith*, edited by Kenneth Kantzer, 143–58. Nashville: Thomas Nelson, 1978.

"People Matter More than Structures." *Crusade* 23, no. 1 (1978): 24–25.

"Situations and Principles" and "Conscience, Character and Choice." In *Law, Morality and the Bible*, edited by Gordon J. Wenham and Bruce Norman Kaye, 151–67, 168–92. Leicester, UK: Inter-Varsity; Downers Grove, IL: InterVarsity, 1978. Translations: Korean, 1978, 1985.

"Uniqueness of Jesus Christ: Some Evangelical Reflections." *Churchman* 92, no. 2 (1978): 101–11.

"What Is the Bible?" In *Introduction to the Bible*. London: Scripture Union, 1978. This is one of five essays in a sixty-two-page booklet.

"Who Is God?" In *Simple Faith: An Exploration of Basic Christian Belief*, edited by Donald Coggan. Berkhamsted, UK: Lion, 1978. This is a thirty-six-page booklet prepared to accompany a BBC series.

Forewords, Introductions, and Prefaces

Introduction to *The Principles of Theology: An Introduction to the Thirty-Nine Articles*, by W. H. Griffith Thomas. London: Vine; Grand Rapids: Baker Academic, 1978. Reprinted as "New Lease of Life: A Preface by James Packer to *The Principles of Theology* by W. H. Griffith Thomas." *Churchman* 92, no. 1 (1978): 44–52.

Preface to *Law, Morality, and the Bible: A Symposium*, edited by Bruce Norman Kaye and Gordon J. Wenham. Downers Grove, IL: InterVarsity; Leicester, UK: Inter-Varsity, 1978. Translations: Korean, 1978, 1985.

1979

Articles, Essays, and Published Lectures

"Battling for the Bible." *Regent College Bulletin* 9, no. 4 (Fall 1979).

"The Gospel: Its Content and Communication." In *Gospel and Culture*, edited by John Stott and Robert Coote, 97–114. Pasadena, CA: William Carey, 1979.

"A Lamp in a Dark Place: 2 Peter 1:19–21." In *Can We Trust the Bible*, edited by Earl D. Radmacher, 15–32. Wheaton: Tyndale, 1979.

Forewords, Introductions, and Prefaces

Foreword to *Does Inerrancy Matter*, by James Montgomery Boice. Oakland, CA: International Council on Biblical Inerrancy; Wheaton: Tyndale, 1979.

Preface to *Holiness: Its Nature, Hindrances, Difficulties, and Roots*, by J. C. Ryle. Welwyn, UK: Evangelical, 1979.

Reviews

Review of *Anselm and Talking About God*, by Gillian R. Evans. *Churchman* 93, no. 2 (1979): 165.

Review of *The Holy Spirit: Activating God's Power in Your Life*, by Billy Graham. *Churchman* 93, no. 2 (1979): 159–60.

Review of *The Mystery of the Incarnation*, by Norman Anderson. *Churchman* 93, no. 1 (1979): 61–62.

1980

Books

Marshall's Bible Handbook. With Merrill Tenney and William White Jr. London: Marshall Morgan and Scott, 1980. Published in the US as *The Bible Almanac*. Nashville: Thomas Nelson, 1980. Reissued in 1997 by Thomas Nelson as *Illustrated Manners and Customs of the Bible*.

Under God's Word. London: Lakeland; London: Marshall, Morgan and Scott, 1980. Published in the US as *Beyond the Battle for the Bible*. Westchester, IL: Cornerstone, 1980.

Articles, Essays, and Published Lectures

"The Adequacy of Human Language." In *Inerrancy*, edited by Norman Geisler, 197–226. Grand Rapids: Zondervan, 1980.

"Charismatic Renewal: Pointing to a Person and a Power." *Christianity Today*, March 7, 1980, 16–20.

"George Whitefield: Man Alive." *Crux* 16, no. 4 (December 1980): 23–26.

"Preaching as Biblical Interpretation." In *Inerrancy and Common Sense*, edited by Roger Nicole and J. R. Michaels, 187–203. Grand Rapids: Baker Academic, 1980.

"Puritanism as a Movement of Revival." *Evangelical Quarterly* 52 (January/March, 1980): 2–16.

"Sacrifice and Satisfaction" and "To All Who Will Come." In *Our Savior God*, edited by James Montgomery Boice, 125–37, 179–89. Grand Rapids: Baker Academic, 1980.

"Theological Reflections on the Charismatic Movement (Part 1)." *Churchman* 94, no. 1 (1980): 7–25.

"Theological Reflections on the Charismatic Movement (Part 2)." *Churchman* 94, no. 2 (1980): 108–25.

Reviews

Review of *Jesus, the Man and the Myth: A Contemporary Christology*, by James P. Mackey. *Churchman* 94, no. 1 (1980): 78–79.

1981

Books

Freedom and Authority. Oakland, CA: International Council on Biblical Inerrancy, 1981. Published in the UK as *Freedom, Authority, & Scripture*. Leicester, UK: Inter-Varsity, 1982.

God's Words: Studies of Key Bible Themes. Downers Grove, IL: InterVarsity, 1981; Leicester, UK: Inter-Varsity, 1981.

A Kind of Noah's Ark: The Anglican Commitment to Comprehensiveness. Oxford: Latimer, 1981. A thirty-nine-page booklet.

Articles, Essays, and Published Lectures

"Is Christianity Credible?" In *Is Christianity Credible?* edited by Peter R. Baelz, 64–72. London: Epworth, 1981.

"The Means of Growth" and "Body Life." *Tenth: An Evangelical Quarterly* (July 1981): 2–11.

"My Path of Prayer." In *My Path of Prayer: Personal Glimpses of the Glory and the Majesty of God Revealed through Experiences of Prayer*, edited by David Hanes, 55–66. Brighton, UK: Walter, 1981.

"Response to Stephen Clark." In *Christianity Confronts Modernity*, edited by Peter Williamson and Kevin Perrotta, 187–93. Ann Arbor, MI: Servant; Edinburgh, UK: Handset, 1981.

"A View from a Jacuzzi." *Regent College Bulletin* 11, no. 4 (Fall 1981).

"Walking to Emmaus with the Great Physician." *Christianity Today*, April 10, 1981, 20–23.

Forewords, Introductions, and Prefaces

Foreword to *Life by His Death! An Easier-to-Read and Abridged Version of the Classic "The Death of Death in the Death of Christ,"* by John Owen. London: Grace Publications Trust, 1981.

Foreword to *No Graven Image: A Novel,* by Elisabeth Elliot. London: Hodder and Stoughton, 1981.

Preface to *Breaking the Prayer Barrier,* by Michael Baughen. Wheaton: Shaw, 1981.

Preface to *The Christian Life,* by Sinclair B. Ferguson. London: Hodder and Stoughton, 1981.

Reviews

Review of *Baptists and the Bible: The Baptist Doctrines of Biblical Inspiration and Religious Authority in Historical Perspective*, edited by L. Russ Bush and Tom J. Nettles. *Southwestern Journal of Theology* 24, no. 1 (Fall 1981): 104–5.

1982

Articles, Essays, and Published Lectures

"God Is" and "The Puritans." In *Eerdmans' Handbook of Christian Belief*, edited by R. Keeley, 126–49 (except pp. 131, 140–41) and 444–45. Grand Rapids: Eerdmans, 1982. Published in the UK as *The Lion Handbook of Christian Belief*, edited by Robin Keeley. Tring, UK: Lion, 1982. Reprinted in the UK as *An Introduction to the Christian Faith*, edited by Robin Keeley. Oxford: Lynx, 1992. Reprinted in the US as Nelson's *Introduction to the Christian Faith*, edited by Robin Keeley. Nashville: Thomas Nelson, 1995.

"Knowing Notions or Knowing God?" *Pastoral Renewal* 6, no. 9 (1982): 65–68.

"The Message Unchanged." *Alliance Witness*, June 23, 1982, 11–14.

"Poor Health May Be the Best Remedy: But if You've Got a Headache Thank God for Aspirin." *Christianity Today*, May 21, 1982, 14–16.

"The Reconstitution of Authority." *Crux* 18, no. 4 (December 1982): 2–12.

"Upholding the Unity of Scripture Today." *Journal of the Evangelical Theological Society* 25, no. 4 (December 1982): 409–14.

Forewords, Introductions, and Prefaces

Foreword to *The God You Can Know*, by Dan DeHaan. Chicago: Moody, 1982.

Foreword to *Know the Truth: A Handbook of Christian Belief*, by Bruce Milne. Downers Grove, IL: InterVarsity; Leicester, UK: Inter-Varsity, 1982.

Preface to *Created for Commitment*, by A. Wetherell Johnson. Wheaton: Tyndale, 1982.

1983

Books

Explaining Hermeneutics: A Commentary. With Norman Geisler. Oakland, CA: International Council on Biblical Inerrancy, 1983. An eighteen-page booklet.

Articles, Essays, and Published Lectures

"Infallible Scripture and the Role of Hermeneutics." In *Scripture and Truth*, edited by D. A. Carson and John Woodbridge, 325–58. Grand Rapids: Zondervan, 1983.

"Lord Send Revival." *The Bulletin* (Winter 1983): 4–5.

"Predestination in Christian History" and "Predestination and Sanctification." *Tenth: An Evangelical Quarterly* (July 1983): 2–16.

"Steps to the Renewal of the Christian People" and "Agenda for Theology." In *Summons to Faith and Renewal,* edited by Peter Williamson and Kevin Perrotta, 107–27. Ann Arbor, MI: Servant, 1983.

Forewords, Introductions, and Prefaces

Introduction to *Sin and Temptation: The Challenge to Personal Godliness*, by John Owen, abridged and edited by James M. Houston. Basingstoke, UK: Pickering and Inglis; Minneapolis: Bethany House; Portland, OR: Multnomah, 1983.

1984

Books

Keep in Step with the Spirit. Leicester, UK: Inter-Varsity; Old Tappan, NJ: Revell, 1984. Revised and enlarged edition published by Revell in 2005. Translations: Korean, 1986; German, 1989; Polish, 1989; Chinese, 1989, 2004, 2007; Portuguese, 1991; Dutch, 1996, 2006; Czech, 1999 (2nd ed.); Korean, 2002.

The Thirty-Nine Articles: Their Place and Use Today. London: Latimer House, 1984.

Articles, Essays, and Published Lectures

"A Christian View of Man." In *The Christian Vision: Man in Society,* edited by Lynne Morris, 101–19. Hillsdale, MI: Hillsdale College Press, 1984.

"Feet in the Clouds." *Regent College Bulletin* 14, no. 1 (Spring 1984).

"John Calvin and the Inerrancy of Holy Scripture." In *Inerrancy and the Church,* edited by John D. Hannah, 143–68. Chicago: Moody, 1984.

"Meeting God." *Spiritual Counterfeits Project Journal* 6, no. 1 (Winter 1984).

"Renewal and Revival." *Channels: Magazine of the Christian Writers' League of America* (Spring 1984).

"Response to Henry Krabbendam: The New Hermeneutic." In *Hermeneutics, Inerrancy and the Bible,* edited by Robert D. Preus and E. Radmacher, 559–71. Grand Rapids: Zondervan, 1984.

Forewords, Introductions, and Prefaces

Foreword to *Fear No Evil: Facing the Final Test of Faith*, by David Watson. London: Hodder and Stoughton, 1984.

Foreword to *Outline Studies in Luke: A Devotional Commentary*, by W. H. Griffith Thomas. Grand Rapids: Kregel, 1984.

Reviews

Review of *Carl F. H. Henry*, by Bob E. Patterson. *Crux* 20, no. 4 (December 1984): 27–28.

1985

Books

Christianity: The True Humanism. With Thomas Howard. Berkhamsted, UK: Word; Waco: Word, 1985. Translations: Korean, 1989, 1990; French: 1990.

Finding God's Will. Downers Grove, IL: InterVarsity, 1985. Translations: Dutch, 2000.

Articles, Essays, and Published Lectures

"Arminianisms." In *Through Christ's Word: A Festschrift for Dr. Philip E. Hughes*, edited by W. Robert Godfrey and Jesse L. Boyd, 121–48. Phillipsburg, NJ: P&R, 1985.

"David Martyn Lloyd-Jones." In *Chosen Vessels,* edited by Charles Turner, 109–23. Ann Arbor, MI: Servant, 1985.

"How to Recognize a Christian Citizen." *Christianity Today*, April 19, 1985, 4–8.

"In Quest of Canonical Interpretation." In *The Use of the Bible in Theology: Evangelical Options,* edited by Robert K. Johnston, 35–55. Atlanta: John Knox, 1985.

"Satan Scores Twice." *Christianity Today*, September 6, 1985, 12.

Forewords, Introductions, and Prefaces

Foreword to *Biblical Revelation: The Foundation of Christian Theology*, by Clark Pinnock. Phillipsburg, NJ: P&R, 1985.

Foreword to *The Mystery of Marriage*, by Mike Mason. Sisters, OR: Multnomah, 1985.

1986

Books

Meeting God: 12 Studies for Individuals or Groups. Lifebuilder Bible Study. Downers Grove, IL: InterVarsity; London: Scripture Union, 1986. Revised edition: Downers Grove, IL: InterVarsity; Milton Keynes, UK: Scripture Union, 2001.

Your Father Loves You: Daily Insights for Knowing God. With Jean Watson. Wheaton: Shaw, 1986. Reprinted as *In God's Presence: Daily Devotions with J. I. Packer.* Wheaton: Shaw, 1998; and *Through the Year with J. I. Packer: Your Father Loves You; Daily Insights for Knowing God.* London, UK: Hodder and Stoughton, 1986.

Articles, Essays, and Published Lectures

"All that Jazz." *Christianity Today*, December 12, 1986, 15.

"A Bad Trip." *Christianity Today*, March 7, 1986, 12.

"'Good Pagans' and God's Kingdom." *Christianity Today*, January 17, 1986, 22–25.

"Great George." *Christianity Today*, September 19, 1986, 12.

"Justification in Protestant Theology." In *Here We Stand: Justification by Faith Today*, edited by David Field, 84–102. London: Hodder and Stoughton, 1986.

"A Kind of Puritan." In *Martyn Lloyd-Jones: Chosen by God,* edited by Christopher Catherwood, 33–57. Crowborough, UK: Highland; Westchester, IL: Crossway, 1986.

"Paths of Righteousness." *Eternity* (May 1986): 32–37.

"Theism for Our Time." In *God Who Is Rich in Mercy: Essays Presented to Dr. D. B. Knox*, edited by Peter Thomas O'Brien and D. G. Petersen, 1–23. Grand Rapids: Baker Academic; Homebush, AU: Lancer, 1986.

"True Guidance." *Eternity* (June 1986): 36–39.

"Steps to the Renewal of the Christian People." *Crux* 22, no. 1 (March 1986): 2–11.

"Understanding the Differences." In *Women, Authority and the Bible*, edited by Alvera Mickelsen, 295–99. Downers Grove, IL: InterVarsity, 1986.

"The Unspectacular Packers." *Christianity Today*, May 16, 1986, 12.

"What Do We Mean When You Say 'God'?" *Christianity Today*, September 19, 1986, 22–25.

"Wisdom Along the Way." *Eternity* (April 1986): 19–23.

Forewords, Introductions, and Prefaces

"Foreword: No Little Person." In *Reflections on Francis Schaeffer*, edited by J. I. Packer and Ronald W. Ruegsegger, 7–17. Grand Rapids: Zondervan, 1986.

"Introduction: Why Preach." In *Preaching: The Preacher and Preaching in the Twentieth Century*, edited by Samuel Logan, 1–29. Darlington, UK: Evangelical, 1986.

Reviews

Review of *The Person of Christ*, by David F. Wells. *Evangelical Review of Theology* 10, no. 1 (1986): 85–86.

1987

Books

The Best in Theology, vol. 1. General editor, with Paul Fromer, editor. Carol Stream, IL: Christianity Today; Waco: Word, 1987.

God in Our Midst: Seeking and Receiving Ongoing Revival. Ann Arbor, MI: Servant, 1987.

Hot Tub Religion: Christian Living in a Materialistic World. Wheaton: Tyndale, 1987. Published in the UK as *Laid-Back Religion.* Leicester, UK: Inter-Varsity, 1989. Translations: Chinese, 1995; Dutch, 1995.

Articles, Essays, and Published Lectures

"An Accidental Author." *Christianity Today*, May 15, 1987, 11.

"Bringing the Bible to Your Life." *Charisma*, January 1987, 43–44.

"Do You Need a Personality Change?" In *Practical Christianity*, edited by LaVonne Neff, Ron Beers, Bruce Barton, Linda Taylor, Dave Veerman, and Jim Galvin, 59–61. Wheaton: Tyndale, 1987. Translations: Korean, 2007.

"The Holy Spirit and His Work." In *Applying the Scriptures,* edited by Kenneth S. Kantzer, 51–76. Grand Rapids: Zondervan, 1987. Also published in *Crux* 23, no. 2 (June 1987): 2–17.

"Inerrancy and the Divinity and the Humanity of the Bible," "Implications for Biblical Inerrancy in the Christian Mission," and "Problem Areas Related to Biblical Inerrancy." In *The Proceedings of the Conference on Biblical Inerrancy 1987*, edited by J. Gregory, 135–51, 205–13, 245–50. Nashville: Broadman, 1987.

"A Modern View of Jesus." *Faith Today*, January 1987, 28–30, 32–33.

"Packer on Preaching." *New Horizons* 8, no. 1 (January 1987): 1–3.

"Right Living: Does It Really Matter?" and "Right Living: Dying Well Is the Final Test." *Eternity* (January 1987): 30.

"Right Living: How Christians Should Understand Themselves." *Eternity* (July 1987): 36.

"Right Living: The Way of the Weak Is the Only Healthy Way." *Eternity* (November 1987): 28.

"The Trinity and the Gospel." In *Good News for All Seasons: Twenty-Six Sermons for Special Days,* edited by Richard A. Bodey, 91–98. Grand Rapids: Baker Academic, 1987.

Forewords, Introductions, and Prefaces

"Foreword: Why We Need the Puritans." In *Worldly Saints*, by Leland Ryken, ix–xvi. Grand Rapids: Zondervan, 1987.

Introduction to *The Best in Theology*, vol. 1, general editor J. I. Packer, with Paul Fromer, editor. Carol Stream, IL: Christianity Today, 1987.

"Introduction: On Being Serious about the Holy Spirit." In *God the Evangelist: How the Holy Spirit Works to Bring Men and Women to the Faith*, by David Wells, xi–xvi. Grand Rapids: Eerdmans, 1987.

Introduction to *Summit III: Application*, International Council on Biblical Inerrancy (ICBI). Walnut Creek, CA: ICBI Press, 1987.

Reviews

Review of *The Cross of Christ*, by John R. W. Stott. *Christianity Today*, September 4, 1987, 35–36.

1988

Books

The Best in Theology, vol. 2. General editor J. I. Packer, with Paul Fromer, editor. Carol Stream, IL: Christianity Today, 1988.

Articles, Essays, and Published Lectures

"Baptism in the Spirit," "Baxter," "Farrer," "Glory of God," "God," "Holiness Movement," "Holy Spirit," "Infallibility and Inerrancy," "Method," "Paradox," "Revival," "Scripture." In *New Dictionary of Theology*, edited by David Wright and Sinclair Ferguson. J. I. Packer, consulting editor. Leicester, UK: Inter-Varsity; Downers Grove, IL: InterVarsity, 1988. Translations: Chinese, 1997; Korean, 2001.

"The Challenge of Biblical Interpretation: Creation," "The Challenge of Biblical Interpretation: Women," and "The Challenge of Biblical Interpretation: Eschatology." In *The Proceedings of the Conference on Biblical Interpretation 1988*, 21–33, 103–15, 191–204. Nashville: Broadman, 1988.

"The Christian and God's World." In *Transforming Our World: A Call to Action*, edited by J. M. Boice, 81–97. Portland, OR: Multnomah, 1988.

"God the Image-Maker." In *Christian Faith and Practice in the Modern World*, edited by Mark Noll and David Wells, 27–50. Grand Rapids: Eerdmans, 1988.

"Jewish Evangelism and the Word of God." *Christian Witness to Israel Herald* (June–August 1988): 15–18.

"John Calvin and Reformed Europe." In *Great Leaders of the Christian Church*, edited by John Woodbridge, 208–15. Chicago: Moody, 1988.

"Right Living: Bringing the Double Mind to a Singleness of Faith." *Eternity* (November 1988): 59.

"Right Living: Christian *Gravitas* in a Narcissistic Age." *Eternity* (July 1988): 46.

"Right Living: Keeping your Balance: A Christian's Challenge." *Eternity* (January 1988): 18.

"Right Living: Soldier, Son, Pilgrim: Christian Know Thy Self." *Eternity* (April 1988): 33.

"Shy Sovereign." *Tabletalk* 12, no. 3 (June 1988): 4.

"What Lewis Was and Wasn't." *Christianity Today*, January 15, 1988, 11.

Forewords, Introductions, and Prefaces

Foreword to *The Unfolding Mystery: Discovering Christ in the Old Testament*, by Edmund P. Clowney. Phillipsburg, NJ: P&R, 1988.

Introduction to *The Best in Theology*, vol. 2, general editor J. I. Packer, with Paul Fromer, editor. Carol Stream, IL: Christianity Today, 1988.

"A Word from J. I. Packer." In *The Gospel in Dostoyevsky: Selections from His Works*, by Fyodor Dostoyevsky, edited by the Bruderhof, illustrations by Fritz Eichenberg, vii. Farmington, PA: Plough Publishing House; Maryknoll, NY: Orbis, 1988.

1989

Books

The Best in Theology, vol. 3. General editor J. I. Packer, with Harold Smith, editor. Carol Stream, IL: Christianity Today, 1989.

Articles, Essays, and Published Lectures

"Christian Morality Adrift." In *Society in Peril,* edited by Kevin Perrotta and John Blattner, 57–76. Ann Arbor, MI: Servant, 1989.

"Godliness in Ephesians." *Crux* 25, no. 1 (March 1989): 8–16.

"History Repeats Itself." *Christianity Today*, September 22, 1989, 22.

"Hype and Human Humbug." *Christianity Today*, February 17, 1989, 11.

"Is Hell Out of Vogue in this Modern Era?" *United Evangelical Action* (September–October 1989): 10–11.

"Is the Charismatic Renewal, Seen in Many Churches Today, from God?" and "Will a Loving God Really Condemn People to Hell? Is Christ the Only Way?" In *Tough Questions Christians Ask*, edited by David Neff. Wheaton: Victor, 1989. "Is the Charismatic Renewal, Seen in Many Churches Today, from God?" was also published as "Piety on Fire." *Christianity Today*, May 12, 1989, 18–23, and *Renewal* (July 1990): 28–32.

"The Means of Conversion." *Crux* 25, no. 4 (December 1989): 14–22.

"The Prayboy Club." *Christianity Today*, October 20, 1989, 11.

Forewords, Introductions, and Prefaces

Introduction to *The Best in Theology*, vol. 3, general editor J. I. Packer, with Harold Smith, editor. Carol Stream, IL: Christianity Today, 1989.

Introduction to *An Exposition of the Prophecy of Hosea*, by Jeremiah Burroughs. Beaver Falls, PA: Soli Deo Gloria, 1989.

Introduction to *Men, Women and Priesthood*, by James Tolhurst. Leominster, Herefordshire, UK; Bloomington, IN: Gracewing, 1989.

"Memoir." In *Rejoice Always! Studies in Philippians 4*, by John Gwyn-Thomas. Carlisle, PA; Edinburgh, UK: Banner of Truth, 1989.

Reviews

Review of *Mysterium and Mystery: The Clerical Crime Novel*, by William David Spencer. *Christianity Today*, April 21, 1989, 51.

1990

Books

The Best in Theology, vol. 4. General editor J. I. Packer, with J. Isamu Yamamoto, editor. Carol Stream, IL: Christianity Today, 1990.

A Quest for Godliness: The Puritan Vision of the Christian Life. Wheaton: Crossway, 1990. Published in the UK as *Among God's Giants: Aspects of Puritan Christianity*. Eastbourne, UK: Kingsway, 1991. Translations: Dutch, 1997 (selections); Korean, 2001.

Articles, Essays, and Published Lectures

"Appendix 2: Pentecostalism 'Reinvented': The Charismatic Renewal." In *Pentecostals from the Inside Out*, edited by Harold B. Smith, 145–49. Wheaton: Victor, 1990.

"Babel." In *Inside the Sermon: Thirteen Preachers Discuss Their Methods of Preparing Messages*, edited by Richard Allen Bodey, 185–200. Grand Rapids: Baker Academic, 1990.

"The Christian's Purpose in Business." In *Biblical Principles and Business: The Practice*, edited by R. C. Chewning, 16–25. Christians in the Marketplace Series, vol. 3. Colorado Springs: NavPress, 1990.

"Evangelicals and the Way of Salvation: New Challenges to the Gospel—Universalism and Justification by Faith." In *Evangelical Affirmations,* edited by Kenneth S. Kantzer and Carl F. H. Henry, 107–36. Grand Rapids: Zondervan, 1990.

"From the Scriptures to the Sermon." *Ashland Theological Journal* 22 (1990): 42–64.

"The Gospel and the Lord's Supper." *Mission and Ministry* 8 (Summer 1990): 18–24.

"An Introduction to Systematic Spirituality." *Crux* 26, no. 1 (March 1990): 2–8.

"The Problem of Eternal Punishment." Leon Morris Lecture 1990. Victoria, AU: Evangelical Alliance Publishing, 1990; *Crux* 26, no. 3 (September 1990): 18–25; and *Evangel* 10 (Summer 1992): 12–19.

"The Reformed Faith in the Modern World: I. Bible." *Evangelical Presbyterian* (December 1990).

"Shepherds after God's Own Heart." *Faith and Renewal* 15, no. 3 (November 1990): 12–17.

"Thirty Years' War: The Doctrine of the Holy Spirit." In *Practical Theology and the Ministry of the Church, 1952–1984: Essays in Honor of Edmund P. Clowney,* edited by Harvie M. Conn, 25–44. Phillipsburg, NJ: P&R, 1990.

"Understanding the Bible: Evangelical Hermeneutics." In *Restoring the Vision: Anglican Evangelicals Speak Out,* edited by Melvin Tinker, 30–58. Eastbourne, UK: Monarch, 1990.

"Westminster and the Roller-Coaster Ride." *Tabletalk* 14, no. 3 (March 1990): 6–10.

"What the Puritans Taught Me." *Christianity Today,* October 8, 1990, 44–47.

"Why I Like My Pie in the Sky." *Christianity Today,* June 18, 1990, 11.

Forewords, Introductions, and Prefaces

Foreword to *After Modernity—What? Agenda for Theology,* by Thomas C. Oden. Grand Rapids: Zondervan, 1990.

Foreword to *Archbishop Cranmer's Immortal Bequest: The Book of Common Prayer of the Church of England: An Evangelistic Liturgy,* by Samuel Leuenberger. Grand Rapids: Eerdmans, 1990.

Foreword to *A Christian Directory,* vol. 1 of *The Practical Works of Richard Baxter.* Morgan, PA: Soli Deo Gloria, 1990.

Foreword to *Surviving a Crisis,* by Paula Michelsen. Wheaton: Tyndale, 1990.

Foreword to *With Heart, Mind and Strength: The Best of Crux,* edited by D. M. Lewis. Langley, BC: Credo, 1990.

Introduction to *The Best in Theology,* vol. 4, general editor J. I. Packer, with J. Isamu Yamamoto, editor. Carol Stream, IL: Christianity Today, 1990.

Introduction to *The Economy of the Covenants between God and Man: Comprehending a Complete Body of Divinity*, by Herman Witsius, translated by William Crookshank. Phillipsburg, NJ: P&R, 1990.

Introduction to *Men, Women and Priesthood*, edited by J. Tolhurst. Leominster, UK: Gracewing, 1990.

1991

Articles, Essays, and Published Lectures

"Authority in Preaching." In *The Gospel in the Modern World: A Tribute to John Stott*, edited by Martyn Eden and David F. Wells, 198–212. Leicester, UK: Inter-Varsity, 1991.

"Evangelical Foundations for Spirituality." In *Gott Lieben und seine Gebote Halten: Loving God and Keeping His Commandments. In memoriam, Klaus Bockmühl.* Edited by M. Bockmühl and K. Burkhardt, 149–62. Giessen/Basel, Germany: Brunnen Verlag, 1991.

"Fan Mail to Calvin." *Christianity Today*, January 14, 1991, 11.

"'Go Fetch Baxter': This Feisty Puritan Spent His Life Quieting the Controversies He Started." With T. Beougher. *Christianity Today*, December 16, 1991, 26–28.

"Is Systematic Theology a Mirage? An Introductory Discussion." In *Doing Theology in Today's World*, edited by John D. Woodbridge and Thomas E. McComiskey, 17–37. Grand Rapids: Zondervan, 1991.

"Let's Stop Making Women Presbyters." *Christianity Today*, February 11, 1991, 18–21.

"The Reformed Faith in the Modern World: II. Gospel." *Evangelical Presbyterian* (March 1991).

"The Reformed Faith in the Modern World: III. Church." *Evangelical Presbyterian* (June 1991).

"Richard Baxter: A Man for All Ministries." London: St. Antholin's Lecture, 1991.

"Scripture, Inerrancy and the Church." *Touchstone* 4 (Fall 1991): 3–4.

"Surprised by Graphics." *Christianity Today*, November 11, 1991, 15.

"Understanding the Lordship Controversy." *Tabletalk* 15 (May 1991): 213–28.

Forewords, Introductions, and Prefaces

Foreword to *The Heart of the Gospel*, by Martyn Lloyd-Jones. Wheaton: Crossway, 1991. Translations: Korean, 1992.

Foreword to *Spiritual Disciplines for the Christian Life*, by Donald S. Whitney. Colorado Springs: NavPress, 1991.

1992

Books

Alive to God: Studies in Spirituality Presented to James Houston. Edited with Loren Wilkinson. Downers Grove, IL: InterVarsity; Vancouver: Regent College Publishing, 1992.

Rediscovering Holiness. Ann Arbor, MI: Vine, 1992. Also published as *A Passion for Holiness.* Cambridge, UK: Crossway, 1992. Translations: Spanish, 1995; Dutch, 1996; German, 1997; Chinese, 2002.

You Know God Is in Control, Don't You? Amityville, NY: Calvary, 1992. This is a ten-page booklet.

Articles, Essays, and Published Lectures

"The Comfort of Conservatism." In *Power Religion,* edited by M. Horton, 283–99. Chicago: Moody, 1992.

"The Empowered Christian Life." *Faith and Renewal* 16, no. 4 (January 1992): 3–9. Also published in *The Kingdom and the Power: Are Healing and the Spiritual Gifts Used by Jesus and the Early Church Meant for the Church Today?* edited by Gary S. Greig, 207–15. Ventura, CA: Regal, 1993.

"Fellowship." In *Reconciliation, Fellowship, and the Grace of God.* Servant's Journal, vol. 2, 96–105. New Lenox, IL: Leadership Resources International, 1992.

"God's Plumber and Sewage Man." *Christianity Today,* April 6, 1992, 15.

"The Inspiration of the Bible." In *Origin of the Bible,* edited by Philip Wesley Comfort, 29–36. Wheaton: Tyndale, 1992.

"The Reality Cure." *Christianity Today,* September 14, 1992, 34–35.

"Richard Baxter on Heaven, Hope and Holiness." In *Alive to God: Studies in Spirituality Presented to James Houston,* edited with Loren Wilkinson, 161–75. Downers Grove, IL: InterVarsity; Vancouver: Regent College Publishing, 1992.

"Rome's Persistent Renewal." *Christianity Today,* June 22, 1992, 19.

"What Holiness Is, and Why It Matters." *Evangel* 11 (August 1992): 84–92.

"The Word of Life." *The Evangelical Catholic* 4, no. 4 (September 1992): 1–8.

Forewords, Introductions, and Prefaces

Foreword to *Can Our Differences Be Settled? A Detailed Response to the Evangelical Feminist Position Statement of Christians for Biblical Equality,* by Wayne Grudem and John Piper. Wheaton: Council of Biblical Manhood and Womanhood, 1992.

Foreword to *The Equipper's Guide to Every-Member Ministry: Eight Ways Ordinary People Can Do the Work of the Church*, by Michael Green, R. Paul Stevens, and Dan Williams. Downers Grove, IL: InterVarsity, 1992.

Reviews

Review of *Spiritual Disciplines for the Christian Life*, by Donald S. Whitney. *Reformation and Revival* 1, no. 1 (Winter 1992): 109–11.

1993

Books

The Church and Homosexuality: A Pastoral Approach. With Ron Barnes, John Briscall, and Ed Hird. Vancouver, BC: Diocese of New Westminster, Anglican Church of Canada, 1993.

Concise Theology: A Guide to Historic Christian Beliefs. Leicester, UK: InterVarsity; Wheaton: Tyndale, 1993. Translations: Hindi, 1997; Portuguese, 1999; Russian, 2001; Swedish, 2002; Chinese, 2005.

Crossway Classic Commentary. 26 vols. Wheaton: Crossway, 1993–2001. Edited with Alister E. McGrath. As series editor, J. I. Packer wrote an introduction to each volume except *Philippians* (1994) and *Colossians and Philemon* (1997).

Articles, Essays, and Published Lectures

"Arts," "Election," "Predestination." In *Dictionary of Biblical Tradition in English Literature,* edited by D. Jeffrey. Grand Rapids: Eerdmans, 1993.

"The Devil's Dossier: Before Christians Engage in Spiritual Warfare, They Should Know Something about the Enemy." *Christianity Today*, June 21, 1993, 24.

"George Whitefield: The Startling Puritan." *Christian History* 12, no. 2 (May 1993): 38–40.

"Holiness." *Faith and Renewal* 17, no. 5 (March 1993): 3–11.

"The Holy Spirit in the Book of Common Prayer." In *The Holy Spirit: A Theological Conference Held at University of King's College, Halifax, Nova Scotia, May 31st–June 3rd, 1992*, edited by Susan Harris, 67–81. Charlottetown, PE: St. Peter, 1993.

"Leisure and Life-Style: Leisure, Pleasure, and Treasure." In *God and Culture: Essays in Honor of Carl F. H. Henry*, edited by D. A. Carson and John D. Woodbridge, 356–68. Carlisle, UK: Paternoster; Grand Rapids: Eerdmans, 1993.

"Packer the Picketed Pariah." *Christianity Today*, January 11, 1993, 11.

"Pleasure Principles: Why the Christian Mission on Earth Is Not Unrelieved Heroic Misery." *Christianity Today*, November 22, 1993, 24–26.

"A Reasonable Faith." *Decision* (December 1993): 13–14.

"The Whale and the Elephant." *Christianity Today*, October 4, 1993, 11.

"Why I Left." *Christianity Today*, April 5, 1993, 33–35.

Forewords, Introductions, and Prefaces

Foreword to *Risking Faith: Personal Answers for Weary Skeptics*, by John Guest. Grand Rapids: Baker Academic, 1993.

Foreword to *Whatever Happened to Hell?* by John Blanchard. Darlington, UK: Evangelical; Wheaton: Crossway, 1993.

Reviews

Review of *Oswald Chambers: Abandoned to God*, by David McCasland. *Christianity Today*, October 4, 1993, 36.

1994

Articles, Essays, and Published Lectures

"Evangelicals and Catholics Together: The Christian Mission in the Third Millennium." With Charles Colson and others. *First Things* 43 (May 1994): 15–22.

"Fear of Looking Forward." *Christianity Today*, December 12, 1994, 13.

"Towards a Systematic Spirituality." *Criswell Theological Review* 7 (Spring 1994): 15–39.

"Why I Signed It: The Recent Statement 'Evangelicals and Catholics Together' Recognizes an Important Truth: Those Who Love the Lord Must Stand Together." *Christianity Today*, December 12, 1994, 34–37.

Forewords, Introductions, and Prefaces

Foreword to *Our Faithful Friend: Building Intimacy with God; Six Studies for Groups or Individuals with Notes for Leaders*, by John D. Sloan. Grand Rapids: Zondervan, 1994.

Foreword to *Our Glorious Lord: Beholding God's Majesty; Six Studies for Groups or Individuals with Notes for Leaders*, by Jack Kuhatschek. Grand Rapids: Zondervan, 1994.

Foreword to *Our Good Provider: Delighting in God's Gifts; Six Studies for Groups or Individuals with Notes for Leaders*, by Lin Johnson. Grand Rapids: Zondervan, 1994.

Foreword to *Our Loving Father: Feeling God's Embrace; Six Studies for Groups or Individuals with Notes for Leaders*, by Jack Kuhatschek. Grand Rapids: Zondervan, 1994.

Foreword to *Our Merciful Judge: Trusting God's Fairness; Six Studies for Groups or Individuals with Notes for Leaders*, by Marshall Shelley. Grand Rapids: Zondervan, 1994.

Foreword to *Our Powerful Helper: Relying on God's Strength; Six Studies for Groups or Individuals with Notes for Leaders*, by Marshall Shelley. Grand Rapids: Zondervan, 1994.

Foreword to *Putting Amazing Back into Grace*, by Michael Horton. Grand Rapids: Baker Books; London: Hodder and Stoughton, 1994.

Reviews

Review of *The Contemporary Christian*, by John R. W. Stott. *Christianity Today*, February 7, 1994, 59.

1995

Books

Knowing and Doing the Will of God. With LaVonne Neff. Ann Arbor, MI: Vine, 1995. Translations: Korean, 1998.

Knowing Christianity. Wheaton: Shaw; Guildford, UK: Eagle, 1995.

Life in the Spirit: A 30-Day Devotional. Wheaton: Crossway, 1995. Translations: Chinese, 2001.

Nelson's Illustrated Encyclopedia of Bible Facts, edited with Merrill Tenney and William White Jr. Nashville: Thomas Nelson, 1995. This is a revised edition of *The Bible Almanac*, 1980. Translations: Spanish, 2002; Polish, 2007.

A Passion for Faithfulness: Wisdom from the Book of Nehemiah. London: Hodder and Stoughton; Wheaton: Crossway, 1995. Translations: Dutch, 1997.

Articles, Essays, and Published Lectures

"Anglicanism Today: The Path to Renewal" and "Jesus Christ, the Only Saviour." In *Anglican Essentials*, edited by George Egerton, 53–63, 98–110. Toronto: Anglican Book Centre, 1995. "Anglicanism Today" was written with Grant Lemarquand, Alister E. McGrath, and John Paul Westin.

"Crosscurrents among Evangelicals." In *Evangelicals and Catholics Together: Toward a Common Mission*, edited by C. Colson and R. J. Neuhaus, 147–74. Dallas: Word; London: Hodder and Stoughton, 1995.

"Higher Criticism." In *New Geneva Study Bible*, 2044–45. Nashville: Thomas Nelson, 1995.

"The Love of God: Universal and Particular." In *The Grace of God, the Bondage of the Will*, vol. 2, edited by Thomas Schreiner and Bruce Ware, 413–27. Grand Rapids: Baker Academic, 1995.

"Never Mind the Quality, Feel the Width: Comprehensiveness in the Church of England." In *The Anglican Evangelical Crisis*, edited by Melvin Tinker, 111–23. Fearn, UK: Christian Focus, 1995.

"The Preacher as Theologian: Preaching and Systematic Theology." In *When God's Voice Is Heard*, edited by John R. W. Stott, Christopher Green, and David Jackman, 79–95. Leicester, UK: Inter-Varsity, 1995. Revised edition: Nottingham, UK: Inter-Varsity, 2003.

"Robert Aitken." In *The Blackwell Dictionary of Evangelical Biography: 1730–1860*, edited by Donald M. Lewis. Oxford: Basil Blackwell, 1995.

"The Spirit with the Word: The Reformational Revivalism of George Whitefield." In *The Bible, The Reformation and The Church: Essays in Honour of James Atkinson*, edited by James Atkinson and W. P. Stephens, 166–89. Sheffield, UK: Sheffield Academic Press 1995.

Forewords, Introductions, and Prefaces

Foreword to *Healing Evangelism: Strengthen Your Witnessing with Effective Prayer for the Sick*, by Don Dunkerley. Grand Rapids: Chosen, 1995.

1996

Books

Commentary on the Montreal Declaration: Anglican Essentials; Reclaiming Faith within the Anglican Church of Canada. Halifax, NS: Essentials, 1996.

The NIV Thematic Study Bible. Edited by Alister E. McGrath and Martin H. Manser. J. I. Packer, consulting editor. London: Hodder and Stoughton, 1996.

Truth and Power: The Place of Scripture in the Christian Life. Wheaton: Shaw, 1996. Translations: Korean, n.d.

Articles, Essays, and Published Lectures

An Anglican to Remember: William Perkins; Puritan Popularizer. London: St. Antholin's Lectureship Charity, 1996.

"The Gospel Bassoon." *Christianity Today*, October 28, 1996, 24.

"Our Lifeline: The Bible Is the Rope God Throws Us in Order to Ensure That We Stay Connected While the Rescue Is in Progress." *Christianity Today*, October 28, 1996, 2–25.

"Theology and Bible Reading." In *The Act of Bible Reading*, edited by Elmer Dyck, 65–87. Downers Grove, IL: InterVarsity, 1996.

"Why We Need the Puritans." *Themelios* 21 (January 1996): 9–13.

Forewords, Introductions, and Prefaces

Foreword and introduction to *The Mortification of Sin*, by John Owen. Fearn, UK: Christian Focus, 1996.

Introduction to *The Life of God in the Soul of Man*, by Henry Scougal. Fearn, UK: Christian Focus, 1996. Also includes the text of *Rules and Instructions for a Holy Life* by Robert Leighton.

1997

Books

Great Grace: A 31-Day Devotional. With Beth Feia. Ann Arbor, MI: Vine, 1997.

A Grief Sanctified: Passing Through Grief to Peace and Joy. With Richard Baxter. Ann Arbor, MI: Vine, 1997.

The Hodder Dictionary of Bible Themes. Edited by Martin H. Manser and Alister E. McGrath. Consulting editor, J. I. Packer. London: Hodder and Stoughton, 1997. Published in the US as *Zondervan Dictionary of Bible Themes.* Grand Rapids: Zondervan, 1999.

Articles, Essays, and Published Lectures

"Assessing the Anglican–Roman Catholic Divide: An Anglican Perspective." *Crux* 33, no. 2 (June 1997): 10–16.

"On from Orr: Cultural Crisis, Rational Realism and Incarnational Ontology." In *Reclaiming the Great Tradition: Evangelicals, Catholics and Orthodox in Dialogue,* edited by James S. Cutsinger, 155–76. Downers Grove, IL: InterVarsity, 1997. Also published in *Crux* 32, no. 3 (September 1996): 12–26.

"Personal Standards." *Churchman* 111, no. 1 (1997): 19–26.

"Thank God for Our Bibles: While Scripture Comes in Many Flavors Today, We Can Still Trust these Translations to Give Us God's Word." *Christianity Today,* October 27, 1997, 29.

"When Prayer Doesn't 'Work.'" *Christianity Today,* January 6, 1997, 29.

Forewords, Introductions, and Prefaces

Introduction to *God the Evangelist: How the Holy Spirit Works to Bring Men and Women to Faith,* by David F. Wells. Carlisle, UK: WEF in association with Paternoster, 1997.

Reviews

Review of *Mansions of the Spirit,* by Michael Ingham. *Crux* 33, no. 4 (December 1997): 28–38.

1998

Books

The Bible Application Handbook. Edited by J. I. Packer and Derek Williams. Guildford, UK: Eagle, 1999.

Celebrating the Saving Work of God: The Collected Shorter Writings of J. I. Packer, vol. 1. Carlisle, UK: Paternoster, 1998.

Serving the People of God: The Collected Shorter Writings of J. I. Packer, vol. 2. Carlisle, UK: Paternoster, 1998.

Articles, Essays, and Published Lectures

"Children of a Larger God: How Good Theology Expands the Soul: An Interview with J. I. Packer." *Leadership* 19, no. 3 (Summer 1998): 108–13.

"The Gift of Salvation: A Statement of Evangelicals and Catholics Together," with others. *First Things* 79 (January 1998): 20–23.

"Living Truth for a Dying World: The Message of C. S. Lewis." *Crux* 34, no. 4 (December 1998): 3–12.

"An Open Letter about *The Gift of Salvation.*" With Timothy George and Thomas Oden. *Christianity Today*, April 27, 1998, 9.

"Richard Baxter." In *The SPCK Handbook of Anglican Theologians*, edited by Alister E. McGrath, 80–82. London: SPCK, 1998.

"A Small Step of Faith: Introduction to *The Gift of Salvation.*" *Touchstone* 11 (January/February 1998): 31.

"Still Surprised by Lewis: Why This Nonevangelical Oxford Don Has Become Our Patron Saint." *Christianity Today*, September 7, 1998, 54–60.

"The Substance of Truth in the Present Age: '. . . The Spirit of Truth, Whom the World Cannot Receive . . .'" *Crux* 34, no. 1 (March 1998): 3–11. Also published as "The Substance of Truth in the Present Age." In *The Way of Truth in the Present Age,* edited by Craig Gay and C. Pete Molloy, 15–29. Vancouver: Regent College Press, 1999.

"Unity and Truth: The Anglican Agony." In *Grace and Truth in the Secular Age*, edited by Timothy Bradshaw, 235–51. Grand Rapids: Eerdmans, 1998.

Forewords, Introductions, and Prefaces

Foreword to *Letters from Heaven*, by Hope MacDonald. Colorado Springs: NavPress, 1998.

Introduction to *The Art of Man-Fishing*, by Thomas Boston. Fearn, UK: Christian Heritage, 1998.

1999

Books

Honouring the People of God: The Collected Shorter Writings of J. I. Packer, vol. 4. Carlisle, UK: Paternoster, 1999.

Honouring the Written Word of God: The Collected Shorter Writings of J. I. Packer, vol. 3. Carlisle, UK: Paternoster, 1999.

J. I. Packer Collection. Selected and introduced by Alister McGrath. Leicester, UK: Inter-Varsity; Downers Grove, IL: InterVarsity, 1999.

Articles, Essays, and Published Lectures

"Can the Dead Be Converted?" *Christianity Today*, January 11, 1999, 82.

"Did God Die on the Cross?" *Christianity Today*, April 5, 1999, 70.

The Pilgrim's Principles: John Bunyan Revisited. London: St. Antholin's Lectureship Charity, 1999.

"Rooted and Built Up in Christ (Col. 2:6–7): The Prayer Book Path" In *The Prayer Book: Yesterday, Today, and Tomorrow*, 27–43. Concord, ON: Toronto Branch, Prayer Book Society of Canada, 1999.

"Some Perspectives on Preaching" and "The Problem of Paradigms." In *Preaching the Living Word: Addresses from the Evangelical Assembly*, edited by David Jackman, 27–44, 45–61. Fearn, UK: Christian Focus, 1999.

"The 'Wretched Man' Revisited: Another Look at Romans 7:14–25." In *Romans and the People of God: Essays in Honor of Gordon D. Fee on the Occasion of His 65th Birthday*, edited by Sven Soderlund and N. T. Wright, 70–81. Grand Rapids: Eerdmans, 1999.

Forewords, Introductions, and Prefaces

Foreword to *Not Ashamed: The Story of Jews for Jesus*, by Ruth Tucker. Sisters, OR: Multnomah, 1999.

Introduction to *I Believe in the Church*, by David Watson. London: Hodder and Stoughton, 1999.

2000

Books

Never Beyond Hope: How God Touches and Uses Imperfect People. With Carolyn Nystrom. Downers Grove, IL: InterVarsity, 2000. Translations: Korean, 2003; Spanish, 2005; Danish, 2006; Romanian, 2008.

The Redemption and Restoration of Man in the Thought of Richard Baxter. Vancouver: Regent College Publishing; Carlisle, UK: Paternoster, 2000. Edited version of 1954 DPhil thesis.

The Way of Wisdom: Essays in Honor of Bruce K. Waltke. Edited with Sven K. Soderlund. Grand Rapids: Zondervan, 2000.

Articles, Essays, and Published Lectures

"Anger" and "Obedience." In *New Dictionary of Biblical Theology,* edited by T. D. Alexander and Brian D. Rosner. Leicester, UK: Inter-Varsity; Downers Grove, IL: InterVarsity, 2000.

"Doing It My Way: Are We Born Rebels?" In *This We Believe: The Good News of Jesus Christ for the World,* edited by John N. Akers, John H. Armstrong, and John Woodbridge, 43–60. Grand Rapids: Zondervan, 2000. Translations: Chinese, 2002.

"For Truth, Unity and Hope: Revaluing the Book of Common Prayer." *Churchman* 114, no. 2 (Summer 2000): 103–13.

"Is Satan Omnipresent?" *Christianity Today,* September 2000, 115.

"Maintaining Evangelical Theology." In *Evangelical Futures: A Conversation on Theological Method,* edited by John G. Stackhouse Jr., 181–89. Grand Rapids: Baker Academic, 2000; Nottingham, UK: Apollos, 2001.

"Theology and Wisdom." In *The Way of Wisdom: Essays in Honor of Bruce K. Waltke,* edited by J. I. Packer and Sven K. Soderlund, 1–14. Grand Rapids: Zondervan, 2000.

"We Can Overcome." Interview with J. I. Packer, Elward Ellis, Robert Franklin, Charles Lyons, and John Ortberg. *Christianity Today,* October 2, 2000, 115.

Forewords, Introductions, and Prefaces

Foreword to *131 Christians Everyone Should Know,* edited by Mark Galli and Ted Olson. Nashville: Broadman and Holman, 2000.

2001

Books

God's Plans for You. Wheaton: Crossway, 2001. Translations: Korean, 2001; Spanish, 2004; Indonesian, 2004; Portuguese, 2004; Dutch, 2007.

The Holy Bible: English Standard Version. General editor, J. I. Packer. Wheaton: Crossway, 2001.

J. I. Packer Answers Questions for Today. With Wendy Murray Zoba. Wheaton: Tyndale, 2001. Translations: Russian, 2002.

Puritan Papers. Vol. 2, 1960–1962. Edited by J. I. Packer. Phillipsburg, NJ: P&R, 2001.

Puritan Papers. Vol. 3, 1963–1964. Edited by J. I. Packer. Phillipsburg, NJ: P&R, 2001.

Articles, Essays, and Published Lectures

"The Content of the Gospel." In *The Mission of an Evangelist: Amsterdam 2000; A Conference of Preaching Evangelists,* 37–38. Minneapolis: Worldwide, 2001. Also published in *Evangelical Review of Theology* 25, no. 1 (January 2001): 16–17.

"Formed in the Wilderness." In *The Desert Experience: Personal Reflections on Finding God's Presence and Promise in Hard Times,* 107–24. Nashville: Thomas Nelson, 2001. Translations: Korean, 2002.

"Hermeneutics and Genesis 1–11." *Southwestern Journal of Theology* 44, no. 1 (Fall 2001): 4–21.

"What Lewis Was and Wasn't" and "The Pilgrim's Regress." In *We Remember C. S. Lewis,* edited by David Graham, 6–8, 29–31. Nashville: Broadman and Holman, 2001.

2002

Books

Faithfulness and Holiness: The Witness of J. C. Ryle: An Appreciation. Wheaton: Crossway; Eastbourne, UK: Kingsway Communications, 2002. Includes the full text of the first edition of J. C. Ryle's *Holiness.*

Articles, Essays, and Published Lectures

"The Bible in Use: Evangelicals Seeking Truth from Holy Scripture." In *Your Word Is Truth,* edited by Richard John Neuhaus and Charles Colson, 59–78. Grand Rapids: Eerdmans, 2002.

"The Glory of the Person of Christ" and "The Glory of Christ's Present Reign." In *The Glory of Christ,* edited by J. Armstrong, 37–56, 115–33. Wheaton: Crossway, 2002.

"Hell's Final Enigma: Won't Heaven's Joy Be Spoiled by Our Awareness of Unsaved Loved Ones in Hell?" *Christianity Today,* April 2002, 84.

"A No to Same-Sex Unions: Why Jim Packer Walked out of the Synod of the Anglican Diocese of New Westminster." *Evangelicals Now* (November 2002).

"A Stunted Ecclesiology?" In *Ancient and Postmodern Christianity,* edited by Kenneth Tanner and Christopher A. Hall, 120–27. Downers Grove, IL: InterVarsity, 2002.

"Text Criticism and Inerrancy." *Christianity Today,* October 2002, 102.

"The Way of Christlikeness." In *Living Like Jesus: Becoming Everything God Wants You to Be,* edited by K. Horn and J. O. Davis, 39–50. Springfield, MO: Onward, 2002.

"Wisdom in a Time of War: What Oswald Chambers and C. S. Lewis Have to Teach Us About Living through the Long Battle with Terrorism." *Christianity Today*, January 2002, 44–49.

"Your Word Is Truth: A Statement of Evangelicals and Catholics Together." With others. *First Things* 125 (August–September 2002): 38–42.

Forewords, Introductions, and Prefaces

Foreword to *The Throne, the Lamb, and the Dragon: A Reader's Guide to the Book of Revelation*, by Paul Spilsbury. Downers Grove, IL: InterVarsity, 2002.

Introduction to *Christ Crucified: A Puritan's View of the Atonement*, by Stephen Charnock. Fearn, UK: Christian Focus, 2002.

Introduction to *The Crook in the Lot: A Puritan's Understanding of That Thorn in Your Side*, by Thomas Boston, edited by Roger N. McDermott. Fearn, UK: Christian Heritage, 2002.

Introduction to *The Heavenly Footman: A Puritan's View of How to Get to Heaven*, by John Bunyan. Fearn, UK: Christian Focus, 2002.

2003

Books

Facing Pluralism Today. Sheffield: Reform, 2003. Only available at http://www.reform.org.uk/pages/bb/facingpluralismtoday.php.

Hope: Never Beyond Hope; 6 Studies for Individuals or Groups with Leader's Notes. With Carolyn Nystrom. Downers Grove, IL: Leicester, UK: Inter-Varsity, 2003.

Articles, Essays, and Published Lectures

"Calvin, *The Institutes* and Me." In *Indelible Ink,* edited by Scott Larsen, 75–89. Colorado Springs: Waterbrook, 2003.

"The Centrality of Holy Scripture in Anglicanism" and "Pastoral Self-Care: Riches from the Anglican Devotional Tradition." In *The Future Shape of Anglican Ministry*, edited by D. M. Lewis, 29–47, 94–115. Vancouver: Regent College Publishing, 2003.

"The Communion of Saints: A Statement of Evangelicals and Catholics Together." With others. *First Things* 131 (March 2003): 26–33.

"Experiencing God's Presents: Is Every Believer Granted at Least One Spiritual Gift?" *Christianity Today*, August 2003, 55.

"Holiness: Separation to God; An Interview with Dr. J. I. Packer." *Cross Point* 16, no. 1 (Winter 2003): 5–13.

"Prayers for Salvation." *Christianity Today*, April 2003, 100.

"Reflected Glory: What Does Genesis Mean by Man Being Made in the Image of God?" *Christianity Today*, December 2003, 56.

"Why I Walked: Sometimes Loving a Denomination Requires You to Fight." *Christianity Today*, January 2003, 46–50.

Forewords, Introductions, and Prefaces

Foreword to *Baptist Sacramentalism*, edited by Anthony R. Cross and Philip E. Thompson. Carlisle, UK; Waynesboro, GA: Paternoster, 2003.

2004

Books

One Faith: The Evangelical Consensus. Selected and arranged with Thomas C. Oden. Downers Grove, IL: InterVarsity, 2004.

Puritan Papers. Vol. 4, 1965–1967. Edited by J. I. Packer. Phillipsburg, NJ: P&R, 2004.

Articles, Essays, and Published Lectures

"The Atonement in the Life of the Christian." In *The Glory of the Atonement*, edited by Frank James and Charles Hill, 409–25. Downers Grove, IL: InterVarsity, 2004.

"The Glory of God and the Reviving of Religion: The Mind of Jonathan Edwards." In *A God-Entranced Vision of All Things*, edited by John Piper and Justin Taylor, 81–108. Wheaton: Crossway, 2004.

"Incarnate Forever: What Is the Scriptural and Theological Support for the Teaching That Jesus, the God-Man, Remains Eternally Incarnate?" *Christianity Today*, March 2004, 72.

"Pilgrim's Progress by John Bunyan (1628–1688)." In *The Devoted Life*, edited by K. M. Kapic and R. Gleason, 183–99. Nottingham, UK: Inter-Varsity; Downers Grove, IL: InterVarsity, 2004.

"Universalism: Will Everyone Ultimately Be Saved?" In *Hell Under Fire*, edited by Christopher W. Morgan and Robert A. Peterson, 169–94. Grand Rapids: Zondervan, 2004.

Forewords, Introductions, and Prefaces

Foreword to *The Saints' Everlasting Rest*, by Richard Baxter, edited by John T. Wilkinson. Vancouver: Regent College Publishing, 2004.

2005

Books

Zondervan Handbook of Christian Beliefs. Consulting editor with Alister McGrath, general editor. Grand Rapids: Zondervan, 2005. Published in the UK as *The New Lion Handbook: Christian Belief*. Oxford: Lion, 2006.

Articles, Essays, and Published Lectures

"All Sins Are Not Equal: Are All Sins Weighed Equally Or Is One More Important than Another?" *Christianity Today*, January 2005, 65.

"The Call to Holiness: A Statement of Evangelicals and Catholics Together." With others. *First Things* 151 (March 2005): 62–69.

"Evangelicals and Catholics: The State of Play." *Books and Culture* 11, no. 2 (March–April 2005): 10–11.

"Mind in Motion." With Jerry Root. *Christian History* 88 (February 2005): 14–18.

"The Ministry of the Spirit in Discerning the Will of God." In *Who's Afraid of The Holy Spirit?* edited by Daniel B. Wallace and M. James Sawyer, 95–110. Dallas: Biblical Studies Press, 2005.

"Salvation sans Jesus." *Christianity Today*, October 2005, 88.

2006

Books

Praying: Finding Our Way through Duty to Delight. With Carolyn Nystrom. Downers Grove, IL: InterVarsity; Leicester, UK: Inter-Varsity, 2006. Translations: Romanian, 2006; Korean, 2008; Afrikaans, 2008.

Taking Faith Seriously. Anglican Agenda Series. Milton, ON: Essentials, 2006. A sixteen-page booklet.

Articles, Essays, and Published Lectures

"God's Triple Team: Preaching the Trinity." *Leadership Journal* 27, no. 4 (Fall 2006): 67–68. An interview.

"Is God Unfair?" *Modern Reformation* 15, no. 5 (September 2006): 16–22.

"Physicians of the Soul." *Christian History & Biography* 89 (Winter 2006): 12–15. An interview.

"A Puritan Perspective: Trinitarian Godliness according to John Owen." In *God the Holy Trinity*, edited by Timothy George, 91–108. Grand Rapids: Baker Academic, 2006.

"Revelation." In *New Dictionary of Christian Apologetics*, edited by W. C. Campbell-Jack, G. J. McGrath, and C. S. Evans. Nottingham, UK: Inter-Varsity, 2006.

"That They May Have Life: A Statement of Evangelicals and Catholics Together." With others. *First Things* 166 (October 2006): 18–25.

Forewords, Introductions, and Prefaces

Foreword to *Battle for the Soul of Canada: Raising up the Emerging Generation of Leaders*, by Ed Hird. Vancouver: Hird, 2006.

2007

Books

Praying the Lord's Prayer. Wheaton: Crossway, 2007.

Taking Christian Unity Seriously. Anglican Agenda Series. Milton, ON: Essentials, 2007.

Taking Doctrine Seriously. Anglican Agenda Series. Milton, ON: Essentials, 2007.

Taking Repentance Seriously. Anglican Agenda Series. Milton, ON: Essentials, 2007.

Articles, Essays, and Published Lectures

"Expository Preaching: Charles Simeon and Ourselves." In *Preach the Word*, edited by Leland Ryken and Todd A. Wilson, 140–54. Wheaton: Crossway, 2007.

Forewords, Introductions, and Prefaces

Foreword to *Communion with God: The Divine and the Human in the Theology of John Owen*, by Kelly M. Kapic. Grand Rapids: Baker Academic, 2007.

Foreword to *Trinitarian Spirituality: John Owen and the Doctrine of God in Western Devotion*, by Brian K. Kay. Bletchley, Milton Keynes, UK; Waynesboro, GA: Paternoster, 2007.

2008

Books

Anglican Evangelical Identity: Yesterday and Today. With N. T. Wright. London: Latimer Trust, 2008.

Guard Us, Guide Us: Divine Leading in Life's Decisions. With Carolyn Nystrom. London: Gardners; Grand Rapids: Baker Books, 2008.

In My Place Condemned He Stood: Celebrating the Glory of the Atonement. With Mark Dever. Wheaton: Crossway, 2008.

Taking the Holy Spirit Seriously. Anglican Agenda Series: Milton, ON: Essentials, 2008.

Articles, Essays, and Published Lectures

"Count Your Surprises: The High Spots of My Life Have Been Anything but Expected." *Christianity Today*, March 2008, 66–67.

Forewords, Introductions, and Prefaces

Foreword to *A Theological Guide to Calvin's Institutes*, edited by David W. Hall and Peter A. Lillback. Phillipsburg, NJ: P&R, 2008.

Appendix B

A Tribute to J. I. Packer

I was a rather quiet and shy student of J. I. Packer at Regent College in the early 1980s. I have remained his student through the years by reading his books and rehearsing what I heard from him in class. On the occasion of this, his eightieth birthday, I offer this hymn, in his honor, as a simple song of praise to God for the impact J. I. Packer has made on my life and on the lives of countless others.

Gary A. Parrett, September 2006
Gordon-Conwell Theological Seminary

As a Witness of Your Grace

For the Gospel of the Lord
I will yield my grateful heart.
God saves sinners, first to last.
God alone can life impart.
As a witness to Your grace,
may I serve You with my heart.

For the life of holiness
I will thirst with all my soul.
May Your Spirit's cleansing font
fill me till I overflow.
As a witness to Your life,
may I serve You with my soul.

For the teachings of God's Word
I will humbly bow my mind.
God Almighty would be known.
Those who seek the Lord shall find.
As a witness to Your truth,
may I serve You with my mind.

For the oneness of the Church
I will work with all my might:
joining Jesus in His pray'r,
loving all for whom He died.
As a witness to Your love,
may I serve You with my might.

Text: Gary A. Parrett / Tune: DIX

To this day, J. I. Packer's introductory essay to John Owen's *Death of Death in the Death of Christ* remains the one piece of writing that has had the greatest impact on my theological landscape. It was wonderfully disequilibrating to me when I read it (and Owen's volume) as a Regent student for a seminar on Puritanism. Packer's exposition of "God Saves Sinners" is still, I believe, the finest and clearest unpacking of the gospel available in print.

In that same seminar, Packer delighted to introduce us all to the Puritans' passionate pursuit of God and of godliness in all spheres of life. He has, of course, put this in print in many places. I remember him telling us that "balance" was not such a good word to the Puritans, because it implied a 50/50 compromise that they would never have affirmed. His introduction to Bishop Ryle's wonderful book *Holiness* is a piece that helped me greatly in my own walk with God.

I rejoice that Packer has left such a deep impression on so many with his love for, and submission to, Scripture. He is a "Bible man" through and through. And he has ever been concerned to make the great truths of Scripture accessible to the church through his teaching and writings. His catechetical commitment has rubbed off on me, as has his love of God's Word.

It is also very clear that Packer has taken deeply to heart Jesus's "high priestly prayer" in John 17:21 (ESV) "that they may all be one . . . Father . . . so that the world may believe that you have sent me." Watching Packer's steadfast commitment to dialogue within the Christian community has challenged me greatly. Like so many other of his passions this too has become one of mine as well.

Notes

Preface *Timothy George*

1. Packer's dissertation was published some fifty years after completion as J. I. Packer, *The Redemption and Restoration of Man in the Thought of Richard Baxter: A Study in Puritan Theology* (Carlisle, UK: Paternoster, 2003).

2. "Statement by nine Anglican Network in Canada clergy to Bishop Michael Ingham." Delivered on April 21, 2008. Statement can be read at the Anglican Network in Canada Web page: http://www.anglicannetwork.ca/clergy_statement_042108.htm. Accessed 5/4/2009.

3. J. I. Packer, *Concise Theology* (Wheaton: Tyndale, 1993), xii.

Chapter 1 The Great Tradition *Alister E. McGrath*

1. J. I. Packer, "On from Orr: Cultural Crisis, Rational Realism and Incarnational Ontology," *Crux* 32, no. 3 (September 1996): 12. For Packer's estimation of Lewis, see his "Living Truth for a Dying World: The Message of C. S. Lewis," *Crux* 34, no. 4 (December 1998): 3–12.

2. Packer's dissertation is now published, fifty years after its completion: J. I. Packer, *The Redemption and Restoration of Man in the Thought of Richard Baxter: A Study in Puritan Theology* (Carlisle, UK: Paternoster, 2003).

3. J. I. Packer, "'Keswick' and the Reformed Doctrine of Sanctification," *Evangelical Quarterly* 27, no. 3 (July 1955): 153–67. The book that was the subject of Packer's criticisms was Steven Barabas, *So Great Salvation: The History and Message of the Keswick Convention* (London: Marshall, Morgan and Scott, 1952). This work is widely regarded, whether by supporters or opponents, as an authoritative exposition of the Keswick view.

4. Packer, "'Keswick' and the Reformed Doctrine of Sanctification," 153, 154.

5. Ibid., 167.

6. In his later work *Keep in Step with the Spirit* (Old Tappan, NJ: Revell, 1984), Packer offers a more irenic and appreciative evaluation of Keswick, which corrects it on several points while remaining appreciative of its intentions. The noticeably more friendly tone of this evaluation reflects Packer's belief that, by this later stage (1984), the Keswick teaching no longer posed the threat that it once did.

7. *The Collected Writings of James Henley Thornwell*, 4 vols. (Richmond: Presbyterian Committee of Publication, 1871–73). Quote is from vol. 1, *Theology*, 34.

8. J. I. Packer, "An Introduction to Systematic Spirituality," *Crux* 26, no. 1 (March 1990): 2–8.

9. Ibid.

10. J. I. Packer, *Truth and Power: The Place of Scripture in the Christian Life* (Downers Grove, IL: InterVarsity, 1999), 110.

11. See J. I. Packer, introduction to *Sin and Temptation: The Challenge of Personal Godliness*, by John Owen, ed. James M. Houston (Portland, OR: Multnomah, 1983), xxv–xxix.

12. J. I. Packer, *A Quest for Godliness: The Puritan Vision of the Christian Life* (Wheaton: Crossway, 1990). Similar themes can be found in *Knowing God*, although Puritan provenance is not given such prominence.

13. See, for example, John Piper and Justin Taylor, eds., *A God-Entranced Vision of All Things: The Legacy of Jonathan Edwards* (Wheaton: Crossway, 2004). For Piper's own approach, see John Piper, *Desiring God: Meditations of a Christian Hedonist* (Sisters, OR: Multnomah, 1996).

14. Packer, "On from Orr," 12–13.

15. See Alister E. McGrath, "Engaging the Great Tradition: Evangelical Theology and the Role of Tradition," in *Evangelical Futures: A Conversation on Theological Method*, ed. John G. Stackhouse Jr. (Grand Rapids: Baker Academic, 2000), 139–58.

16. J. I. Packer, "The Comfort of Conservatism," in *Power Religion*, ed. M. Horton (Chicago: Moody, 1992), 283–99.

17. Ibid., 290.

18. Ibid., 289.

19. Ibid., 283.

20. Ibid., 288.

21. Ibid., 289.

22. Packer, *Truth and Power*, 110.

23. Ibid., 116–18.

Chapter 2 The Gifts of J. I. Packer *Edith M. Humphrey*

1. This translation is from the 1962 Canadian Book of Common Prayer, "Psalm 133: *Ecce, quam bonum!*"

2. J. I. Packer, "On from Orr: Cultural Crisis, Rational Realism and Incarnational Ontology," in *Reclaiming the Great Tradition: Evangelicals, Catholics and Orthodox in Dialogue*, ed. James S. Cutsinger (Downers Grove, IL: InterVarsity, 1997), 156.

3. Ibid., 160.

4. Ibid., 157.

5. Ibid.

6. J. I. Packer, *Commentary on the Montreal Declaration: Anglican Essentials; Reclaiming Faith within the Anglican Church of Canada* (Halifax, NS: Essentials, 1996). The declaration itself emerged from the essentials gathering in Montreal in 1995 and was followed by the *Commentary* in 1996.

7. Ibid., 3.

8. Ibid., 49.

9. Ibid., 42–43.

10. "The Church's One Foundation," lyrics by Samuel J. Stone in *The Book of Common Praise* (Toronto: Anglican Book Centre, 1938), hymn 561.

11. Packer, "On from Orr," 176.

12. Carl Tuttle, "I Worship You" (South Hampshire: Mercy/Vineyard Publishing, 1982).

13. J. I. Packer, *Knowing God* (Downers Grove, IL: InterVarsity, 1977), 41.

14. R. T. Beckwith with G. E. Duffield and J. I. Packer, *Across the Divide* (Basingstoke, UK: Lyttelton, 1977), 59.

15. J. I. Packer, *A Quest for Godliness* (Wheaton: Crossway, 1990), 13.

16. Alister McGrath, *J. I. Packer: A Biography* (Grand Rapids: Baker Books, 1997), 257.

17. For the gist of Packer's commencement address, see Alister McGrath, *J. I. Packer: A Biography* (Grand Rapids: Baker Books, 1997), 257.

18. My italics here indicate the surprise of the phrase, which we would anticipate as "Systematic *Theology*." The address is published in *Crux* 26, no. 1 (March 1990): 2–8.

19. McGrath, *J. I. Packer*, 288.

20. J. I. Packer, "Anglican-Methodist Unity," in *Fellowship in the Gospel: Evangelical Comment on Anglican-Methodist Unity and Intercommunion Today* (Abingdon, UK: Marcham Manor, 1968), 26.

21. Bradley Nassif, "An Eastern Orthodox Response," in Cutsinger, *Reclaiming the Great Tradition*, 177.

22. Packer, "On from Orr," 175.

23. See the principles articulated in Packer, "Anglican-Methodist Unity," in *Fellowship in the Gospel*, 9–38.

24. Packer, "On from Orr," 157.

25. Ibid.

26. Beckwith with Duffield and Packer, *Across the Divide*, 13.

27. Ibid., 15.

28. "The Doxology," originally the seventh and last stanza of "Glory to Thee, My God, This Night," a hymn of evening worship written by Ken Thomas in 1674, usually sung to the tune of *Old One Hundredth* in Anglican worship and found in Anglican hymnbooks.

Chapter 3 Pumping Truth *David Neff*

1. J. I. Packer, "Fundamentalism: The British Scene," *Christianity Today*, September 29, 1958, 3–6. All quotations pertaining to this article are taken from p. 5.

2. Phyllis Elaine Alsdurf, "*Christianity Today* Magazine and Late Twentieth-Century Evangelicalism" (PhD diss., University of Minnesota, 2004).

3. "CT Predicts More of the Same," editorial in *Christianity Today*, December 6, 1999, 36.

4. J. I. Packer, "Hype and Human Humbug," *Christianity Today*, February 17, 1989, 11.

5. J. I. Packer, "What the Puritans Taught Me: They Kept Their Eyes on Heaven as Pilgrims Traveling Home to the Celestial City," *Christianity Today*, October 8, 1990, 44–47. Quotations pertaining to this article are taken from p. 46. The article is a condensed excerpt from J. I. Packer, *A Quest for Godliness: The Puritan Vision of the Christian Life* (Wheaton: Crossway, 1990).

6. J. I. Packer, "The Gospel Bassoon," *Christianity Today*, October 28, 1996, 24.

7. J. I. Packer, "An Accidental Author," *Christianity Today*, May 15, 1987, 11.

8. J. I. Packer, "Surprised by Graphics," *Christianity Today*, Novermber 11, 1991, 15.

9. Ibid.

10. J. I. Packer, "Still Surprised by Lewis: Why This Nonevangelical Oxford Don Has Become Our Patron Saint," *Christianity Today*, September 7, 1998, 54–60. All quotations pertaining to this article are taken from p. 57.

11. J. I. Packer, "All That Jazz," *Christianity Today*, December 12, 1986, 15.

12. Packer, "Fundamentalism," 4.

13. J. I. Packer, "Why I Walked: Sometimes Loving a Denomination Requires You to Fight," *Christianity Today*, January 2003, 49.

14. J. I. Packer, "Wisdom in a Time of War," *Christianity Today*, January 7, 2002, 44.

15. Ibid.

16. J. I. Packer, "A Bad Trip," *Christianity Today*, March 7, 1986, 12.

17. J. I. Packer, "Packer the Picketed Pariah," *Christianity Today*, January 11, 1993, 11.

18. J. I. Packer, "The Prayboy Club," *Christianity Today*, October 20, 1989, 11.

19. J. I. Packer, "Why I Signed It: The Recent Statement 'Evangelicals and Catholics Together' Recognizes an Important Truth: Those Who Love the Lord Must Stand Together," *Christianity Today*, December 12, 1994, 34–37.

20. The statement was published in *Christianity Today* (June 14, 1999) and is available online at http://www.christianitytoday.com/ct/2000/106/53.0.html.

21. J. I. Packer, "Why I Like My Pie in the Sky," *Christianity Today*, June 18, 1990, 11.

22. Timothy Beougher and J. I. Packer, "'Go Fetch Baxter': This Feisty Puritan Spent His Life Quieting the Controversies He Started," *Christianity Today*, December 16, 1991, 26–28.

23. J. I. Packer, "History Repeats Itself," *Christianity Today*, September 22, 1989, 22.

24. Packer, "Wisdom in a Time of War," 47, 49.

25. J. I. Packer, "How Will I Be Remembered?" *Christianity Today*, June 24, 1991, 11.

Chapter 4 J. I. Packer's Theological Method *Donald J. Payne*

1. This chapter is a revised and condensed version of chapter 8, "Theological Method," in Donald J. Payne, *The Theology of the Christian Life in J. I. Packer's Thought: Theological Anthropology, Theological Method, and the Doctrine of Sanctification* (Carlisle, UK: Paternoster, 2006). Reprinted with permission from Paternoster.

2. David F. Wright, "Recovering Baptism for a New Age of Mission," in *Doing Theology for the People of God: Studies in Honor of J. I. Packer*, ed. Donald Lewis and Alister McGrath (Downers Grove, IL: InterVarsity, 1996), 52.

3. R. Steer, *Guarding the Holy Fire: The Evangelicalism of John R. W. Stott, J. I. Packer, and Alister McGrath* (Grand Rapids: Baker Academic, 1999), 216.

4. J. I. Packer, "Method, Theological," in *New Dictionary of Theology*, ed. Sinclair B. Ferguson, David F. Wright, and J. I. Packer, 424–26 (Leicester, UK: Inter-Varsity, 1988), 425.

5. Ibid.

6. Ibid.

7. Alister McGrath, *To Know and Serve God: A Life of James I. Packer*, with a foreword by J. I. Packer (London: Hodder and Stoughton, 1997), 213–18.

8. Ibid., 218.

9. J. I. Packer, "Infallible Scripture and the Role of Hermeneutics," in *Scripture and Truth*, ed. D. A. Carson and John D. Woodbridge (Grand Rapids: Zondervan, 1983), 346.

10. J. I. Packer, "Understanding the Bible: Evangelical Hermeneutics," in *The Collected Shorter Writings of J. I. Packer*, vol. 3, *Honouring the Written Word of God* (Carlisle, UK: Paternoster, 1999), 158.

11. For example, see his three published addresses to the Conference on Biblical Inerrancy, entitled "The Challenge of Biblical Interpretation: Creation," "The Challenge of Biblical Interpretation: Women," and "The Challenge of Biblical Interpretation: Eschatology," in *Shorter Writings*, vol. 3, 171–212.

12. J. I. Packer, "In Quest of Canonical Interpretation," in *Shorter Writings*, vol. 3, 221.

13. J. I. Packer, *Truth and Power: The Place of Scripture in the Christian Life* (Wheaton: Shaw, 1996), 91.

14. J. I. Packer, "The Adequacy of Human Language," in *Inerrancy*, ed. Norman Geisler, 197–226 (Grand Rapids: Zondervan, 1980), 201.

15. Packer, "Method, Theological," 424–25.

16. Ibid., 425. He states, "Believers who define 'unprejudiced', 'open-minded' and 'scientific' as meaning 'determined by the object of study itself' rather than 'shaped by the anti-Christian positivism of some natural and historical scientists', and who go on to recognize that the central object of study is in fact the living creator, self-revealed in Scripture as triune personal Subject, have already in principle overcome this tension."

17. J. I. Packer, "Upholding the Unity of Scripture Today," in *Shorter Writings*, vol. 3, 141. Packer's insistence that inerrancy is a fact and a logical necessity must be qualified by his admis-

sion that "inerrancy ought always to be held as an article of faith not capable of demonstrative proof but entailed by dominical and apostolic teaching about the nature of Scripture." But he believes that the unity of Scripture is now a demonstrable possibility, claiming that "we have now reached a point in technical evangelical scholarship at which the possibility of an entirely harmonious exegesis of the whole Bible has been shown in such conclusive detail that the century-old liberal assertion that this position cannot be held with intellectual integrity may safely be dismissed as refuted."

18. I develop this claim at length and also attempt to lay the groundwork for how Packer's theological anthropology affects his theological method in chapter 7 of *Theology of the Christian Life*, 183–214.

19. J. I. Packer, "Inerrancy and the Divinity and the Humanity of the Bible," in *The Proceedings of the Conference on Biblical Inerrancy 1987*, ed. J. Gregory (Nashville: Broadman, 1987), 138.

20. Packer, "Infallible Scripture," 334–35.

21. Ibid., 328–32.

22. Ibid., 349f. See also *Truth and Power*, 134–36; and J. I. Packer, *"Fundamentalism" and the Word of God: Some Evangelical Principles* (London: Inter-Varsity, 1958), 94–101.

23. J. I. Packer, "Encountering Present-Day Views of Scripture," in *Shorter Writings*, vol. 3, 21–22.

24. Packer, *Truth and Power*, 134.

25. Ibid., 98.

26. Ibid., 52.

27. Packer, "Infallible Scripture." He claims that "the Scriptures are the products of a single divine mind" (350). See also J. I. Packer, "Upholding the Unity of Scripture Today," *Journal of the Evangelical Theological Society* 25 (December 1982). Here Packer affirms the traditional view of the "internal coherence" of Scripture, stating, "As law codes are to be presumed consistent, so all the contents of Scripture, originating as they were held to do from God's mind as their single source, were to be treated as harmonious and were to be interpreted in terms of the principle that the Reformers called the analogy of Scripture or the analogy of the faith (*analogia fidei*)" (409).

28. Packer, *"Fundamentalism" and the Word of God*. He states, "The infallibility and inerrancy of biblical teaching does not, however, guarantee the infallibility and inerrancy of any interpretation, or interpreter, of that teaching; nor does the recognition of its qualities as the Word of God in any way prejudge the issue as to what Scripture does, in fact, assert" (96).

29. Packer, "Infallible Scripture," 351–52.

30. Ibid., 350.

31. Packer, *Truth and Power*, 103.

32. See B. A. Demarest, "Analogy of Faith," in *Evangelical Dictionary of Theology*, ed. Walter A. Elwell (Grand Rapids: Baker Academic, 1984), 44. Demarest points out that Augustine used the principle of "analogy of faith" in reference to the Apostles' Creed as a hermeneutical safeguard. In *Truth and Power*, Packer claims, "The phrase *analogy of faith* stands for the principle of interpreting Scripture harmoniously, letting what is basic and clear illuminate what is peripheral and obscure" (243).

33. J. I. Packer, "On Covenant Theology," in *The Collected Shorter Writings of J. I. Packer*, vol. 1, *Celebrating the Saving Work of God* (Carlisle, UK: Paternoster, 1998), 9.

34. Ibid., 12, 13, 15.

35. Packer, "In Quest of Canonical Interpretation," 217.

36. Packer, "On Covenant Theology," 21.

37. Packer, "Arminianisms," in *The Collected Shorter Writings of J. I. Packer*, vol. 4, *Honouring the People of God* (Carlisle, UK: Paternoster, 1999), 305.

38. J. I. Packer, *Concise Theology: A Guide to Historic Beliefs* (Wheaton: Tyndale, 1993), see the table of contents. Packer begins his theological structure with the doctrine of Scripture, then addresses "Interpretation" and "General Revelation." He includes more categories than the Confession but follows the order of "Creation," "Sovereignty," "Predestination," and "Trinity" (with various related themes interspersed). See also *The Westminster Confession of Faith: An Authentic Modern Version*, rev. 2nd ed. (Signal Mountain, TN: Summertown, 1979), v. The order of the Confession begins with "Holy Scripture," "God and the Holy Trinity," "God's Eternal Decrees," "Creation," and "Providence."

39. Packer, "In Quest of Canonical Interpretation." He states, "The first thing to say is that I perceive the sixty-six books of the Protestant canon to be the Word of God given in and through human words. Canonical Scripture is divine testimony and instruction in the form of human testimony and instruction" (214–15). Interestingly, Packer appears to send mixed signals about the value of experience in validating and interpreting the text of Scripture. He contends that the cumulative experience of the church is a source of validation for the canon. "Then, theologically, I see the attestation of the Protestant canon by the Holy Spirit growing stronger year by year as more and more Bible readers have the sixty-six books authenticated to them in actual experience" (216). Yet in the same article he disallows experience as a criterion for interpretation, stating, "The truth of theological assertions should be decided by asking whether they faithfully echo Scripture, not whether God has blessed folk who have held them" (214). At best, this presents an unclear picture of exactly what experience can and cannot accomplish in regard to Scripture.

40. J. I. Packer, "Understanding the Differences," in *Women, Authority and the Bible*, ed. Alvera Mickelsen (Downers Grove, IL: InterVarsity, 1986), 296.

41. Packer, "In Quest of Canonical Interpretation," 223.

42. Packer, "Upholding the Unity of Scripture Today," 137. Packer applauds the efforts of Karl Barth and T. F. Torrance in attempting to counter "the liberal idea of an ultimate evolutionary pluralism in Scripture" with a "theologically unitive hermeneutics based on Chalcedonian Christology."

43. Packer, *Truth and Power*, 121. It could be asked whether it is fair to polarize the positions in this manner. Is it logically necessary that taking Jesus Christ's humanity as a starting point for understanding his nature results in compromising the nature of his divinity?

44. Ibid., 192.

45. J. I. Packer, "Aspects of Authority," in *Orthos*, no. 9 (papers from Fellowship of the Word and Spirit, n.d.), 16.

46. J. I. Packer, "Why Preach?" in *Shorter Writings*, vol. 3, 252–53.

47. Stephen Neill, review of *Knowing God*, by J. I. Packer, *Churchman* 88, no. 1 (1974): 77.

48. See Edward A. Dowey Jr., *The Knowledge of God in Calvin's Theology* (New York: Columbia University Press, 1952). Packer's attempt to be christological appears to resemble Dowey's description of Calvin's christocentrism. Dowey states, "The center of Calvin's thought, around which all else moves, is the divine provision for and the divine accomplishment of the salvation of sinful humanity through Jesus Christ to the glory of God alone. That is to say, Calvin's thought has a *soteriological center* which dominates all his theology, but not all elements equally. Although Calvin's soteriology proper is profoundly Christocentric, it is not strictly accurate to say that his thought or theology as a whole is Christocentric. This is true because there is an inherent dialectic within his soteriology by which it is related to and is set within non-soteriological elements upon which it depends for its meaning" (246–47, italics in original).

49. See Anthony C. Thiselton, *New Horizons in Hermeneutics* (Grand Rapids: Zondervan, 1992). Thiselton draws attention to the work of Ernst Fuchs and J. L. Austin in which "they rightly focussed on the capacity of language *to perform acts*: in the case of some parables, to *make pledges or offers,* to *effect acts of forgiveness,* to *subvert* institutional assumptions, and

so forth" (16, italics in original). Packer apparently ascribes to Scripture a more descriptive than performative character.

50. A sharp distinction between interpretation and application is not uniformly upheld, even by evangelical theologians. H. M. Conn contends that understanding the original meaning of a text is impossible apart from personal response to it. Conn, a Reformed missiologist, challenges the history of theological method characteristic of his own tradition, claiming that it has departed from John Calvin's theological method. See Harvie M. Conn, *Eternal Word and Changing Worlds: Theology, Anthropology, and Mission in Trialogue* (Grand Rapids: Zondervan, 1984), 220.

51. Packer, "Infallible Scripture and the Role of Hermeneutics," 345.

52. Packer, "The Adequacy of Human Language," 27.

53. Packer, "Infallible Scripture and the Role of Hermeneutics," 338–39.

54. Packer, *Truth and Power*, 147. While here Packer subsumes the act of exegesis under the heading of hermeneutics, he elsewhere relates the two terms in the opposite manner, placing hermeneutics as a discipline within the activity of exegesis. See also J. I. Packer, "Maintaining Evangelical Theology," in *Evangelical Futures: A Conversation on Theological Method*, ed. John G. Stackhouse Jr. (Grand Rapids: Baker Academic, 2000), 185.

55. Packer, "Infallible Scripture and the Role of Hermeneutics," 348. Interestingly, Packer's use of the phrase "hermeneutical spiral" in this 1983 publication predates Grant Osborne's use of the same phrase as the title of his 1991 book.

56. Ibid., 350.

57. Ibid., 337.

58. Packer, "The Adequacy of Human Language," 34–35. It must be noted that Packer does recognize the category of performative language as one type of language used in the Bible, along with imperative, illuminative, and celebratory language. Performative language, to Packer, is used by God when, by making covenants (e.g., with Abram in Genesis 17:2–4), God "causes the state of affairs spoken of to exist." This usage within Scripture is not the same, however, as Scripture itself functions as a performative act with the reader. Rather, in Packer's schema Scripture serves as descriptive language to report on God's performative language in another setting.

59. Packer, "Understanding the Bible: Evangelical Hermeneutics," 150.

60. Packer, *Truth and Power*, 149.

61. Packer, "Maintaining Evangelical Theology," 184.

62. Ibid., 185.

63. J. I. Packer, "Theology and Wisdom," in *The Way of Wisdom: Essays in Honor of Bruce K. Waltke*, ed. J. I. Packer and Sven K. Soderlund (Grand Rapids: Zondervan, 2000), 1.

64. Packer, "Maintaining Evangelical Theology," 186.

65. Ibid., 186–88.

66. See J. I. Packer, "Theology and Bible Reading," in *The Act of Bible Reading*, ed. Elmer Dyck (Downers Grove, IL: InterVarsity, 1996). He states, "Theology, with its network of internal linkages, has sometimes been described as a circle or (better) a rising spiral, the thought being that until you have toured the whole of which each item is a part, your understanding of that item is certainly deficient. But when you come back to it after making the tour, you understand it at least a little better than you did before" (67). See again his description of the hermeneutical act as that of a rising spiral in "Infallible Scripture and the Role of Hermeneutics," 338.

67. Packer, "Theology and Bible Reading," 68–71.

68. Ibid., 69–70. He states,

Systematic theology gathers to itself the findings of exegesis, biblical theology and historical theology in a watershed discipline. . . . Systematic theology thinks through the material that biblical and historical theology present in order to find a way of stating the whole faith today, topic by topic and in all its fullness, that will show its coherence and cogency in relation to current interests, assumptions, questions, doubts and challenges, both outside and inside the churches. Some have chosen to call the discipline dogmatic theology on the grounds that it deals with the defined faith (the dogmas) of the church, but 'systematic' says more about its scope and is therefore preferable. . . . When properly managed, it appears as a discipline of declaratory and applicatory biblical interpretation which merits the description 'systematic' not because it imposes a speculative system (it does not) but because it links biblical themes together in the way that Scripture itself does and sets forth each as part of a God-centered, thought-out, self-consistent whole. Good systematic theology always commends itself as a testimony to the God of the gospel, the triune Creator-Redeemer, and as a transcript of this God's self-disclosure and of the revelation of his mind as set forth in the Bible. (69–70)

69. See chap. 7 of Payne, *Theology of the Christian Life.*

70. Packer, "Theology and Bible Reading," 67.

71. Ibid. He states, "Without the ministrations of theology challenging us again and again not to force what we read into an anthropocentric, egocentric mold, we are in danger of missing the life-changing impact of this emphasis and ending up among those whose reading of the Bible never brings them to embrace the Bible's point of view" (84).

72. Ibid., 85.

73. J. I. Packer, foreword to *After Modernity—What? Agenda for Theology,* by Thomas Oden (Grand Rapids: Zondervan, 1990), 10.

74. Packer, *Truth and Power,* 98. See also J. I. Packer, "God's Plumber and Sewage Man," *Christianity Today,* April 6, 1992, 15.

75. J. I. Packer, "Paradox in Theology," *New Dictionary of Theology,* 491.

76. Ibid.

77. Ibid., 492.

78. Packer, "What Did the Cross Achieve? The Logic of Penal Substitution" in *Shorter Writings,* vol. 1. He claims that "ordinary language is used to speak intelligibly of a God who is partly like us (because we bear his image) and partly unlike us (because he is the infinite Creator while we are finite creatures). All theological models, like the non-descriptive models of the physical sciences, have an analogical character; they are, we might say, analogies with a purpose" (92–93). See also J. I. Packer, "God," *New Dictionary of Theology,* 274–77. Here he admits that as Christian thought progressed it made use of Greek philosophical categories, particularly those found in Plato, Aristotle, and the Stoics. He questions whether those categories were the best fit for the biblical ideas in view but insists that "those who used them from the 2nd to the 20th century have never let them obscure the fact that God is personal, active and very much alive" (276).

79. Packer, "Theology and Bible Reading," 75.

80. Ibid., 76.

81. Ibid.

82. Ibid.

83. Ibid., 77.

84. Packer admires the theological method of Scottish theologian J. Orr, and uses Orr's theological work as a model for challenging cultural drifts in which authoritative revelation from God is ignored. Packer specifically makes use of Orr's appeal to doctrine and dogma as, respectively, the coherent strands of God's revelation and the conclusions developed in response to that organic revelation. See J. I. Packer, "On from Orr: The Cultural Crisis, Rational Realism and Incarnational Ontology," *Crux* 32, no. 3 (September 1996), 12–26.

85. Packer, *Truth and Power,* 110.

Chapter 5 God Has Spoken *Paul R. House*

1. J. I. Packer, *God's Words: Studies of Key Bible Themes* (Downers Grove, IL: InterVarsity, 1981), 15.

2. J. I. Packer, *Knowing God* (1973; twentieth anniversary edition, Downers Grove, IL: InterVarsity, 1993).

3. For evidence of this point see J. I. Packer, *Honouring the Written Word of God: The Collected Shorter Writings of J. I. Packer*, vol. 3 (Carlisle, UK: Paternoster, 1999). This collection does not include every academic piece Packer wrote on the subject of Scripture, but it offers an excellent selection of representative works.

4. J. I. Packer, "Inerrancy and the Divinity and Humanity of the Bible," in *Honouring the Written Word of God*, 162. This article was originally presented as a lecture at the 1987 Conference on Biblical Inerrancy sponsored by the Southern Baptist Convention.

5. For an explanation of Baxter's pastoral catechizing, see Richard Baxter, *The Reformed Pastor* (Richmond: John Knox, 1956).

6. J. I. Packer, *Truth and Power: The Place of Scripture in the Christian Life* (Wheaton: Shaw, 1996), 98.

7. J. I. Packer, *"Fundamentalism" and the Word of God: Some Evangelical Principles* (Grand Rapids: Eerdmans, 1958), 22.

8. The overlap in the first two eras is because Packer received his doctorate in 1954 and published his first significant article on the Bible the same year.

9. Packer, *Truth and Power*, 99.

10. Ibid.

11. Ibid.

12. Alister McGrath, *J. I. Packer: A Biography* (Grand Rapids: Baker Books, 1997), 26–28.

13. Ibid., 34–39.

14. See his comments on how John Owen helped in this regard in his comments in the introduction to John Owen, *Sin and Temptation: The Challenge to Personal Godliness*, abr. and ed. James M. Houston (Portland: Multnomah, 1983), xxv–xxix.

15. J. I. Packer, *A Quest for Godliness: The Puritan Vision of the Christian Life* (Wheaton: Crossway, 1990), 98.

16. McGrath, *Packer*, 46–49, 59–69.

17. See ibid., 49–54. Many of the presentations from these conferences have been gathered in *Puritan Papers: Five Volumes* (Phillipsburg, NJ: P&R, 2000–2006). These volumes cover the years 1956–69, which are the years Packer participated. D. Martyn Lloyd-Jones edited the first volume and Packer edited the final four volumes.

18. For Packer's sense of the theological context in Britain at this time see Packer *"Fundamentalism,"* 9–23, 146–68, and "Inerrancy and the Divinity and Humanity of the Bible," 161–63.

19. Packer, *Truth and Power*, 107.

20. J. I. Packer, "Revelation and Inspiration," in E. F. Kevan et al., eds., *The New Bible Commentary*, 2nd ed. (London: Inter-Varsity, 1954), 12–18.

21. Ibid., 12–17.

22. Ibid., 12–13.

23. Ibid., 13–17.

24. Ibid., 17.

25. Ibid., 16.

26. Ibid.

27. Ibid., 17.

28. Ibid.

29. Ibid.

30. Ibid.

31. Ibid.

32. Ibid., 17–18.

33. Ibid., 18.

34. Ibid.

35. Gabriel Hebert, *Fundamentalism and the Church of God* (London: SCM, 1957).

36. Packer, "*Fundamentalism*," 15.

37. Ibid., 17.

38. Ibid.

39. Ibid., 18.

40. Ibid.

41. Ibid., 21–23.

42. Ibid., 24–40.

43. Ibid., 41–74.

44. Ibid., 75–114.

45. Ibid., 115–25.

46. Ibid., 126–45.

47. Ibid., 146–68.

48. Ibid., 21.

49. Ibid., 21–22.

50. J. I. Packer, *God Has Spoken*, 5th ed. (London: Hodder and Stoughton, 2005), 12.

51. Ibid.

52. McGrath, *Packer*, 197. For Packer's reflections on this conference, see *Truth and Power*, 104–5.

53. Harold Lindsell, *The Battle for the Bible* (Grand Rapids: Zondervan, 1976).

54. See "*Fundamentalism*," 20, where he asserts, "Only truth can be authoritative; only an inerrant Bible can be used, as we shall hope to show, in the way that God means Scripture to be used." See also pp. 94–101 in the same volume.

55. J. I. Packer, "Inerrancy and the Divinity and Humanity of the Bible," in *Honouring the Written Word of God*, 164.

56. Ibid., 162. See also Packer, "*Fundamentalism*," 20, 96.

57. Packer, "Inerrancy and the Divinity and Humanity of the Bible," 164.

58. See Packer, *Truth and Power*, 105.

59. Ibid.

60. McGrath, *Packer*, 199, and Packer, *God Has Spoken*, 134, 151. See also Packer, *Truth and Power*, 105–6.

61. Packer, "Inerrancy and the Divinity and Humanity of the Bible," 164.

62. Ibid., 165.

63. J. I. Packer, "Understanding the Bible: Evangelical Hermeneutics," in *Honouring the Written Word of God*, 153–57.

64. J. I. Packer, "Upholding the Unity of Scripture Today," in *Honouring the Written Word of God*, 137–43, and J. I. Packer, "In Quest of Canonical Interpretation," in *Honouring the Written Word of God*, 213–29.

65. See "Inerrancy and the Divinity and Humanity of the Bible," 161–69, quote from p. 164.

66. See ibid., 171–212. These pages reproduce lectures he gave to Southern Baptists at the 1987 Conference on Biblical Inerrancy. He also used his exegetical skills in *A Passion for Faithfulness: Wisdom from the Book of Nehemiah* (Wheaton: Crossway, 1995).

67. I regret that one of the choices I felt I had to make in this chapter was to leave out a discussion of Packer's views on expository preaching as a natural result of his theological method. Interested readers should consult *Honouring the Written Word of God*, 239–336, and J. I. Packer, "Authority in Preaching," in *The Gospel in the Modern World: A Tribute to John Stott*, ed. Martyn Eden and David F. Wells (Leicester, UK: Inter-Varsity, 1991), 198–212.

68. Packer, "Understanding the Bible," 153–57.

69. J. I. Packer, "Encountering Present-Day Views of Scripture," in *Honouring the Written Word of God*, 7–18. This article, written in 1978, in many ways updates the 1959 article, "Contemporary Views of Revelation," in *Honouring the Written Word of God*, 65–80.

70. Packer, "Encountering Present-Day Views of Scripture," 12–15.

71. Ibid., 15.

72. Packer, *Truth and Power*, 118–19.

73. Ibid., 119.

74. Payne, *Theology of the Christian Life*, 245.

75. See, for example, *"Fundamentalism,"* 115–45 for an extended treatment of the subject.

76. The English Standard Version is a revision of the Revised Standard Version. The translation was prepared by members of the oversight committee, reviewed by biblical scholars, and confirmed by action of the oversight committee, which met for several sessions from 1999–2001 and for one session in 2005. Members of the translation oversight committee were Lane Dennis, J. I. Packer, Wayne Grudem, Vern Poythress, William Mounce, Robert Mounce, Bruce Winter, Jack Collins, Gordon Wenham, Paul House, Kent Hughes, and Leland Ryken.

77. J. I. Packer, "Crosscurrents among Evangelicals," in Charles Colson and Richard John Neuhaus, eds., *Evangelicals and Catholics Together: Toward a Common Mission* (Dallas: Word, 1995), 171.

78. See J. I. Packer, "The Centrality of Holy Scripture in Anglicanism," *Crux* 40, no. 1 (March 2004): 9–18.

79. Packer, *"Fundamentalism,"* 119.

80. Ibid., 123.

81. Ibid., 131.

82. Ibid., 136.

83. Ibid., 142.

84. Ibid., 144.

85. Ibid., 59.

86. Ibid., 69.

Chapter 6 J. I. Packer and Pastoral Wisdom from the Puritans *Mark E. Dever*

1. Thomas Babington Macaulay, *History of England*, vol. 1 (Lurgen: Ulster Society for the Promotion of Ulster-British Heritage and Culture, 1989), chap. 3.

2. Garrison Keillor, quoted on his *Prairie Home Companion* Radio Show (August 7, 2003) and cited at http://www.qotd.org/archive/2003/08/07.html. Accessed 8/28/2007.

3. J. I. Packer, *A Quest for Godliness* (Wheaton: Crossway, 1990).

4. J. I. Packer, *"Fundamentalism" and the Word of God: Some Evangelical Principles* (London: Inter-Varsity, 1958), 49.

5. Ibid., 173.

6. Mark Twain, quoted in George Bainton, ed., *The Art of Authorship*, 1st American ed. (New York: Appleton, 1898).

7. Richard Sibbes, "Soul's Conflict with Itself," in *Works of Richard Sibbes* (Edinburgh, UK; Carlisle, PA: Banner of Truth, 1979), 1:273–74.

8. Ibid., 286.

9. J. I. Packer, *Knowing God* (Downers Grove, IL: InterVarsity, 1973), 89.

10. Ibid., 254.

11. J. I. Packer, "Introductory Essay," in John Owen's *The Death of Death in the Death of Christ* (Edinburgh: Banner of Truth, 1959), 2–3.

12. Cited in ibid., 10–11.

13. J. I. Packer, "What Did the Cross Achieve? The Logic of Penal Substitution," *Tyndale Bulletin* 25 (1974), 3–45.

14. Ibid., 45.

15. Quoted in J. I. Packer, *A Grief Sanctified: Passing Through Grief to Peace and Joy* (Ann Arbor, MI: Vine, 1997), 119–20.

16. Packer, *"Fundamentalism,"* 175.

17. Christopher Catherwood, *Martyn Lloyd-Jones: A Family Portrait* (Grand Rapids: Baker Books, 1995), 71.

18. Packer, *"Fundamentalism,"* 45.

19. J. I. Packer, "Fundamentalism: The British Scene," *Christianity Today*, September 29, 1958, 5.

20. J. I. Packer, "Why I Signed It" *Christianity Today*, December 12, 1994, 36. This is expressed clearly in the 2003 Evangelicals and Catholics Together Statement on the Communion of Saints: "Our historical circumstance makes our common witness increasingly urgent," *First Things* (March 2003): 27.

21. See *The Joint Declaration on the Doctrine of Justification in Confessional Lutheran Perspective* (The Lutheran Church–Missouri Synod, 1999).

22. Packer, "Why I Signed It," 36–37.

23. Jonathan Edwards, "Treatise on Justification," in *Works of Jonathan Edwards*, vol. 1 (New Haven: Yale University Press, 1957), 654. John Owen expressed similar thoughts: "Men may be really saved by that grace which *doctrinally they do deny*; and they may be justified by the imputation of that righteousness which *in opinion they deny to be imputed*. For my part, I must say, that notwithstanding all the disputes that I see and read about justification, I do not believe but that the authors of them . . . do really trust unto the Mediator of Christ for the pardon of their sins, and for acceptance with God, and not unto their own works or obedience. Nor will I believe the contrary, until they expressly declare it," John Owen, *The Doctrine of Justification by Faith*, in *Works*, vol. 5 (Edinburgh: Banner of Truth, 1965), 163–64, italics in original. Thanks to Ligon Duncan, who, in turn, thanked Justin Taylor, for this Owen reference.

24. J. I. Packer and others, *Here We Stand: Justification By Faith Today* (London: Hodder and Stoughton, 1986), 5.

25. Packer, "Justification in Protestant Theology," in *Here We Stand*, 101–2.

26. Sibbes, "Soul's Conflict," 185–86.

27. J. I. Packer, *The Redemption and Restoration of Man in the Thought of Richard Baxter* (Vancouver: Regent College Publishing, 2003), 406.

Chapter 7 Retrieval and Renewal *D. Bruce Hindmarsh*

1. Marcellino D'Ambrosio, "*Ressourcement* Theology, *Aggiornamento*, and the Hermeneutics of Tradition," *Communio viatorium* 18 (Winter 1991): 532.

2. Ibid., 537.

3. Packer quoted in Alister McGrath, *J. I. Packer: A Biography* (Grand Rapids: Baker Books, 1997), 252.

4. Quoted in D'Ambrosio, "*Ressourcement*," 540.

5. C. S. Lewis, "On the Reading of Old Books," in *God in the Dock: Essays on Theology and Ethics* (Grand Rapids: Eerdmans, 1970), 201–4.

6. J. I. Packer, "On from Orr," *Crux* 32, no. 3 (September 1996): 12–13.

7. *Documents of Vatican II*, ed. A. P. Flannery (Grand Rapids: Eerdmans, 1975), 686.

8. See further his personal remarks in this regard in the introduction to J. I. Packer, *Among God's Giants: The Puritan Vision of the Christian Life* (Eastbourne, UK: Kingsway, 1991), 11–18.

9. See W. R. Ward's reference in "Power and Piety," in *Faith and Faction* (London: Epworth, 1993), 75.

10. John Newton, *Works*, 6 vols. (London, 1808), 6:271.

11. On the genealogical and theological continuities in the history of evangelicalism, see Mark A. Noll, *The Rise of Evangelicalism: The Age of Edwards, Whitefield, and the Wesleys* (Leicester, UK: Inter-Varsity, 2004).

12. Walter Truett Anderson, *Reality Isn't What It Used to Be* (San Francisco: Harper & Row, 1990), 188.

13. John Telford, ed., *Wesley's Veterans*, 7 vols. (London, 1912–14), 1:210.

14. Margaret Austin to Charles Wesley, ALS, May 19, 1740, Early Methodist Volume, John Rylands Library, Manchester.

15. John Newton and William Cowper, *Olney Hymns* (London, 1779; facsimile reprint, Olney, 1984), 234.

16. Erik Routley compares hymns to folk songs as different from professional or art songs. Hymns are "communal song," songs for unmusical people to sing together, and poetry for unliterary people to utter together. See further Routley's *Christian Hymns Observed* (Princeton: Prestige Publications, 1982), 1–6.

17. Quoted in Bruce Hindmarsh, *The Evangelical Conversion Narrative: Spiritual Autobiography in Early Modern England* (Oxford: Oxford University Press, 2005), 143.

18. Ibid., 144.

19. Cf. Andrew Walls, "The Evangelical Revival, The Missionary Movement, and Africa," in *Evangelicalism*, ed. Mark Noll, David Bebbington, and George Rawlyk (New York: Oxford University Press, 1994), 310–30. Walls writes, for example, "The evangelicalism of the period takes its identity from protest, and in effect from nominal Christianity. Evangelical religion presupposes Christendom, Christian civil society" (312).

20. Donald Davie, *Purity of Diction in English Verse* (London: Chatto & Windus, 1952), 79.

21. Charles Wesley, Hymn 374, in *A Collection of Hymns for the Use of the People Called Methodists*, ed. Franz Hildebrandt, Oliver A. Beckerlegge, and James Dale, vol. 7 of *Works*, 547.

22. Stephen Gunter, *The Limits of "Love Divine": John Wesley's Response to Antinomianism and Enthusiasm* (Nashville: Abingdon, 1989), 270–76.

23. Frank Baker, *William Grimshaw* (London: Epworth, 1963), 74.

24. Newton, *Works*, 1:419.

25. Ibid., 1:171–91.

Chapter 8 J. I. Packer *Carl R. Trueman*

1. Throughout the essay, I use both of the terms *English* and *British*. This choice is deliberate. The division between Packer and Lloyd-Jones impacted evangelicals across Britain, especially in England and Wales, though much less so in Scotland and Northern Ireland. Yet its impact in England was different from that in Wales because of the relative strength of Anglican evangelicalism in England, the peculiarly strong tradition of revival (and its concomitant mysticism) in Wales, and the increasingly dominant, if not almost messianic role played by Lloyd-Jones amongst Welsh ministers in particular.

2. I am aware of, and very sympathetic to, the pleas of scholars such as D. G. Hart for the addition of *confessional* as a third category necessary for a properly nuanced model for analyzing American Protestantism in the early twentieth century. The category is not so helpful in the Anglo-Welsh context where confessional churches (primarily Lutheran, Presbyterian, and Reformed) have not been a strong force as *confessional* churches. For an example of how this category can be fruitfully used in historical analysis, see D. G. Hart, *Defending the Faith: J. Gresham Machen and the Crisis of Conservative Protestantism in Modern America* (Grand Rapids: Baker Academic, 1995).

3. See Iain H. Murray, *D. Martyn Lloyd-Jones: The Fight of Faith, 1939–1981* (Edinburgh: Banner of Truth, 1990), 187–88.

4. Ibid., 226–27.

5. The address is published under the title "Evangelical Unity: An Appeal" in D. Martyn Lloyd-Jones, *Knowing the Times* (Edinburgh: Banner of Truth, 1989), 246–57. See also Murray, *Lloyd-Jones*, 513–32; John Brencher, *Martyn Lloyd-Jones (1899–1981) and Twentieth Century Evangelicalism* (Carlisle, UK: Paternoster, 2002), 92–106.

6. This is the basic position of Iain Murray; see his *Evangelicalism Divided* (Edinburgh: Banner of Truth, 2000).

7. See Brencher, *Martyn Lloyd-Jones*, 83–92.

8. See "Luther and His Message for Today" in D. Martyn Lloyd-Jones, *Unity in Truth* (Darlington, UK: Evangelical, 1991). The penultimate paragraph on p. 43 is eloquent: "What then are we as evangelicals to do in this situation? I reply by saying that we must heed a great injunction in Revelation 18:4: 'Come out of her, my people, that ye be not partakers of her sins, and that ye receive not of her plagues.' Come out of it!"

9. J. Gresham Machen, *Christianity and Liberalism* (Grand Rapids: Eerdmans, 1996), 171.

10. Ibid., 50.

11. Lloyd-Jones, *Knowing the Times*, 254.

12. J. I. Packer, "Martyn Lloyd-Jones," in *The Collected Shorter Writings of J. I. Packer*, vol. 4, *Honouring the People of God* (Carlisle, UK: Paternoster, 1999), 79.

13. See Murray, *Lloyd-Jones*, 656, 658.

14. Gaius Davies, "Physician, Preacher and Politician: Dr. D. Martyn Lloyd-Jones (1899–1981)," in *Genius, Grief and Grace: A Doctor Looks at Suffering and Success* (Fearn, UK: Christian Focus, 2001), 325–69, esp. 358–60.

15. Davies speaks of Packer's "scurvy treatment by Dr. Lloyd-Jones and his like-minded colleagues," and of him being "cold shouldered and rejected by people with whom he had worked closely," ibid., 358–59.

16. More perplexing than Packer, of course, are the Anglicans who stayed in and yet had no ecclesiology ("It's the best boat to fish from"—as if ecclesiology can be reduced to evangelistic opportunity) and for whom answering Lloyd-Jones's call would scarcely have involved compromise of ecclesiastical principle; their legacy continues to shape great swaths of the antitheological world of much of Anglican evangelicalism to its lasting weakness and detriment; but critiquing them, while surely necessary at some point, is beyond the scope of this particular essay.

Chapter 9 Packer, Puritans, and Postmoderns *Charles W. Colson*

1. Stanley Fish, "Condemnation without Absolutes," *New York Times*, October 15, 2001, http://www.nytimes.com/2001/10/15/opinion/condemnation-without-absolutes.html. Accessed 4/2/2009.

2. *The Passion of the Christ*, a film directed by Mel Gibson (2004), depicts the last twelve hours of Jesus Christ's life.

3. Charles W. Colson, *In Search of the Good Life* (Wheaton: Tyndale, 2006).

4. Barry W. Lynn is the executive director of Americans United, an independent 501 (c)(3) organization for separation of church and state. See http://www.au.org. Accessed 8/31/2008.

5. For more on the lawsuit and Prison Fellowship programs, see Bill Berkowitz, "Charles Colson's prison project on trial in Iowa," November 2, 2005, at http://mediatransparency.org/story.php?/storyID=91. Accessed 4/6/2009. For further reading on IFI ruling information, visit http://www.ifiprison.org/generic.asp?ID=7277&print=1. Accessed 4/6/2009.

6. Barna Group, "Most adults feel accepted by God, but lack a biblical worldview," August 9, 2005, http://www.barna.org. Accessed 4/8/09.

7. For more on the Back to Jesus movement see Peter M. Warren, "Thousands Accept Jesus into Their Hearts on Infield," *New York Times*, August 15, 1997.

8. Andy Crouch, "The Emergent Mystique," *Christianity Today*, November 2004, 38. Quote comes from interview of Rob Bell and his wife, Kristen, after Sunday services at Mars Hill Bible Church, Grand Rapids, MI.

9. Ibid.

10. Laurie Goodstein, "Disowning Conservative Politics, Evangelical Pastor Rattles Flock," *New York Times*, July 30, 2006.

11. For further reading, see Aaron Milavec, *The Didache: Faith, Hope and Life of the Earliest Christian Communities* (Mahwah, NJ: Paulist Press, 2003).

12. René Descartes, French mathematician, philosopher, and scientist, 1596–1650. Internet resource: http://thinkexist.com/quotes/rene_descartes. Accessed 8/31/2008.

13. For more on Plantinga's views on God, see "The Reformed Objection to Natural Theology," *Christian Scholar's Review* 11 (1982); and "On Reformed Epistemology," *The Reformed Journal* 32 (January 1982): 17.

14. See Charles Colson and Nancy Pearcey, *How Now Shall We Live?* (Wheaton: Tyndale, 1999).

15. See further discussions of presuppositionalism and Cornelius Van Til (1895–1987) at "Thinking Biblically: An Introduction to Presuppositionalism," by Nathan Pitchford, http://strangebaptistfire.wordpress.com/2008/08/17/thinking-biblically-an-introduction-to-presuppositionalism/. Accessed 8/31/2008. See also Cornelius Van Til, "Why I Believe in God," http://www.reformed.org/apologetics/why_I_believe_cvt.html. Accessed 8/31/2008.

16. Lee Strobel, *The Case for Christ* (Grand Rapids: Zondervan, 2001).

17. J. Budziszewski, *What We Can't Not Know: A Guide* (Dallas: Spence, 2003).

18. Marc Hauser, *Moral Minds* (New York: Ecco, 2006).

19. Timothy George, *Is the Father of Jesus the God of Muhammad?* (Grand Rapids: Zondervan, 2002).

20. Samuel Huntington, *The Clash of Civilizations and the Remaking of World Order* (New York: Touchstone, 1997). Princeton professor Bernard Lewis, probably the world's greatest authority on Arabic cultures and Middle Eastern religions and beliefs, actually coined the phrase *clash of civilizations*. Lewis first used the term in a Washington meeting in 1997 where it was recorded (Bernard Lewis, interview by Ruthie Blum, "One on One: 'When Defeat Means Liberation,'" *Jerusalem Post,* 1997).

21. Francis Fukuyama, *The End of History and the Last Man* (New York: Free Press, 1992).

22. Quoted by Harold Myra and Marshall Shelley in "Leading with Love," *Today's Christian,* September/October 2005, http://www.christianitytoday.com/tc/2005/005/2.40.html. Accessed 8/31/08. For further reading on love, see Martin Luther King Jr., *Strength to Love* (Philadelphia: Fortress, 1963, 1981), esp. chaps. 4, "Love in Action," and 5, "Love your Enemy," pp. 39–58.

Chapter 10 Christ without Culture *Richard John Neuhaus*

1. Alister McGrath, *J. I. Packer: A Biography* (Grand Rapids: Baker Books, 1997), 56.

2. Augustine, "On the Predestination of Saints," in *Selected Writings of Saint Augustine,* ed. Roger Hazelton, 129–30 (New York: World Publishing Co., 1962).

3. From an interview with Richard John Neuhaus, Joan Chittister, Michael Lerner, John Meacham, Seyyed Hossein Nasr, and Joel Osteen by Tim Russert on MSNBC's *Meet the Press,* April 16, 2006. For a transcript go to http://www.msnbc.msn.com/id/12283802. Accessed 4/15/09.

4. William James, *The Varieties of Religious Experience: A Study in Human Nature; Being the Gifford Lectures On Natural Religion Delivered at Edinburgh in 1901–1902* (New York: Modern Library, 1902).

5. Harold Bloom, *The American Religion: The Emergence of the Post-Christian Nation* (New York: Simon & Schuster, 1992), 37.

6. See Augustine, *The City of God* (New York: Modern Library, 1950).

7. C. S. Lewis, "Christian Apologetics," in *God in the Dock: Essays in Theology and Ethics,* ed. Walter Hooper (Grand Rapids: Eerdmans, 1970), 101.

Chapter 11 On Knowing God *James Earl Massey*

1. Raymond E. Brown, *The Gospel According to John (XIII–XXI)* (Garden City, NY: Doubleday, 1970), 748.

2. See esp. J. I. Packer, *Knowing God* (London: Hodder and Stoughton; Downers Grove, IL: InterVarsity, 1973); J. I. Packer, "On Knowing God," in *Our Sovereign God,* ed. James M. Boice (Grand Rapids: Baker Academic, 1977), 61–76.

3. For the full text of these hymns, see *Pilgrim Hymnal* (New York: Pilgrim, 1958), hymns 333, 429, 334, and 7, respectively.

4. Charles Wesley, "I Do Believe," *Melodies of Zion* (Anderson, IN: Gospel Trumpet, 1926), hymn 301.

5. Samuel Rodigast, "Whate'er Our God Ordains Is Right," trans. by Catherine Winkworth, *Trinity Hymnal* (Philadelphia: Orthodox Presbyterian Church, 1961), hymn 96.

6. D. O. Teasley, "God Is Love," *Hymnal of the Church of God* (Anderson, IN: Warner, 1953), hymn 96.

7. Roger Hazelton, *The God We Worship* (New York: Macmillan, 1946), 91.

8. H. Ernest Nichol, "We've a Story to Tell to the Nations," *Worship the Lord: Hymnal of the Church of God* (Anderson, IN: Warner, 1989), hymn 298.

Chapter 12 *Unde, Quonam, et Quemadmodum?* *Timothy George*

1. J. I. Packer, "Richard Baxter," in *The Collected Shorter Writings of J. I. Packer,* vol. 4, *Honouring the People of God* (Carlisle, UK: Paternoster, 1999), 79.

2. Edward John Carnell, *The Case for Orthodox Theology* (Philadephia: Westminster, 1959), 113.

3. John Calvin, *Institutes of the Christian Religion,* 1.5.8; 1.14.20; 2.6.1.

4. Philip Jenkins, *The Next Christendom* (New York: Oxford University Press, 2003).

5. Karl Barth, *Fragments Grave and Gay,* ed. Martin Rumscheidt (Glasglow: Collins, 1971), 116–17.

Chapter 13 Reflection and Response *J. I. Packer*

1. John Masefield, *The Everlasting Mercy,* in *The Oxford Book of English Mystical Verse,* ed. D. H. S. Nicholson and A. H. E. Lee (Oxford: Clarendon, 1917), http://www.bartleby.com/236. Accessed June 7, 2007.

2. *The Collected Letters of C. S. Lewis,* vol. 2, *Books, Broadcasts and the War, 1931–1949,* ed. Walter Hooper (San Francisco: HarperSanFrancisco, 2004), 674; cited in Alan Jacobs, *The Narnian: The Life and Imagination of C. S. Lewis* (San Francisco: HarperSanFrancisco, 2005), 236.

3. Charles Williams, *Many Dimensions* (Grand Rapids: Eerdmans, 1949).

4. Charles Wesley, *The Methodist Hymnal* (Nashville: Methodist Publishing House, 1966), 341.

5. Isaac Watts, *The Methodist Hymnal,* 9.

6. Richard Baxter, *Dying Thoughts* (Edinburgh: Banner of Truth, 2004), 218.

7. See Thomas Oden and J. I. Packer, *One Faith* (Downers Grove, IL: InterVarsity, 2004).

8. John Newton, "Amazing Grace," *The Baptist Hymnal* (Nashville: Convention, 1991), 33.

9. John Telford, *The Life of John Wesley* (London: Epworth, 1947), 307.

10. Francis A. Schaeffer, *The Complete Works of Francis A. Schaeffer: A Christian Worldview,* vol. 1 (Westchester: Crossway, 1982), 140.

Index

abortion, 53
Abortion and the Early Church (Gorman), 53
Achtemeier, Elizabeth, 31
addresses and lectures
   "An Introduction to Systematic *Spirituality*,"
     38
   Sangwoo Youtong Chee Professor of Theology
     inaugural address (1989), 22–23, 38
advocacy journalism, 44–45
Alarm to the Unconverted (Alleine), 104
Alsdurf, Phyllis, 45
American Christianity, 146–47, 149, 150–51,
   245n2
*American Religion: The Emergence of the Post-
   Christian Nation, The* (Bloom), 150
analogy, 66–67, 240n78
Anglican Communion, 11, 30
Anglicanism, and nonconformity, 116–29
anthropocentrism, 66
Anyabwile, Thabiti, 97
apostolic succession, 184
"As a Witness of Your Grace" (hymn), 231–32
Association of Theological Schools, 167
Augustine, 57, 237n32
Aulen, Gustaf, 92
Austin, Margaret, 106, 107

Banner of Truth Trust, 118, 119, 124
Barth, Karl, 57, 81–82, 169
Bash Camps, 118
Battle for the Bible, The (Lindsell), 78
Baxter, Richard, 20, 36–37, 53, 70, 73, 93, 97,
   118, 167, 175, 178

Bebbington, David, 179
Bell, Nelson, 45
Benedict XVI, 149, 151–52
Bible
   authorial intent, 62–64, 237n27
   Barth's exegesis of, 82
   canonical character of, 60–61, 80–81, 85,
     238n39
   christological focus of, 61–62
   covenantal framework of, 59–60
   postmodern views of, 135
   unity of, 80
Bible Church Missionary Society, 165
biblical authority, 23, 50, 56, 58, 74, 89, 179
biblical inerrancy, 57–59, 76, 78, 79–83, 86,
   236–37n17, 237n28, 238n39
Billy Graham London Crusade (1954), 75
Bloom, Harold, 150–51
Borg, Marcus, 34
Boyd, Gregory, 135
British Evangelical Council, 124
Bruce, F. F., 117
Budziszewski, J., 137
Bunyan, John, 88, 92

Calvin, John, 57, 72, 174, 238n48
Calvinism, 60, 91
Case for Christ, The (Strobel), 137
catechesis, 174–77
Chambers, Oswald, 53
charismaticism, 118, 125
charity, 169
Christ and Culture (Niebuhr), 144

Christianity
  Christian life, 92–93, 168
  Christian unity, 52, 83–84, 87, 93–96
  and culture, 144–53
  global, 144
Christianity and Liberalism (Machen), 120,
  121, 135
Christianity Today, 11, 43–54, 165
Christians in Complete Armor (Gurnall), 92–93
Christocentrism, 238n48
Christology, 61–62, 81, 118
Christus Victor (Aulen), 92
Chrysostom, 57
church centrality, 180–81
Church Missionary Society, 165
Church of England, 116, 149
clash of civilizations, 247n20
*Clash of Civilizations and the Remaking of
  World Order, The* (Huntington), 140
Coleridge, Samuel Taylor, 101
Colson, Charles W., 13
communion, 181
community and individual, 105–8
Conn, H. M., 239n50
covenant theology, 59–60
criticism, 51–52
culture, 144–53

death, 177–78
Death of Death in the Death of Christ, The
  (Owen), 91, 95, 119, 167
Dever, Mark E., 13
discipleship, 58
discipleship of the mind, 21
Dowey, Edward A., 238n48
Doxology, the, 41, 235n28
doxology, 181

Edwards, Jonathan, 24, 95–96, 104, 244n23
Elliott, Charlotte, 172
End of History and the Last Man, The
  (Fukuyama), 140
England, class and conformity, 116–17,
  245nn1–2
English Standard Version (ESV), 83, 84, 243n76
epistemology of engagement, 57
"Eternal Father, Strong to Save" (hymn), 156
eternal life, 159–60
eucharistia, 30
Evangelical Alliance, 165
Evangelicals and Catholics Together (ECT), 52,
  83, 94, 131

evangelical theology
  attentiveness to past in, 20–21
  and value of tradition, 24–25
evangelicalism
  ahistorical nature of, 99
  doctrinal enumeration, 179–81
  future of, 84–86, 183–85
  and gospel, 108–9
  hermeneutical principles, 80
  individual and community in, 105–8
  mission and, 109–11
  in 1960s, 78
  nonconformist, 116–28
  origins, 103–5
  Packer on, 178–83
  personality cult in, 54
  as renewal movement, 99–114, 166, 182–83
  transformation and consummation, 112–14
  worship, 111–12
Everlasting Mercy, The (Masefield), 172–73
experience, 238n39
expository preaching, 242n67

faith, 84–85, 180
  analogy of, 59, 237n32
  unity of, 38
"Father Almighty, Bless Us with Thy Blessing!"
  (hymn), 156
Fellowship of Independent Evangelical
  Churches, 124
Fish, Stanley, 132–33
Foxe, John, 96
Fuller Seminary, 78
Fundamentalism and the Church of God
  (Hebert), 50, 76, 89

Gadamer, Hans-Georg, 56, 63
George, Timothy, 13–14, 139
Gnosticism, 151, 184
God, identities of, 156–59
Goodwin, Thomas, 89
Gorman, Mike, 53
gospel, 91–92, 108–9
Grace Baptists, 124
Graham, Billy, 44, 45–46, 75, 78, 89, 165–66
Great Tradition, 38–39, 89, 102
Gregory of Nazianzus, 174
Grimshaw, William, 104, 113
Gurnall, William, 92–93

Harris, Howell, 110
Hart, Darryl, 45

Hauser, Marc, 137
Hebert, Gabriel, 50, 76, 89
Hendriksen, William, 57
Henry, Carl, 45
Henry, Matthew, 57
hermeneutics, 56–64, 239nn54–55
Hindmarsh, D. Bruce, 14
historical-critical biblical interpretation, 75
Hodge, Charles, 57
holiness, 180
Holy Spirit, 62–64, 73, 84
*Holy Spirit in Puritan Faith and Experience,
    The* (Nuttall), 92
homophobia, 138–39
Horton, Michael, 52
House, Paul R., 14
How Now Shall We Live? (Colson), 137
Hughes, Philip E., 117
humility, 169
Humphrey, Edith M., 14–15
hymnody, 111–12, 155–59, 172, 245n16

"Immortal, Invisible, God Only Wise," 156–57
incarnation, 61–62
individual and community, 105–8
individualism, 25
inerrancy, biblical, 57–59, 78, 79–83, 86,
    236–37n17, 237n28, 238n39
Inner-Change Freedom Initiative (IFI), 134
In Search of the Good Life (Colson), 133
inspiration, 73, 74–75
interfaith concerns, 38–39
International Council on Biblical Inerrancy,
    79–80, 82
Inter-Varsity Christian Fellowship, 73, 89, 117
Islam, 139–40, 145
Is the Father of Jesus the God of Muhammad?
    (George), 139

James, William, 150
Jenkins, Philip, 168
Jesus, 160–61, 180
"Jesus! The Name High Over All" (hymn), 177
J. I. Packer: A Biography (McGrath), 37
John Paul II (pope), 148
Jones, Bob, Sr., 108
justification, 93–96, 244n23

Keswick Convention, 21–22, 233n6
Know the Truth (Milne), 125, 129

language, 239n58
Latimer House, Oxford, 77

Lausanne II, 52
Lewis, Bernard, 247n20
Lewis, C. S., 10, 50, 53, 101–2, 152, 167, 175
liberalism, 73, 77, 135
Lindsell, Harold, 78
Lloyd-Jones, Elizabeth, 10, 119
Lloyd-Jones, Martyn, 96, 116, 117, 118, 119–28
"Love Divine, All Loves Excelling" (hymn),
    112–13
Lutheranism, American, 78
Lynn, Barry, 134

Machen, J. Gresham, 120, 121, 135
*Mark of Jesus: Loving in a Way the World Can
    See, The* (George and Woodbridge), 169
Mascall, E. L., 123
Masefield, John, 172–73
Massey, James Earl, 15
McGrath, Alister, 9, 15, 37, 56
mere Christianity, 101–2
Methodism, 106
mission, 109–11
Moody, Dale, 164
Moore College, 125–26
Moral Minds (Hauser), 137
Murray, Iain, 124
Myra, Harold, 46

National Evangelical Anglican Congress (1967),
    123
National Evangelical Anglican Congress (1977),
    56
Neff, David, 16
neoorthodoxy, 81–82
Neuhaus, Richard John, 16, 152–53
New Bible Commentary, The, 73
New Evangelicalism, 45–46
new theology, 100
Newton, John, 104, 106, 113
Next Christendom, The (Jenkins), 168
Niebuhr, H. Richard, 144
nonconformity, 116–29
North American evangelicalism, 25, 165–66
Nuttall, Geoffrey, 92

Olivers, Thomas, 106
Onesimus, 163
Orr, James, 31, 240n84
orthodoxy, 67
Owen, John, 23–24, 53, 57, 88, 91, 95, 119, 127,
    244n23

Packer, J. I.
  birth and early life, 10
  as catechist, 174–77
  and *Christianity Today*, 43–54
  communication skills, 48–49
  contributions to theological literature, 117–19
  conversion, 172
  education, 164–65
  influences, 56–57
  and Martyn Lloyd-Jones, 119–28
  1944–1954, 71–73
  1954–1976, 73–78
  1977–1996, 79–83
  1997–2006, 83–84
  positions held, 20, 70
  self-identification of, 19
  shaping of early theology, 23–24
  summary of ministry, 70
  theological growth, 173
  tradition in theology of, 24–27
  vocational sense, 173–74
  See also works of J. I. Packer
Parrett, Gary A., 231–32
Pascal, Blaise, 152
pastoral intentions, 64–65
patience, 51–52
Pawson, John, 104
Payne, Don, 16, 82
Pelagianism, 21–22
penal substitution, 92
performative language, 239n58
personality cult, 54
Pietism, 22
Pilgrim's Progress (Bunyan), 92
Plantinga, Alvin, 136
pneumatology, 118
political parties, 117
postmodernism, 131–41
prayer, 155–59
Presbyterianism, 88
Presbyterianism, American, 78
priesthood, 40
Prison Fellowship, 134
Proclamation Trust, 125
Psalm 133, 29–30
Puritan and Reformed Studies Conference, The, 73, 88
Puritans/Puritanism
  catechetical nature of, 176
  on Christian life, 92–93
  on Christian unification, 93–96

defined, 166
  on God, 90–91
  on the gospel, 91–92
  introduction to, 87–88
  on justification, 93–96
  and *Knowing God*, 90
  Packer's regard for, 21, 24, 44, 47, 53, 70, 72–73
  on Word of God, 88–90
Puritan Studies Conference, 118, 119, 124

rationality, human, 57–59, 236n16
Reformed Pastor (Baxter), 37, 175
Reformed tradition, 116, 126–27
Regent College, Vancouver, 20, 37, 79
relativism, 132–33
religion, 146
revelation, 73–74
role models, 21
Roman Catholicism
  Evangelicals and Catholics Together (ECT), 52, 83, 93–96, 131
  regard for, 52
  sacramentalism, 26

Saints' Everlasting Rest, The (Baxter), 53
sanctification, 21
Schaeffer, Francis, 185
Scripture
  analogy of, 59
  authorial intent, 62–64, 237n27
  authority of, 25–26
  biblical inerrancy, 57–59, 76, 78, 79–83, 86, 236n17, 237n28, 238n39
  and context of tradition, 41, 56, 100–101
Second National Assembly of Evangelicals (1966), 119–22
self, religion of the, 150–51
Sibbes, Richard, 90
sin, 23–24
Sisoes, St., 36–37
sloth, 169
Smith, Harold, 46
Smith, Timothy, 53
Southern Baptists (US), 78
sovereignty, 180
spirituality, 22–23, 47
Spurgeon, Charles Haddon, 20
Steer, Roger, 55
Stott, John, 34–35, 117, 118, 119–20, 123
Strobel, Lee, 137
synaxis, 30

terrorism, 51, 53
theology
  covenant theology, 59–60
  evangelical interest in, 21
  Packer's approach to, 22–23, 64–67
  paradox in, 66
  as rising spiral, 239n66
  teaching of, 19–20
  ten disciplines of, 65
  theologoumena, 32
  undergraduate years, 23–24, 71–73
Thiselton, Anthony, 56, 238n49
Thomas Aquinas, 23, 66–67
Thornwell, James Henley, 22
tradition
  Great Tradition, 38–39, 89, 102, 181–82
  historical retrieval, 99–114
  importance of, 24–27, 54
transformation and consummation, 112–14
trinitarian theocentricity, 31
Trinity, 179–80
Trinity College, Bristol, 20
Trueman, Carl J., 16–17
truth, 46–47, 53–54, 86, 132–36
Tyndale Fellowship, 73, 165
Tyndale Hall, Bristol, 20, 27, 75, 77

Varieties of Religious Experience, The (James),
  150
Vatican II, 100, 149

Waters, Maxine, 137
Watts, Isaac, 177–78
Wenham, John, 117
Wesley, Charles, 107, 108, 109, 111, 112–13, 177
Wesley, John, 104, 109–10, 184
Westminster Conference, 124
Westminster Confession, 60
What We Can't Not Know (Budziszewski), 137
Whitefield, George, 20, 106, 107, 109, 110
Wiles, Maurice, 123
wisdom, 65
women's ordination, 40
Woodbridge, John, 52

works of J. I. Packer
  Across the Divide, 36
  "The Adequacy of Human Language,"
    239n58
  "A Bad Trip," 51
  in *Christianity Today*, 43–54
  "The Comfort of Conservatism," 25
  *Commentary on the Montreal Declaration:
    Anglican Essentials*, 32–33
  Concise Theology, 60, 238n38
  Evangelism and the Sovereignty of God, 10,
    93, 164
  "Fundamentalism: The British Scene," 43–44,
    50
  "Fundamentalism" and the Word of God, 10,
    50, 76–77, 89, 117–18
  God Has Spoken, 77, 81, 82
  God's Words: Studies of Key Biblical Themes,
    81, 118
  "The Gospel of Jesus Christ: An Evangelical
    Celebration," 52
  "Hype and Human Humbug," 46–47
  "Inerrancy and the Divinity and Humanity of
    the Bible," 81
  Keep in Step with the Spirit, 118, 233n6
  Knowing God, 10, 21, 22, 34–35, 62, 70, 81,
    90, 118, 129, 144
  "Packer the Picketed Pariah," 52
  A Quest for Godliness, 24, 37, 88, 91
  "Resolutions for Roman Catholic and Evan-
    gelical Dialogue," 51
  "Revelation and Inspiration," 73–75
  "Saved by His Precious Blood," 91, 95, 119,
    168
  "Theology and Bible Reading," 239n66
  Truth and Power, 82, 239n54
  "What Did the Cross Achieve? The Logic of
    Penal Substitution," 92, 240n78
  "Why I Signed It," 52, 95
  "Why We Need the Puritans," 103
worship, 32–33
Wright, David F., 55